Overcoming
Endometriosis

Overcoming Endometriosis

*New Help from the American
Endometriosis Association*

Edited by

**Mary Lou Ballwegg
and
Susan Deutsch**

*Arlington Books
King St, St James's
London*

OVERCOMING ENDOMETRIOSIS
First published in Great Britain 1988 by
Arlington Books (Publishers) Ltd
15–17 King St, St James's
London SW1

© 1987 The Endometriosis Association
Foreword to British Edition
© 1988 The Endometriosis Society

Typeset by Profile Information, London
Printed and bound by
Billing & Sons Ltd, Worcester

British Library Cataloguing-in-Publication Data

Ballwegg, Mary Lou
Overcoming endometriosis
1. Women, Endometriosis.
I. Title II. Deutsch, Susan
618.1'4

ISBN 0–85140–729–3

Dedicated to women with endometriosis
—together we will overcome this disease

Contents

Working Together in Britain—The Endometriosis Society

By Lesley Mabbett

'*Suddenly the horror of what had happened to us as young women and the negligence of it all made us realise that there was a real need for a self-help group and that a lot of work was needed to bring sufferers of endometriosis together to try and help themselves . . .*

I continue with my full-time job in the Civil Service, where I've worked over the years, as well as being 'taken over' and working almost full-time(!) on the Society work—the Society is still based at my home—doing the administration, the accounts, opening and answering the mail, preparing the newsletter, etc. etc. It's all work I love doing.' Ailsa Irving, founder of the Endometriosis Society.

'*Due to the small notices that have been in the papers, I have had women from all over Scotland writing to me and to date have received about 30 letters. All this is keeping me busy but I enjoy every minute of it. I feel if I can help someone by writing a letter or listening to them on the 'phone then it is worth it. I know that the day I heard about the Society and wrote to you was the best thing that ever happened to me.*' Margaret Lilley, leader of the new Lanarkshire group.

DIFFERENCES BETWEEN BRITAIN AND THE UNITED STATES (AND MANY SIMILARITIES)

This book summarises the work of the US–Canadian Endometriosis Association, in helping women with the condition since 1979. In many ways the experiences of American women parallel those of women in Britain. In particular:

- The range of symptoms suffered (and often not described in the medical literature) are very similar (see page 253).
- We all have difficulties in getting doctors to take our problems seriously so that the disease is diagnosed.
- On both sides of the Atlantic we are trying to cope with taking difficult life-decisions with inadequate information and often unhelpful medical attitudes.
- We have to cope with similar surgery and treatments.
- Both British and American women feel extremely isolated with the illness, which is often not understood by family or friends.
- The Association and the Society have both immediately tapped a huge reservoir of need among sufferers from the disease.

There are a number of differences in experience, however, caused by the variations in medical systems on either side of the Atlantic and by the different ways in which self-help groups have developed:

- The National Health Service ensures that British women do get medical treatment, regardless of ability to pay, since payment has already been made through taxation. This means that while our sisters in the United States are battling to be able to afford their treatment, especially when they are too disabled by Endometriosis to work, we in Britain are concerned about the ways in which under-funding of the Health Service means long delays and waiting lists and the non-availability of some treatments.

- Laser surgery is, in general, not available for Endometriosis in Britain. At present there is only one gynaecologist (in Guildford) able to offer laser treatment on the NHS, though other doctors are trying to acquire the equipment and the skills to use it.
- Under the NHS system, we have a very limited ability to choose our doctors. It usually requires a letter from our Family Doctor before we get to see a Gynaecologist. It is not easy to change GP's but the local Community Health Council or Family Practitioner Committee may be able to help. We do not have an automatic right to a second opinion (but it's always worth asking.)
- In general, more hysterectomies are performed in the United States than in Britain.
- British doctors appear to prescribe a wider range of hormone treatments for Endometriosis, In America, there seems to be a greater reliance on danazol (trade-named Danol in Britain). Though this is

widely prescribed here, women are also often treated with progestogens such as norethisterone (Primolut N) and dydrogesterone (Duphaston). Though these may be somewhat less effective at treating the disease, they do suit some women well and the side-effects are generally not so devastating as those of danazol.

- The British Endometriosis Society has been particularly interested in discovering alternative and complementary treatments for the disease and much of the material on alternative medicine in this book is derived from their work.

- The Endometriosis Society has adopted the policy of charging women contacting them as little as possible, its annual subscription barely covering the cost of producing and posting newsletters. Thus its work is carried out purely on a voluntary basis, with no paid staff. Its acheivements have been made possible by the generosity of sufferers who have been able to contribute both money and time.

The Endometriosis Society began in 1981 in Britain when, after years of trying to get her condition diagnosed and then coping with the treatment necessitated by the years of neglect, Ailsa Irving met another sufferer by chance in a hospital waiting room. She writes, 'neither of us realised until that day that our host of peculiarities were all something to do with this thing called endometriosis . . .' An advertisement in the Personal column of the Guardian led to contacts with other sufferers, the first small meeting and the first newsletter of the Endometriosis Self-Help group, dated February 1981.

The group continued to meet in London, sharing experiences and gathering information on case-histories, treatments and research. They rapidly discovered many more common symptoms than are reported in the medical literature, including constant fatigue, bowel problems, a tendency to sore throats, depression, emotional fluctuations and premenstrual tension. They discovered many contacts with a history of glandular fever (such as Ailsa herself), low body temperatures (about one degree below normal), low blood sugar levels, low blood pressure and insomnia. Members found that the difficulties they had experienced in dealing with the medical system and in coping with treatment were by no means unique and that in general both doctors and women themselves were ignorant about the disease.

In March 1982, Jill Rakusen wrote an article in *Good Housekeeping* which resulted in about 1000 replies to the Society. Many people wanted to help and Ailsa suggested that they form groups locally.

In September 1982, the group, renamed the Endometriosis Society, became registered charity no. 326222, administered by a committee of trustees. Its aims are:

- To encourage self-help and mutual support amongst endometriosis sufferers.
- To encourage greater awareness of endometriosis, its symptoms and its consequences amongst the medical profession and the general public.
- To encourage further research into better treatments for endometriosis and its associated infertility and to assist where possible.
- To encourage further research into the epidemiology of endometriosis, to improve the recognition of 'at risk' groups and encourage earlier diagnosis.

The Society continues to operate on a voluntary basis, supported by members' contributions with some fund-raising from industry and local Councils. The number of local groups grows all the time, but it can be difficult finding people to help with the central organisation, which is based at Ailsa's house where she provides the backbone of the Society and does much of the administrative work. At times reduced to three, the trustees now number six, and are always looking for others with the time to help. Decisions are taken by consensus at long meetings held in London each 4–6 weeks, with each woman offering her particular skills in research, medical matters, letter-writing, management, fund-raising etc. Ailsa comments 'We've been extremely lucky with our team of trustees and we all work well together as well as being really good friends.' It is hoped eventually to establish a staffed office, if a grant can be obtained to provide financial stability, since the Society does not wish to charge fees which would discourage the most needy from seeking help.

New Contacts with The Society

National publicity and word-of-mouth continue to bring in letters from sufferers every day and the Society has been in contact with over 15,000 women in its seven years. Almost all the popular women's magazines have now run articles on Endometriosis and Society members have twice appeared on Woman's Hour on Radio 4. There have been items in the national press and in nurses' magazines as well as a Thames Television 'Help' programme.

All new contacts are sent a preliminary pack including basic information about Endometriosis, a list of local groups which they can contact, details of more specific information which they can request and alternative medicines and publications supplied by the Society, plus an invitation to join the Society and subscribe to the bi-monthly newsletter. In 1987, the subscription system was computerised, which allows the Society to provide a better distribution process and keep in contact with members. Previously there had been no formal membership and all who sent in stamped, addressed envelopes received newsletters.

The bi-monthly bulletin, of which there have now been 45, contains news about research and treatments, publications and local groups, Society activities and international contacts. Two regular features, designed to lighten the hopelessness which can so often swamp women in their struggle against Endometriosis, are news of pregnancies, births and adoptions among members and 'How I got better' stories. The latter are not tales of miracle cures, since all too often 'getting better' comprises finding effective ways of minimising and coping with a disease which is likely to be around for a long time. However, such solutions are likely to have something which can be duplicated by some of the readers. Women have found help through many different routes—conventional medicine, complementary therapies, psychotherapy, diet, and religion—even running! The common feature with them all is that women have taken their healing into their own hands and made their own decisions. We feel that the resulting confidence not only enables women to cope with the variety of circumstances with which Endometriosis faces them, but has a direct effect on the disease process itself.

'HOW I GOT BETTER'—SOME EXAMPLES FROM NEWSLETTERS

'*I must tell you how much better I have been since taking Selenium ACE. I had severe Endometriosis and had a hysterectomy and removal of one ovary in 1983. After a few months I became very unwell again with frequent and very painful muscular spasms of the bowel and violent diarrhoea plus all the other usual symptoms. After various unpleasant tests Endometriosis was thought to be the cause again and I was put on a course of danazol. As soon as I stopped taking the Danol, the pain and diarrhoea started again. I was reluctant to have the other ovary removed and the consultant was reluctant to operate again. However, after 4 months on Selenium the pain is much relieved, the diarrhoea has stopped and I feel very much better in myself. The consultant is delighted and has suggested that I keep as far away from him as possible!*'

Cilla, Hertfordshire

'*I have been meaning to write my 'How I got Better' story ever since I came 342nd in our local 10 mile race. For me that day represented my fight to come to terms with my laparoscopy, laparotomy and the subsequent 15 months of hormones as well as the two stone I'd put on in weight. My body had been hurt and confused. I then felt distorted by the treatment. All the pain I'd had and then the surgery and drugs told me that I was ill but when I started to run I began to feel strong and healthy—better than I'd ever done before! I was learning to listen to my body, respect it and appreciate it ... When I talk to women facing similar problems now I get echoes of my own frustration and anger during the long months of diagnosis and treatment. You want to have faith each time round, but it is so hard. Why me? Can I cope? What if? In the end I did find the right treatment for me (a high dose of Primolut N). The ones that didn't help me have helped others ... Through my running I was trying to come to terms with my experiences of pain, disability and depression in my own way. Other women have found other ways to deal with the perfectly natural feelings that Endometriosis arouses. I hope that we can continue to share these experiences and help each other through the Society. We may only be 342nd at the end of the journey but we'll get there in the end!'*

Caroline, York

Sometimes it is necessary for the newsletter to record unforeseen disappointments and discouragements. In the newsletter for March/April 1984, Ailsa wrote 'Of the several thousand endometriosis sufferers who've now been in contact with us, we cannot recall hearing from anyone in dire trouble after the natural menopause because of Endometriosis.' However, the Cambridge group soon began to tell us that, contrary to received medical opinion, they had members who still had problems after the menopause. Others had had both ovaries removed and were still suffering. At first the Society couldn't see how Endometriosis could continue with no oestrogen to sustain it, but after a while we began to realise that there were other factors involved. If a little ovarian tissue remains after oophorectomy, or if hormone replacement therapy is given, this may start off the Endometriosis. However, pain may also be due to all the internal organs being stuck together by adhesions caused by both years of Endometriosis and surgical interventions. We discovered through Dr Brush that a number of women felt awful because their thyroid levels were low, and taking thyroxin (though probably for life) helped enormously. This left a small group of women whose Endometriosis is probably sustained because their bodies continue to produce oestrogen in small amounts after the ovaries cease working at the menopause. In their case, steroids produced by the adrenal glands are metabolised into oestrogen by the body's fat deposits (not that they're fat) and this keeps the disease going. For many women this means that the natural menopause is trouble-free, but for some with Endometriosis it can, rarely, make things hard, especially when their doctors do not see that it is possible. It may be that alternative therapies offer the best hope in this sad situation.

Twice a year the Society holds a workshop for 40–50 members. These have mostly been at the King's Fund Centre in London, but in 1987 we had a successful day in York. Participants enjoy the friendly atmosphere and the support of other Endometriosis sufferers as well as talks from practitioners of both orthodox and alternative medicine. There is also the opportunity to buy publications, including books not easily available, and useful vitamin, mineral or herbal remedies, such as Selerium ACE, Efamol, Agnus Castus and D-L phenylanine—a natural painkiller—which the Society is able to supply at a reduced price.

Information

Over the years the Society has produced a number of leaflets and information sheets for members and professionals. These include general information and specific sheets on topics such as Infertility, Danazol, Hormone Replacement Therapy, *in vitro* Fertilisation, Hysterectomy, Alternative Medicines, Yoga, Covenant-giving and lists of penpals, useful books and people willing to discuss particular experiences.

There is also information on the Society and its work, an annual report and advertising material. Most recently, recognising that her GP is usually the first point of call for a woman seeking diagnosis for the condition, the Society's Coventry group has published a collection of short scientific papers, specially commissioned, and aimed at providing professionals with more up-to-date information about Endometriosis, so that they can recognise when their patients may have it. It has been distributed free to G.P.s in a number of areas and, since the first print-run of 4000 has now all been sent out, is being reprinted for further distribution.

A display on Endometriosis and the work of the Society commissioned in 1986 has been well-received at exhibitions and talks, such as a study-day on Endometriosis for the Royal College of Nursing.

Local Groups

For many women, their main contact with the Society is through one of the 60 or more local contacts and affiliated groups. These vary considerably—from one woman in a rural area keeping in touch with local women by telephone or letter, to large groups with 200 or more members in Lincoln and Coventry. Often they are started and maintained by the enthusiasm of one or two women and their activities may fluctuate according to their state of health. One group leader writes 'I admit that sometimes the tremendous amount of work that goes into running the group gets on top of me, especially when feeling ill, but . . . I must admit to feeling pleased with what has been achieved in the past year.'

The most common activity for local groups are meetings in which Endometriosis sufferers can share their experiences and offer mutual support. Members are recruited through local hospitals and doctor's surgeries, and publicity in local press and radio. Groups have become involved in campaigns to inform women about the disease, to raise awareness among doctors and nurses and to distribute locally-based information. Some have held workshops, while others have established strong relationships with supportive consultants and G.Ps, sometimes helping to raise money for much-needed hospital equipment or campaigning against the loss of NHS facilities.

Leaders of local groups are supported as much as possible by the small central organisation of the Society. They are provided with a Starter Pack of suggestions on running a group, invited to occasional Organisers' workshops and can always find helpful advice from Ailsa at the end of the telephone. Leaders of officially affiliated groups can also now be supplied with up-to-date lists of members in their area, through the computerised system. The conscientious work of many women allows the local groups to provide a network of mutual support to sufferers throughout Great Britain. Indeed, three of the national trustees are now women who are also deeply involved in the Coventry and Lincoln groups, bringing together local and national concerns.

Research

From its earliest days, like the American Association, the Endometriosis Society has had a concern for improving research into the disease and its treatment, causing questions to be asked in Parliament about the lack of work being done. Over the years, the Society has made contact with most of the doctors in this country concerned about research into Endometriosis, and many have spoken at our workshops. Through the newsletters sufferers have been recruited to take part in trials of new drugs such as Gestrinone and the GnRH analogues discussed in this book. (At the moment this is usually the only way that women who have had no success with other drug treatments, or who cannot tolerate their side-effects, have access to these therapies.) We hope that a trial on the effectiveness of Efamol will start soon. In addition to research into treatments, there is also a need to investigate the basic causes of Endometriosis and its adverse effects on patients. Accordingly, the Society has established a small fund to help finance basic research. At the moment it is helping to support a research student, working with Dr Michael Brush, a biochemist at St Thomas's Hospital, looking into the prostaglandin content of Endometriosis tissue and its role in causing inflammation, adhesions and pain in the sufferer. (Dr Brush has already published work on the large proportion of women with auto-antibodies to thyroid hormone among Endometriosis sufferers from the Society.) Other research projects are being considered for support.

The Society has been collecting information on members' experiences of the disease and its treatment from its beginning, the most recent survey being the computer analysis of 726 questionnaires.

THE BRITISH ENDOMETRIOSIS SOCIETY: SELECTED QUESTIONNAIRE RESULTS

As the article here describes, the British Endometriosis Society distributed questionnaires asking women with endometriosis about their experiences with the disease and its treatment. In the January/February 1986 newsletter, the Society reported these findings from 726 questionnaires:

- 94% of the 726 mentioned they had painful periods. (97% of the American Endometriosis Association sample from Data Study I of 365 women reported pain with their menstruation.)
- 66% of these reported the pain as severe; 22% as moderate; only 6% as mild. (The E.A. questionnaire was more graduated: severe, 34%; moderate to severe 23%; moderate, 21%; mild to moderate, 3%; mild, 6%; mild to severe, 13%.)
- 57% experienced pain at any time, not just at the time of their periods. (62% of the E.A. group reported this.)
- 55% reported painful sex. (59% of the E.A. sample reported painful sex.)
- 37% reported back pain during periods and 42% reported it most of the time. (48% of the E.A. group reported lower back pain.)
- 41% suffered problems with infertility. (47% of the E.A. group reported this.)

77% reported swollen abdomen; 77% experienced painful ovulation; 72% loss of stale brown blood during periods; 67% premenstrual tension; 63% depression; 62% loss of large clots during period; 26% painful urination; 21% insomnia and 32% sleeplessness due to pain; painful defaecation was reported by 48%. (The latter symptoms are not directly comparable to the American results because of differences in the questionnaires.)

Subsequent newsletters have carried further reports on women's experiences of treatments for the disease, their side-effects and the process of medical consultation. Questionnaires are no longer being distributed to first-time enquirers, but more data remains to be derived from the analysis of these 726.

The Society's results paralleled the results from the Association's data registry and the Australian Association's study, (see Table p. 253) in finding that women had symptoms at a much younger age than is, in general, noted in the medical literature, with British and Australian women reporting their first experience of the disease at an even younger age than the Americans. The British and Australian data also show the very distinct pattern of how diagnosis follows the beginning of symptoms by many years.

Such findings have led the Society to question the common medical view (still taught to medical students) that endometriosis is primarily a disease of white, middle-class women in their 30's, who have delayed having children. (The so-called 'Career-Woman's Disease.') The gap between age of onset and age at diagnosis is a measure of the difficulty women experience in getting the condition properly identified. In Britain this depends on one's ability to persuasively and persistently use the medical system. This may effectively deny access to adequate diagnosis and care to black, teenaged and other less-advantaged women. The medical stereotype so created helps to further discriminate against recognition of endometriosis in these sufferers.

Other studies have been on particular topics, such as the effects of pregnancy and breast-feeding on remission of endometriosis. (Our research so far would not support the idea that having a baby is an instant cure!) One of the trustees is painstakingly collecting information on uncommon but damaging side-effects of danazol, such as permanent problems with joints, and the possibility of polycythaemia—a dangerous increase in the number of red blood cells. This reflects the Society's concern for the very widespread use of an extremely powerful but not completely understood drug, sometimes without a proper respect for the patient's circumstances, contraindications or adverse effects experienced. A further study is on the possible reason for the severe pain in the left-hand side of the rib-cage often reported by women with Endometriosis. Research into cyclic variation in body temperature is also underway.

Other Activities

The Endometriosis Society maintains links with sufferers from the disease all over the world and values its connection with the US. Association and the Australian group. It also has contact with many other support associations, setting up all over the world, in places as far afield as Bermuda, New Zealand and West Berlin. Links with the medical communities in other countries were considerably strengthened when 4 of the trustees, with help from sponsors, were able to attend the first International Medical Symposium on Endometriosis at Clermont-Ferrand, France in Nov. 1986. A great deal was learnt from the 70 or more leading researchers who contributed to the event. However, the Society was also able to demonstrate the contribution that can be made by self-help organisations, by presenting three papers in the subsidiary programme (on some of our survey results, the work of self-help groups and emotional aspects of Endometriosis) and a display of the Society's work. We were also participators in the discussions and questions throughout the event. We hope that some members will be able to attend the next symposium in Houston, Texas in 1989 and we look forward to meeting more of our sisters from the US–Canadian Endometriosis Association at that time. In the Spring of 1984 we were delighted to meet Carol Levantrosser who presented us with a copy of Julia Older's book 'Endometriosis', inscribed 'Presented as a small token of our appreciation for your work. In sisterhood, the Endometriosis Association.' We hope to be able to strengthen these links and to re-echo Carol in saying, 'I can hardly express the excitement I felt in being in another country where I could meet with a sister organisation devoted to the support of women with Endometriosis.'

Lesley Mabbett has been involved with the Endometriosis Society since its inauguration and is one of the trustees. She has studied Microbiology, has a Master's degree in Community Medicine and has worked as a Health Education Officer, co-ordinated a mental health charity and been active in planning and campaigning for improved health services. She is currently expecting her second child.

Foreword

By Camran Nezhat, M.D., F.A.C.O.G.

Endometriosis is a common disease, affecting approximately 5.5 million women in the United States and Canada and millions more around the world. The symptoms, including pain, nausea, vomiting, diarrhoea, fatigue, and low-grade fever, can be severe. In addition, endometriosis is one of the major causes of infertility in the world today. When left untreated, the consequences of the disease can be devastating, including the sorrow of not being able to have a child, ruined relationships, and limited financial resources.

In medicine today it sometimes seems as if we are able to do the impossible. Just a few years ago conquering endometriosis *did* seem impossible. Now, to some extent, it has yielded to us, though not completely. But with intense commitment and lots of hard work we shall get there!

When Mary Lou Ballweg, President of the U.S.–Canada Endometriosis Association, asked me to write the Foreword to this excellent volume, I wondered how best to do it. I have decided to share with you some of my current ideas about endometriosis and then to tell you about my involvement with the Endometriosis Association—how it started, why it is so important to me, and what I believe the Endometriosis Association stands for. Some of my ideas are new and may seem to be revolutionary. Some may even fly in the face of the medical establishment and step on some toes. But then just a short time ago no one believed that Stage IV disease and large endometrial cysts could be treated through the laparoscope, and we now do these things routinely in my practice. And if the Endometriosis Association had not flown in the face of the medical establishment on several issues, it would not have made the excellent progress that it has made.

There is still a great deal of debate going on about the aetiology (cause) of endometriosis. As you may know, there are three main theories. The most widely accepted and attractive theory is that of retrograde menstruation. This theory states that the retrograde (back through the fallopian tubes) flow of menstrual blood causes a spread of endometrial cells in the pelvis and abdomen. These cells then implant, and under the influence of the body's hormones, grow and produce symptoms of endometriosis. This theory has been supported by several lines of experimentation: (1) In monkeys, when the cervix was transposed, menstrual flow found its way into the peritoneal cavity. Months later, endometriosis was found in these monkeys. (2) In some women back flow of menstrual blood into the pelvis has been observed through the fallopian tubes during laparoscopy. (3) Fragments of endometrium are viable (alive) and can grow. This has been proven by experiments with these fragments in tissue culture.

It is my belief that the theory of retrograde menstruation does not explain *all* cases of endometriosis, but it *does* explain cases of superficial endometriosis of the organs or endometriosis that arises later in life. In my opinion, this type of endometriosis responds well to hormonal therapy and pregnancy.

A second theory explaining the onset of endometriosis is that the coelomic epithelium (tissue in the embryo which develops into the lining of the pelvis) becomes transformed into endometrial-type glands, or even that there is a congenital presence of endometrial glands (i.e., these glands were present, in rudimentary form, since birth). Under the influence of certain substances (e.g., steroids), this tissue is stimulated to grow and bleed. I believe that this type of endometriosis responds very well to surgical removal and very poorly to medical therapy and pregnancy.

Finally, a third theory of the cause of endometriosis is that endometrial tissue travels through the bloodstream or the lymphatic system to various sites of the body—even distant sites such as the lung and nose. My belief is that this type of endometriosis is more unpredictable but usually responds well to both medical and surgical therapy.

So, while many of us have believed for several years that treatment of endometriosis needs to be tailored to the needs of the patient—e.g., childbearing wishes, severity of disease, etc.—maybe the specific mode of therapy needs also to be tailored to the aetiology of the endometriosis in that specific patient.

One of the pearls of wisdom that should be remembered about endometriosis is that it can be managed far better if it is diagnosed early and evaluated properly. Thus, both the patient and the physician should be on the lookout for signs and symptoms of the disease. Any of the following symptoms should be taken seriously: lower abdominal pain; dyspareunia (painful intercourse); progressively worsening dysmenorrhoea (painful periods); pain at the time of bowel movement, especially if cyclical with the menstrual cycle; lower back pain. Of course, infertility also should be evaluated thoroughly. While pain is usually most severe during the menses, it may also be present throughout the month. Some women have significant amounts of pain every day. The pain is probably due to stretching of the tissue of the peritoneal surfaces following bleeding into the cavities or by stretching due to gradual growth of the glands. Often, the degree of pain is disproportionate to the extent of the disease. Women with minimal amounts of disease may have excruciating pain, while those with large endometriomas (chocolate cysts) may be symptom-free. In many infertile couples, the only reason for the infertility is the presence of endometriosis. Some of these women have painful periods, while others have no pain. Their endometriosis is found at the time of a diagnostic evaluation of their infertility using the laparoscope.

A word must be said here about endometriosis in teenagers. Some people believe, erroneously, that endometriosis occurs only in older women. Nothing could be further from the truth. There are many very young women who suffer severely and remain undiagnosed because of the myth that endometriosis is the 'career woman's disease.' If so, I have seen several 14-, 15-, and 16-year-old 'career women' who have suffered unnecessarily for years, some of them since the onset of puberty. It is understandable that a physician may be reluctant to laparoscope a very young woman—for one thing, if the diagnosis is negative, the hospital review board may object strenuously. Hopefully, in the very near future, we will have a blood test for endometriosis that has a high degree of accuracy. Until then, I believe that young women with severe menstrual pain should be evaluated thoroughly for endometriosis, including the use of laparoscopy.

As with most other areas concerning the disease, the treatment of endometriosis has been the subject of a great deal of controversy: When should medical therapy alone be used? When should medical therapy be combined with surgery? When should laparotomy be performed, and when can the disease be treated effectively through the laparoscope? And even, should a patient with mild to moderate disease be treated at all if it does not cause infertility?

First, let me say that I believe that endometriosis should *not* be left untreated no matter how 'mild.' And here we come to another interesting question. Is 'mild' *really* mild? Much of the confusion concerning proper treatment of the disease may result from the fact that the current system of classification (American Fertility Society, 1985, revised from 1979) puts very heavy emphasis on ovarian disease and tubal scarring and very light emphasis on disease of the bowel and other organs. For example, a 3 cm endometrioma receives 20 points according to this classification scheme, while a lesion 6 cm or greater on the bowel receives only 6 points. A patient could have extensive involvement of the bladder, rectum, and pelvic and abdominal wall and still be classified as *mild*. In my opinion this is very misleading. Deep involvement of the rectum and bladder is severe disease and should be treated as such. So maybe it is time for the classification scheme to be revised once again.

To emphasize something I said earlier, proper treatment of endometriosis begins with thorough evaluation and should be individualized according to the needs of the patient. At the present time excellent diagnostic laparoscopes are available to all physicians. Both typical and atypical patches of endometriosis can be visualized clearly with these scopes and should be treated. Fibrous tissue (so-called 'burned-out' endometriosis) should not be ignored but should be treated surgically. I am not going to discuss treatment extensively here. Many of the pages of this volume provide an excellent discussion of the available modes of therapy. Once again, however, I would like to make a special remark about the young woman with endometriosis. After diagnosis and possible laparoscopic treatment of the disease (via laser, knife, or cautery) I believe that her cycle should be suppressed medically until she is ready for childbearing. Perhaps, in this way, we can avoid the many heartbreaking cases of infertility in women in their twenties who have had endometriosis since their teenage years.

So far I have discussed many areas of confusion and controversy. Is there any good news about endometriosis? Actually there is, and that good news is the Endometriosis Association. I believe that the Endometriosis Association has been one of the major factors in the education of patients, the general public, and even (in some cases) physicians.

My involvement with the Endometriosis Association began in April 1985, when Dr Maria Menna Perper, former president of the Greater New York Chapter, invited me to New York to speak about my work with videolaseroscopy. Much of what I know about the Association comes from my close contact with this chapter and its former president, from my conversations with Mary Lou Ballweg, and from the newsletter, many examples of which are included in this volume.

The Endometriosis Association stands for a high degree of professionalism in its efforts to promote education and support. It stands for improving the doctor-patient relationship—making it truly a partnership so that the best treatment decisions can be made. And it stands for providing empathetic and compassionate support at all times for its members, their families, and even their medical advisors. (When Mary Lou Ballweg very kindly asked me to write this Foreword, there was a very tight deadline, and I had several travel commitments. Dr Perper has provided extensive help with the writing and editing of this Foreword as she did with the article on laser laparoscopy, which was written under similar circumstances and appears later in this volume.) And, finally, the Endometriosis Association stands for *not* standing still for the status quo. Conventional medical treatment is not good enough just because it is conventional. When new treatments come along, even if they are unorthodox, the Association educates about them if they work.

All in all, the Endometriosis Association stands for everyone working together to find the best answer for the disease. The recent media campaign has brought the message about endometriosis to millions of people. Almost every woman now has heard of the disease and knows where to get information about it. One of the biggest contributions of the Association is the newsletter. Recent research developments are brought to the members of the Endometriosis Association almost before they are received by many physicians.

This book, which contains many articles from previous newsletters, provides an overview of selected topics on the diagnosis and treatment of endometriosis. It should help patients become better partners with their physicians in conquering the disease and brings closer the day when we can put endometriosis to an end.

Dr Nezhat is a widely known Atlanta physician who uses video laser laparoscopy to treat endometriosis, from mild to severe cases. He has given numerous talks on the subject in the U.S., Canada, and Europe and has been conducting workshops for years to train gynaecologists in using video laser laparoscopy. Dr Nezhat is the director of the Fertility and Endocrinology Center in Atlanta and has been an advisor to the Endometriosis Association since mid-1985.

Authors' Note

The Endometriosis Association is an independent organization for those with the disease, governed primarily by those with the disease, and independent of vested interests. The contents of this book are not to be construed as medical advice, nor is the book a substitute for proper medical treatment. Unless clearly stated as such, treatment options are not recommended by the Endometriosis Association. The Association does not promote any drugs, treatments, or specific theories about endometriosis unless clear evidence of their efficacy emerges.

Letters published reflect the experience and/or opinions of the writers. Publication in the text does not constitute endorsement of the letter writers' opinions or verification of their experiences. Likewise, articles published in the text reflect the research, experience, and opinions of the individual authors. The Endometriosis Association neither endorses nor disclaims specific theories or treatment recommendations in the articles unless such endorsement or disclaimer is specifically stated. 'Alternative' therapies are included so as to present all possible treatment options to the readers. No endorsement is intended, nor should an 'alternative' therapy be undertaken without consultation with a qualified medical practitioner.

Acknowledgements

To Mary Lou Ballweg and Carolyn Keith for founding the Association; Bread and Roses Women's Health Clinic, Milwaukee, for their assistance in the early years; Dr Karen Lamb, the fairy godmother who helped us establish the data registry from which so much of our information on endometriosis came. Also, to our advisors—gynaecologists Rita Marino, M.D.; Harold Borkowf, M.D.; the late Richard Mattingly, M.D.; W. F. (Dub) Howard, M.D.; Lyle J. Breitkopf, M.D.; Robert W. Kistner, M.D.; and Camran Nezhat, M.D.; preventive medicine and self-help specialist Ric Biek, M.D.; medical sociologist Suzanne Morgan, Ph.D.; and Karen Lamb, R.N., Ph.D.

We would also like to acknowledge the Medical College of Wisconsin, which provided tremendous support in our research programme, and GeorgAnna and Joseph Uihlein, Jr., who partially supported our research through a philanthropic award to the Medical College of Wisconsin.

We deeply appreciate the critical financial support of the following in our early years: Mary Lou Ballweg, who contributed thousands of volunteer hours in the first 2½ years of developing the Association and then left her own business to work for the Association at low pay (and sometimes no pay at all!); Jim Dorr, who, along with Mary Lou, contributed the office space at the headquarters so no rent was needed; and once again, Dr Karen Lamb, whose tireless efforts and ability to obtain resources helped in so many ways.

To Winthrop Laboratories, Inc., for a number of outreach grants and an advertising campaign that has helped us reach thousands of women; to our wonderful lifetime member, Tracy Dickinson, and the Fairchild Foundation for helping with timely and important financial support. And to the hundreds of women with endometriosis who made contributions year after year. They will never know how much their $10, $20, and $50 donations kept us going and our spirits up during the hard times!

We also wish to acknowledge the efforts of our early steering committees and the U.S. and Canadian board members who have served over the years, and our great chapters and support groups. We also gratefully acknowledge the contribution of Jayne Kennedy, actress and TV host, in the making of our public service announcement and other efforts to help us educate the public about endometriosis. And we would like to thank Nancy Surdy and the staff of the Endometriosis Association over the years, who worked to assist women with endometriosis under sometimes difficult conditions.

In the production of the book, numerous wonderful people were invaluable. First, the book would not exist without the ongoing efforts of Mary Lou Ballweg, who wrote many of the articles under her byline on weekends and evenings and was involved in the development and editing of almost all the other articles in the book. She also worked hundreds of hours in negotiating the book contract, working out copyright permissions, organizing the materials, editing, and attending to hundreds of other details too numerous to mention. Others who made a special contribution to the book include Dr Camran Nezhat, who, in addition to his magnificent and miraculous work with lasers for women with endometriosis, took time to prepare the foreword for this book with the assistance of Maria Menna Perper, Ph.D. Maria is a past president of the New York City chapter of the Association and former member of the U.S.–Canadian Board. We were also blessed with special volunteers such as Suzanne McDonough, who read all of the materials for the book and provided tremendous help in organizing the materials, as well as writing her wonderful column, 'Research Recap'; Lorraine Ashmore, who did endless hours of work on the index for this book and whose professional expertise as a librarian and indexer is deeply appreciated; Jody Ranbarger, who literally volunteered days (and nights!) of her time to help us with the difficult task of last-minute editing and proofreading; Sue Martell, who also helped with this job; and Sandy Hintz, member of the Association and literary agent, and Ellen Kozak, attorney, for their assistance on the contract and copyright issues. Finally, we'd like to extend our appreciation to the people at Contemporary Books for their work with us in producing this book.

Endometriosis Association

Section I. Introduction

Why the Endometriosis Association Was Started

By Mary Lou Ballweg, Cofounder and President

In 1978, I was flying high—travelling all over the U.S. on fascinating assignments as a freelance consultant for two communications/audiovisual/management consulting firms in Washington, D.C. After college, I'd been a feature writer and then, at the age of 24, the managing editor of *Investor, Wisconsin's Business Magazine*. Then I'd spent a year learning film making and audiovisual production. Next, launching out on my own, I'd been able to build a national business in communications, specializing in human relations.

Now I was doing wonderful assignments such as editing a speech for Buckminster Fuller; media travel tours in which I'd carry a story to every TV station, radio station, and newspaper in a city, a different city every day for weeks (what a great way to see the U.S.!); and troubleshooting on assignments for the U.S. Department of Housing and Urban Development.

I had a marvelous job offer to manage communications productions for one of the consulting firms I worked with at a great salary. (I knew they were very serious about hiring me when they showed me my very own parking spot next to our office building!) But I hesitated about moving. There were professional reasons, but there were also nagging personal reasons. There seemed to be something wrong with my health.

It had started in the fall, when my cat had infested my apartment with fleas (which was especially strange because he was an indoor cat

1

and never went outside). I'd wake up in the mornings with as many as 20 flea bites on my legs. The apartment had been sprayed with insecticides several times. Since then, exhaustion had overtaken me, and even a vacation hadn't helped.

Somehow, it seemed, something related to the fleas, the insecticides, and the exhaustion had upset the balance in my body. (And my cat's, too, for in a few months he died of feline leukaemia.) Besides the fatigue, there were no clues about what was wrong except for the return of menstrual pain, a problem I'd had since the age of 15–16. (In my twenties, after years of careful attention to nutrition, exercise, and all-around healthy living, my menstrual problems had subsided.) I was chagrined at their return.

Then, suddenly, at the end of 1978, right after Christmas, I was sick. It didn't seem serious—sore throat, cold, and an intensification of the fatigue that had been plaguing me for months now. Little did I know that soon I was to be so utterly exhausted that taking a shower in a day would become an accomplishment. I slept endlessly, much as I had during my four-month battle with mononucleosis in college. It seemed as if I had been suddenly plunged into a dark closet without a clue as to what had happened, where I might find a crack of light or the door, or if there even was a door!

As the malaise continued and I sought medical answers, I was tested for mononucleosis, hepatitis, cat-scratch fever, and a number of other illnesses suggested by the symptoms of low-grade fever and swollen lymph glands throughout my body. But when these tests came back negative, the intern suggested I needed a vacation. 'A vacation?!' I said. 'I haven't worked for six weeks. What I need is to get back to work, not a vacation!'

If he and the other doctors I saw were at a loss to explain my illness, why not just say so instead of making me, already fearful and vulnerable, feel worse with the sly blaming and impugning of character? Couldn't they just say they didn't know? Why wasn't there a profession called 'medical detective' who'd help me track down the problem?

It was luck that at about that time I had my routine yearly pelvic exam. Because the swelling in my lymph glands in most parts of my body had begun to subside but not in my groin, I was beginning to feel this problem had something to do with my earlier health problems with my periods. I started reading up on women's health problems. Fortunately, I had good general resources because of my involvement some years earlier in helping to start a women's reproductive health clinic. In my reading and in meeting with my gynaecologist, the word 'en-dough-metree-o-sis' came up. I began to believe this long, ominous-sounding word might have something to do with me.

My gynaecologist didn't have much to say about it except that my symptoms were not typical of *en-do-me-tri-o-sis*, and besides, even if I did have it, there wasn't anything to be done for it except to put me back on the pill. (I'd been put on the pill before because of my severe menstrual pain, but serious and ongoing side effects always drove me off them again.)

I pushed for a laparoscopy to determine if it was endometriosis. After all, I couldn't go on without explanation, living on my disability insurance money of $250 a month and my dwindling savings! I felt alone and lost. My family, friends, and clients were concerned but as puzzled as I was. It seemed that as far as most of the healthy world was concerned, a person suddenly sick without answers could just slip off the edge of the world. To see such an active, alive, happy person suddenly become bedridden was too much for some of those around me—if something so befuddling could befall someone like me, they seemed to feel, something inexplicable and awful could happen to them, too. To accept the randomness and inability to explain such things was too fear-provoking. For example, a sister found solace in the belief that something like this could never happen to her because, as in the book *Getting Well Again*, she had complete control over her body via her mind. That hurt me deeply because she seemed to be saying I had allowed this disease into my body. A boyfriend, after asking if what I had was contagious, literally backed away from me and never called again to see me. Some friends, while understanding that I was sick, couldn't understand the *consequences* of being sick: exhaustion and pain can give no break for socializing; sleep becomes a precious commodity; and, for a while, you need others to help even though you might not be able to give back. These experiences superimposed more isolation and hurt on that already imposed by the physical illness.

I promised myself that when I was well again I'd do something to change that. How many others were out there like me, shut off from the active, healthy world, feeling lost and afraid, confused, unable to get help from the medical world, which seemed, at best, indifferent and, at worst, bent on demolishing one's self-respect along with one's health?

Finally, months into this puzzling illness, the laparoscopy was done. Yes, I had endometriosis. Finally I had a name for my problem.

But the relief of having a label for the problem didn't last long. The more I read on endometriosis, the more I realized there were far more questions in this label than answers. In fact, there was almost nothing to read about it except in gynaecological textbooks and a smattering of small research studies, many so skimpy and conducted with so few research subjects that they wouldn't stand up to research standards in other fields (nor in endometriosis now, only seven years later). The texts and studies documented a history of confusion around the disease. They would state that a drug was beneficial for alleviating the disease in one edition, only to state in a later edition that it should not be used. It seemed that any hormonal drug that came on the market had been used for the disease—DES, methyltestosterone, Enovid, high-dose birth control pills, progestins, and now a testosterone-based drug, danazol. At least the last had been developed for endometriosis—previously the drugs were simply carried over from other areas and tried, for lack of anything else, on women with endometriosis. The chain of textbooks contradicted each other—use high doses of oestrogen; no, use low doses of oestrogen; no, use progestins; no, surgery is the only answer; no, pregnancy is the cure. Where science (what little there was of it for this disease) left off, speculation began.

It seemed, according to the texts, the disease afflicted white, well-educated, perfectionistic, thin 'career women'. My years of work on black/Hispanic issues and in the women's movement and my own experience in trying to obtain a diagnosis made me instantly doubt this. *White* women? Well, had they looked for it in black women and other women of colour? A review of research materials available showed they had not. (A 1982 study by Drs. Donald Chatman and Anne Ward disproved this stereotype with its findings of endometriosis in black teenagers.)

'Well educated'? I doubted it—if a woman like me, who perhaps fit the stereotype, had had to push for a diagnosis of this disease, how was it going to get diagnosed in women who didn't fit the stereotype?

'Perfectionistic'? Had they done psychological testing on these women? And even if they had, if only certain women were being diagnosed, how were they controlling for this diagnostic bias? I could find no studies—the 'psychological' profile of women with endometriosis was unsubstantiated speculation by a few doctors. Their speculations were picked up as 'truth' by media, and myth had begun.

'Thin'? Had any studies been done? After all, it's pretty easy to weigh people, and medical charts contain weight—a retrospective study could easily document the weights versus heights of women diagnosed as having endometriosis. Curiously, even such a simple thing had not been studied. Yet the statements were made as if this had been studied and documented. (In fact, the first study tracking height/weight in women with endometriosis was not published until 1986, and no difference in weight was found between women with endometriosis and those without it.)

'Career women'? It seemed this idea came out of the observation that endometriosis symptoms abated during pregnancy. (Of course—no periods!) From that observation to a belief that pregnancy would *prevent* it was a leap of faith. The belief that a state of pregnancy alleviated the disease was the reason doctors put women with endometriosis on the birth control pill—to induce a state of pseudopregnancy. But I had been on the pill for a total of nearly 5 years since the age of 19—the equivalent of 6.6 pregnancies.

And what about all those symptoms from the age of 15–16? Was I a 'career woman' at 16? And what if I *had* tried to get pregnant at 20? All the textbooks were clear on the fact that infertility was frequent in endometriosis. How did the doctors who started this 'career woman' idea know whether there weren't lots of women out there with the disease who had greatly wanted children and hadn't been able to get pregnant? And who knew whether there weren't thousands of homemakers hiding out at home, so to speak, with symptoms, who had been treated as I had—like a hypochondriac.

As I read I felt that the pieces of this puzzle just did not fit. I was determined to figure it out—I *had* to, after all. My doctor (thank heavens she was more informed than most) told me that I could expect more trouble with this disease in the future and put me on the birth control pill again.

By June, I was able to start working some again. The old problems I'd always had with the pill returned, but at least I wasn't confined to bed and my home most of the time. Things were looking up, and then I suffered a near-stroke. I was told that I could never again take the pill. Feeling desperate—but at least now with enough health to do something about the situation—I started searching for other women with endometriosis. I felt sure that some of them must have figured this out, could give me guidance, tell me the truth about pregnancy, the hormones used for the disease, and other aspects of it.

I asked everyone I knew if they knew anyone with endometriosis. Most people had never heard the word.

In the summer of 1979 my dearest friend, Jim Dorr, a trained group facilitator, started a self-help health support group in part to try to help me. I was the only one in the group who had a serious health problem. The group was a valuable experience for me, particularly the exposure to the self-help health philosophy of Dr Ric Biek, but participation in the group itself was emotionally devastating. For example, when exploring the importance of exercise, the group went to one of Milwaukee's beautiful parks containing a 'Vita-Course'—a series of exercises and exercise equipment placed throughout the park, complete with instructions. To my horror, I found that my once-strong body was still weak from the bout I'd just been through. I could do few of the exercises. But what hurt even more were the well-meaning statements from others in the group urging me on, telling me to try harder, and clearly indicating that they thought simple willpower could make my body do the exercises. I went home and wept. Healthy people, who probably took their health for granted just as I had before I was sick, seemed to regard their health as a matter of personal accomplishment. While this belief was comforting for *them*, it created more pain for those unfortunate enough, like me, not to be healthy.

I decided only a group of other women who'd 'been there' was likely to understand and provide the emotional support I needed to come to terms with this baffling experience of endometriosis. In the autumn of 1979, Carolyn Keith, also a member of the Feminist Writers Guild and then health education coordinator at Bread and Roses Women's Health Clinic in Milwaukee, asked me to do an in-service training session on endometriosis for the clinic staff. I described my experiences earlier in the year and what I'd learned about endometriosis in studying the medical and research literature. At the end of my talk, I said what I had really needed in my bout with endometriosis earlier in the year was a support group of women with endometriosis. Carolyn and Fran Kaplan, founder and director of Bread and Roses, said they'd help me start one.

And the rest, as the saying goes, is history. The group was an instant success. Within the first six months, word-of-mouth was spreading the news that there was a group of women with endometriosis in Milwaukee. Mail started coming in from all over the U.S. (and then from Canada and later other countries as well). The women poured out their hearts and souls in the letters and confirmed how devastating and misunderstood the disease had been for them, too. To keep up with the volume of mail, we started publishing pamphlets and articles that answered the most commonly asked questions, at least where there was any kind of 'answer.'

To find answers for the unanswerable questions (of which there were and still are dozens!), the group determined to push for research, even if we had to do it ourselves. By August we had our now-famous yellow brochure entitled *What Is Endometriosis?* in circulation as well as our comprehensive questionnaire for information gathering. This questionnaire, completed by over 300 women by October of 1980, represented more data than had ever been gathered on women with endometriosis! That so much could be done so fast showed not only the determination of this group of Milwaukee women but also how little had been done previously. Armed with solid information on the disease, we began to work to educate ourselves, other women with the disease, the public, and the medical community.

Key in this work (which continues to this day, of course) were wonderful people like the real-life fairy godmother, Dr Karen Lamb, whose work in helping us establish the data registry for research in endometriosis at the Medical College of Wisconsin is documented later in this book. Others who helped us tremendously were our medical advisors—people such as the late Dr Richard Mattingly, who at first told me on the phone, when he heard of the group, 'Aren't you women making a mountain out of a molehill?' He said pretty soon there would be a support group for people with fallen arches! However, when we invited him to come to speak to the group (he was, after all, author of one of the gynaecological textbooks in widespread use and internationally known as a professor of gynaecology) and he saw and heard the women and their husbands, he began to reassess the impact of endometriosis on people's lives. Eventually he became very supportive and helpful. Others were the wonderful, soft-spoken Milwaukee gynaecologist Dr Rita Marino, who in her quiet way helped us with her belief in us; the dedicated Dr Harold Borkowf; and, of course, Dr Ric Biek, whose leadership and concepts of self-help health were very important in developing our philosophy.

As we helped women around the U.S. and Canada, they, in turn, asked us how to set up support groups and chapters in their cities. Gradually, a network of members of the Association grew so that today women diagnosed with endometriosis need never feel all alone with the disease, as I did in 1979. Similar groups have sprung up in Britain and Australia, so women in those countries too now have help.

'So what happened to you with *your* endometriosis?' I can hear women with the disease ask. Back to the fall of 1979 to fill in necessary details. In fall 1979, Jim and I decided to buy a house and found a big, once-beautiful but now dilapidated one that intrigued Jim (an architect and builder) with its fix-up possibilities. The house gradually became a focal point for the Association because my office was there and there was ample room for steering committee meetings, volunteer activities, and, later, staff.

Despite a homoeopathic remedy I tried for six months, by the spring, as my doctor had indicated, the disease was indeed back. As the year wore on, the pain and disability increased. To make matters worse, my doctor had left the health maintenance organization in which I was insured.

Because of our endometriosis group, I now knew who the good

specialists in Milwaukee were for endometriosis, and they were not in my plan. However, I could not get out of my plan because no other insurance company, to my horror, would insure me, and the doctors in the plan would not refer me!

I started searching for information on coping with the situation, sought information on the doctors that it seemed I was going to have to work with, and spent time with a professional counsellor to sort out childbearing issues.

By the end of the summer, I was in extremely poor health again and this time with pain so bad that many times I couldn't get up and down the stairs in my house. Additional problems developed, including intestinal bleeding with my periods. A variety of procedures, including a colonoscopy, were done to explore whether endometriosis had invaded my intestines, but the results were inconclusive. By this time I had become so financially destitute that, at the urging of friends (who quite logically insisted I could not get well if I didn't eat), I went on food stamps. It was an intensely frustrating and embarrassing experience for someone raised, as I was, to be independent.

That memory and one of another day when I ran out of an over-the-counter painkiller (before I'd found my new doctor and got a prescription for codeine) still stand out as among the most painful memories in my bouts with endometriosis. Being broke and in excruciating pain, I called Jim at work and asked if he had any money in the house I could borrow. 'Only in my penny jar,' he said and told me that I was welcome to take whatever I needed. So, with several dollars worth of pennies, I went up to the checkout line in the grocery store. I was in such pain I couldn't stand up straight, and beads of sweat stood out on my face (a typical prostaglandin-induced symptom of dysmenorrhoea). I nearly broke down sobbing with pain and humiliation when the gal at the counter said she wouldn't take my pennies and sent me to the service desk!

Late in the summer, I tried danazol but unfortunately had to stop due to highly unusual side effects—intense trembling and shaking after every dosage and migraine headaches.

We began to move toward my first major surgery, at the end of September 1980. One diseased ovary and tube and extensive endometriosis were removed in the surgery. Through this terrible time in my life, the support and love of Jim kept me going. Our friendship blossomed into romance. The surgery got me back on my feet, and, although I was still in some pain, I found that ibuprofen (better known now by the trade names Motrin, Advil, Nuprin) reduced the level of pain so that I could work and carry out normal activities again.

I was taking this daily, as OK'd by my doctor, when—miracle of miracles—in January 1981 I became pregnant! I was overjoyed! Six weeks into the pregnancy, all the remaining pain was gone, and, despite five-and-a-half months of morning sickness, it was one of the most exciting and joyous times of my life. Our little daughter was born in October.

Despite breastfeeding, ovulation and pain returned in about two months. Rather than become completely disabled again, I had a hysterectomy and removal of my remaining ovary when our baby was six months old.

Although my doctor objected, I took no oestrogen replacement for the first eight-and-a-half months after the surgery. By this time, 1982, we knew all too many women in the Association with severe cases like mine who'd had a continuation or recurrence of the disease after hysterectomy and removal of the ovaries if they took hormone replacement immediately after the surgery. I was determined not to be one of them. Surgical menopause can be very immediate and difficult for many young women, but fortunately for me, I did not experience menopausal symptoms until nearly six months after the surgery, possibly due to carefully planned regimens of diet, exercise, and vitamins.

Eight-and-a-half months after the surgery, I started hormone replacement gradually so I could watch what was happening closely. First I used vaginal oestrogen cream and then graduated into oral tablets. At one point, I tried progesterone supplementation but found I didn't do well on it, possibly because of problems with *Candida albicans*, which emerged full-blown for me about three years after the hysterectomy. (Articles on this problem, common in women with endometriosis, appear in this book.)

Obviously, if my experiences had not also been that of thousands and thousands of other women, I wouldn't be writing this introduction to this book today. Even today, as hundreds of letters come to the Association every week, I still find it hard to believe that all this need, frustration, and pain was and is occurring and is so routinely ignored. I still find it hard to understand and believe that an estimated 70 percent of the women who come to us have been told at one time or another, in one form or another, that their symptoms are in their heads: 'psychosomatic,' 'hypochondriac,' 'frigid,' 'You're just the nervous type,' and so on and on.

The letters and accounts of experiences with endometriosis keep me motivated. And, if that wasn't enough, the fear that my daughter, who's had severe candidiasis problems since before the age of two, might develop endometriosis later is compelling motivation indeed! (If I had a son, I'd be concerned, too, as the types of immune system problems being found in women with endometriosis and the familial links in the disease, mean sons are likely to have some effects, too.)

I've been privileged to travel and meet many women with endometriosis all across the U.S. and Canada. One of the most beautiful trips was one I took in autumn 1986 to give a series of speeches and media appearances starting near the southern border of the U.S. at San Diego and going all the way up the West Coast to Seattle. On the flight from Milwaukee to San Diego, we flew over the plains and farmland of the middle of the U.S., then the sharp green and white peaks of the Rockies, then the softer rounded brown peaks of Utah, the rock spires jutting out of the Arizona desert, over the sharp ridge of the Sierras rising out of cloud cover to the lush beauty of San Diego just on the other side. But most exquisite of all was the Grand Canyon, its delicate pale pink and green ribbons of rock ringing the canyon. I thought back to the terrible pain when sometimes I hadn't wanted to live anymore because life had been so painful. And how glad I was to be alive at this moment! How I wished all women with endometriosis could be with me at this moment, I thought, seeing this beauty and realizing that life could be and would be this beautiful for them again, too. I thought of how the river in the canyon had cut away the rock to form the canyon. And I thought about how we, the women with endometriosis, are like that river.

Alone, we are powerless against this disease and the 'rock of ages' of taboo about women's bodies. We are but one drop of water. But *together* we're the river that can carve out the Grand Canyon, cutting through the walls of prejudice and taboo and ignorance. *Together* we can overcome endometriosis!

Mary Lou Ballweg began the Endometriosis Association, the first organization for women with endometriosis in the world, with Carolyn Keith in 1980. She serves as its president and executive director, a staff position she took on after giving more than 2,300 volunteer hours in starting the Association. She previously was one of the founders of the Margaret Sanger Community Health Clinic in Milwaukee and was managing editor of a business magazine and scriptwriter/director at a film production and public relations company. She operated her own business in writing, public relations, and filmmaking for seven years, managing numerous state and national accounts. Before endometriosis disabled her, she was a consultant for two East Coast firms and travelled extensively on national business.

The Endometriosis
Association: Who We Are

The Endometriosis Association is a self-help organization of women with endometriosis and others interested in exchanging information about endometriosis, offering mutual support and help to those affected by endometriosis, educating the public and medical community about the disease, and promoting research related to endometriosis. Ending the feeling of being alone, sharing with others who understand what one is going through, counteracting the lack of information and misinformation about endometriosis, and learning from each other are ways those affected by the disease help each other.

The Association is a single corporation with headquarters in Milwaukee, Wisconsin (U.S.A.), and members, chapters, and activities located throughout the U.S. and Canada. Elected officers guide the Association, with help and suggestions from an advisory board of medical professionals and others. The Association was the first group in the world dedicated to helping women with endometriosis. Similar groups have now started in Great Britain and Australia.

Meetings are held according to the wishes of the local chapter. Usually, some are planned to allow informal information sharing about endometriosis and support and help with problems arising from it. Other meetings offer speakers and presentations on endometriosis, self-help care, infertility, medical research, and so on.

Literature on endometriosis and related concerns is published regularly. A small library of materials on endometriosis is maintained.

And a data registry of individuals' experiences with endometriosis is maintained for research. The data registry is compiled of the detailed answers to a questionnaire about an individual's endometriosis history, treatments and results, and experiences with the disease. Members and subscribers receive a newsletter six times a year, and formal and informal Crisis Call listening/counselling services are available—members who are willing to listen and offer suggestions and help during times of pain, difficult decisions, or other crises due to endometriosis.

The Association also conducts research on endometriosis and serves as a clearinghouse for information on endometriosis. Researchers interested in working with the Association data registry (housed at the Medical College of Wisconsin) should write the Research Review Panel, Endometriosis Association, at the headquarters office, P.O. Box 92187, Milwaukee, WI 53202.

Section II. Treatments for a Stubborn Disease

'Can endometriosis be treated?' This is one of the first questions most women ask their doctors after being diagnosed as having the disease. The answer to the question is 'yes.' Treatment for endometriosis has varied over the years, but no cure has yet been found. Painkillers, hormonal treatments, and surgery all provide some remedy. This section of the book tells you about some of the current methods of treatment.

Chapter 1 introduces the readers to the basic facts known today about endometriosis. Pain is the most common symptom of the disease. Learning how to control pain safely and adequately is an important adjunct to a programme of treatment for endometriosis. Chapter 2 will help you work with your doctor on finding the most effective format for alleviating pain.

There are many myths surrounding the use of hormones in the treatment of endometriosis. Since hormonal treatments are an important part of the current treatment arsenal, it is essential that you learn to separate fact from fiction. Armed with the information in Chapter 3, you will be able to work with your doctor in making the necessary treatment decisions. You will also learn about the latest in research on the new drug GnRH.

The word *surgery* often inspires fear. But women with endometriosis now have more options than in the past for surgical treatment, as explained in Chapter 4, and hysterectomy is just one of them. Fertility problems related to endometriosis are discussed in Chapter 5.

Finally, alternative treatments are discussed in Chapter 6. No particular claims are made for such remedies, but the chapter completes the picture of the current treatment options available. Indeed, the purpose of this section is to give you all the information needed to make informed choices.

"I am not Well enough to Work."

How often these significant words are spoken in our great mills, shops, and factories by the poor girl who has worked herself to the point where nature can endure no more and demands a rest! The poor sufferer, broken in health, must stand aside and make room for another.

The foreman says, "If you are not well enough to work you must leave, for we must put some one in your place."

Standing all day, week in and week out, or sitting in cramped positions, the poor girl has slowly contracted some deranged condition of her organic system, which calls a halt in her progress and demands restoration to health before she can be of use to herself or any one else.

To this class of women and girls Mrs. Pinkham proffers both sympathy and aid. When these distressing weaknesses and derangements assail you, remember that there is a remedy for them all. We have on record thousands of such cases that have been absolutely and permanently cured by **Lydia E. Pinkham's Vegetable Compound**, restoring to vigorous health and lives of usefulness those who have been previously sorely distressed. Here is one of them.

Miss Junglas' First Letter.

"DEAR MRS. PINKHAM:—As I have heard and read so much about your wonderful medicine I thought I would write to you and tell you about my sickness. I have been sick for four years with womb trouble, have whites, sick headache, pain in my back, and in right and left side of abdomen, feeling of fullness in vagina, am dizzy, weak and nervous. I have used many patent medicines, but found very little relief. Please give me your advice."—MISS KATIE P. JUNGLAS, New Salem, Mich. (May 4th, 1898.)

Miss Junglas' Second Letter.

MISS KATIE P. JUNGLAS

"DEAR MRS. PINKHAM:—I write to thank you for the good Lydia E. Pinkham's Vegetable Compound and Sanative Wash have done me. It is now six years since I was taken sick. I had falling of the womb and ovarian trouble, I suffered untold pains, sometimes was so bad that I thought I could not live. I used the Vegetable Compound faithfully and am now well. If you like, you may use my letter for the benefit of others."—MISS KATIE P. JUNGLAS, New Salem, Mich. (May 12th, 1900.)

$5000 REWARD

Owing to the fact that some skeptical people have from time to time questioned the genuineness of the testimonial letters we are constantly publishing, we have deposited with the National City Bank, of Lynn, Mass., $5,000, which will be paid to any person who will show that the above testimonial is not genuine, or was published before obtaining the writer's special permission.—LYDIA E. PINKHAM MEDICINE Co.

1
Endometriosis: The Basics

WHAT IS ENDOMETRIOSIS?
By Mary Lou Ballweg

Endometriosis is a puzzling disease affecting women in their reproductive years. The name comes from the word *endometrium*, which is the tissue that lines the inside of the uterus and builds up and sheds each month in the menstrual cycle. In endometriosis, tissue like the endometrium is found outside the uterus, in other areas of the body. In these locations outside the uterus, the endometrial tissue develops into what are called *nodules, tumours, lesions, implants*, or *growths*. These growths can cause pain, infertility, and other problems.

The most common locations of endometrial growths are in the abdomen—involving the ovaries, the fallopian tubes, the ligaments supporting the uterus, the area between the vagina and the rectum, the outer surface of the uterus, and the lining of the pelvic cavity. Sometimes the growths are also found in abdominal surgery scars, on the intestines or in the rectum, on the bladder, vagina, cervix, and vulva (external genitals). Endometrial growths have also been found outside the abdomen, in the lung, arm, thigh, and other locations, but these are uncommon.

Endometrial growths are generally not malignant or cancerous—they are a normal type of tissue outside the normal location. (However, in recent decades there has been an increased frequency of malignancy occurring or being recognized in conjunction with endometriosis.) Like the lining of the uterus, endometrial growths usually respond to the hormones of the menstrual cycle. They build up tissue each month, break down, and cause bleeding.

However, unlike the lining of the uterus, endometrial tissue outside the uterus has no way of leaving the body. The result is internal bleeding, degeneration of the blood and tissue shed from the growths, inflammation of the surrounding areas, and formation of scar tissue. Other complications, depending on the location of the growths, can be the rupture of growths (which can spread the endometriosis to new areas), the formation of adhesions, intestinal bleeding or obstruction (if the growths are in the intestines), interference with bladder function (if the growths are on or in the bladder), and other problems. Symptoms seem to worsen with time, though cycles of remission and recurrence are the pattern in some cases.

SYMPTOMS

The most common symptoms of endometriosis are pain before and during periods (usually worse than 'normal' menstrual cramps), pain during or after sexual activity, infertility, and heavy or irregular bleeding. Other symptoms may include fatigue, painful bowel movements with periods, lower back pain with periods, diarrhoea and/or constipation and other intestinal upset with periods. However, some women with endometriosis have no symptoms. The amount of pain is not always related to the extent of visible endometrial growths according to medical textbooks. Some women with extensive visible growths have no pain; others with a few small growths have incapacitating pain. This is one of the many puzzles of endometriosis and an indication of the lack of understanding of the actual disease process of endometriosis. Not all women with endometriosis are infertile, though infertility is a common result with the progression of the condition.

THEORIES ABOUT THE CAUSE OF ENDOMETRIOSIS

The cause of endometriosis is not known. A number of theories have been advanced, but no one of them seems to account for all cases. One theory is the retrograde menstruation or transtubal migration theory—that during menstruation some of the menstrual tissue backs up through the fallopian tubes, implants in the abdomen, and grows. Some experts on endometriosis believe all women experience some menstrual tissue backup and that an immune system problem and/or hormonal problem allows this tissue to take root and grow in women who develop endometriosis. Another theory suggests that the endometrial tissue is distributed from the uterus to other parts of the body through the lymph system or the blood system. A genetic theory suggests that it may be carried in the genes of certain families or that certain families may have predisposing factors to endometriosis.

Another theory suggests that remnants of tissue from when the woman was an embryo may later develop into endometriosis or that some adult tissues retain the ability they had in the embryo stage to transform into reproductive tissue under certain circumstances. Surgical transplantation has also been cited as a cause in cases where endometriosis is found in abdominal surgery scars, although it has also been found in such scars when direct accidental implantation seems unlikely. Other theories are being developed by the Association and others researching endometriosis.

DIAGNOSIS

Diagnosis of endometriosis is generally considered uncertain until proven by laparoscopy. Laparoscopy is a minor surgical procedure done under anaesthesia in which the patient's abdomen is distended with carbon dioxide gas to make the organs easier to see and a laparoscope (a tube with a light in it) is inserted into a tiny incision in the abdomen. By moving the laparoscope around the abdomen, the surgeon can check the condition of the abdominal organs and see the endometrial implants, if care and thoroughness are used.

A doctor can often feel the endometrial implants upon palpation (pelvic examination by the doctor's hands), and symptoms will often indicate endometriosis, but medical textbooks indicate it is not good practice to treat this disease without confirmation of the diagnosis through laparoscopy. Ovarian cancer sometimes has the same symptoms as endometriosis, and hormonal treatment (particularly oestrogen), which is common in treating endometriosis, could cause a cancer to grow even faster. A laparoscopy also indicates the locations, extent, and size of the growths and may help the doctor and patient make better-informed, long-range decisions about treatment and pregnancy.

TREATMENT

Treatment for endometriosis has varied over the years, but no definitive cure, other than hysterectomy and removal of the ovaries, has yet been found. Painkillers are usually prescribed for the pain of endometriosis. Treatment with hormones aims to stop ovulation for as long as possible and can sometimes force endometriosis into remission during the time of treatment and some months or years afterward. The disease recurs in most women, however.

Hormonal treatments include oestrogen and progesterone, progesterone alone, a testosterone derivative (danazol), and a new drug, GnRH, gonadotropin releasing hormone. Early study results indicate that GnRH, like other treatments for endometriosis, is not a cure, unfortunately. Side effects are a problem for some women with all hormonal treatments.

Because pregnancy often causes a temporary remission of symptoms and because it is believed that infertility is more likely the longer the disease is present, women with endometriosis are often advised not to postpone pregnancy. However, there are numerous problems with the 'prescription' of pregnancy to treat endometriosis. The woman might not yet have made a decision about childbearing, certainly one of the most important decisions in life. She might not have critical elements in place to allow for childbearing and childrearing (partner, financial means, etc.). She may already be infertile.

Other factors may also make the pregnancy decision and experience harder. Women with endometriosis have higher rates of ectopic pregnancy and miscarriage, and one study has found they have more difficult pregnancies and labours. Research also shows there are family links in endometriosis, increasing the risk of endometriosis and related health problems in the children of women with the disease.

Conservative surgery, either major surgery or through the laparoscope, involving removal and cauterization (burning) of the growths, is also done and can relieve symptoms and allow pregnancy to occur in some cases. As with other treatments, however, recurrences are common. A new surgical technique is laser laparoscopy, in which small incisions are made in the abdomen and a laser is used through the laparoscope to vaporize growths, cut adhesions, etc. Radical surgery, involving hysterectomy and removal of all the growths and the ovaries (to prevent any further hormonal stimulation), becomes necessary in cases of longstanding, troublesome endometriosis.

Menopause also generally ends the activity of mild or moderate endometriosis. Even after radical surgery or menopause, however, a severe case of endometriosis can be reactivated by oestrogen replacement therapy or continued hormone production after menopause. Some authorities suggest no replacement hormone be given for a short period (three to nine months) after hysterectomy and removal of the ovaries for endometriosis.

A NOTE ON THE PAST/FUTURE

We've come a long way in a relatively few years. It's hard to imagine a leading gynaecologist telling the Association today that we are making a mountain out of a molehill. Equally hard to imagine is the National

Institutes of Health setting aside money for clinical research on endometriosis, as they did in the early '80s, and having no researchers file proposals to utilize the money!

But we still have a long way to go. Treatments are far from easy to tolerate and afford. Support outside the Association can be hard to find. And research, while under way, is really just beginning.

Still, looking back at women 100 years ago, who had only Lydia Pinkham's Vegetable Compound or the doctor's leeches and opiates to 'help' them, we can see progress. Imagine what women 100 years from now will think when they read about us. Those women, our great-great-great-granddaughters, will find it hard to believe what we endured.

Nervous Breakdown

"I am so nervous it seems as though I should fly"—"My nerves are all on edge"—"I wish I were dead." How often have we heard these expressions or others quite as extravagant from some loved one who has been brought to this state by some female trouble which has slowly developed until the nerves can no longer stand up under it. No woman should allow herself to drift into this condition without giving that good old-fashioned root and herb remedy Lydia E. Pinkham's Vegetable Compound a trial.

Read the Letters of These Two Women.

North East, Md.—"I was in ill health four or five years and doctored with one doctor after another but none helped me. I was irregular and had such terrible pain in my back, lower part of my body and down each side that I had to go to bed three or four days every month. I was very nervous, tired, could not sleep and could not eat without getting sick. A friend asked me to take Lydia E. Pinkham's Vegetable Compound and I am sorry I did not take it sooner for it has helped me wonderfully. I don't have to go to bed with the pain, can eat without being sick and have more strength. I recommend your medicine and you are at liberty to publish my testimonial."—ELIZABETH WEAVER, R. R. 2, North East, Md.

Minneapolis, Minn.—"I was run down and nervous, could not rest at night and was more tired in the morning than when I went to bed. I have two children, the youngest three months old and it was drudgery to care for them as I felt so irritable and generally worn out. From lack of rest and appetite my baby did not get enough nourishment from my milk so I started to give him two bottle feedings a day. After taking three bottles of Lydia E. Pinkham's Vegetable Compound I felt like a new woman, full of life and energy. It is a pleasure to care for my children, and I am very happy with them and feel fine. I nurse my baby exclusively again, and can't say too much for your medicine."—Mrs. A. L. MILLER, 2633 E. 24th St., Minneapolis, Minn.

Nervous, Ailing Women Should Rely Upon

Lydia E. Pinkham's Vegetable Compound

LYDIA E. PINKHAM MEDICINE CO., LYNN, MASS.

2
Pain Medications for Endometriosis

By Patricia Doyle-Gordon, R.Ph.

'After 15 years of excruciating menstrual cramps and severe endometriosis, I have found relief for the menstrual cramps in an antiprostaglandin drug.'   Heidi, Bedford, Texas

'These past 10 months have been a total hell for me and my family and friends as well. They don't and can't understand . . . A lot of people think that I couldn't possibly have that much pain, but you and I know better. The sleepless nights, the crying, the pain pills, etc. Every so often the pain gets too bad for the pain pills to work, and I go to the emergency room, and they give me a shot of Demerol and send me home . . .

'I used to be so active. But not anymore; this disease is eating me and my personality alive.'   Christine, Connecticut

Various groups of medications are prescribed to relieve the pain and dysmenorrhoea that may accompany endometriosis. The use of pain relievers only alleviates symptoms. It does not treat the cause of the disease or change its course. Pain experienced by each woman varies and is not necessarily proportional to or a measure of the extent of the disease. When a physician diagnoses and treats the underlying endometriosis, he or she may also prescribe an analgesic (a drug to relieve pain) or an anti-inflammatory. Anti-inflammatories relieve pain by inhibiting the synthesis of chemicals involved in the intensity and frequency of uterine contractions and in causing pain. The purpose of this article is to discuss three major categories of drugs commonly prescribed or used in treating the pain of endometriosis as noted in the first 365 questionnaires in the Association's data registry housed at the Medical College of Wisconsin. These drugs are (1) aspirin and mild analgesics, (2) narcotics and related drugs, (3) nonsteroidal anti-inflammatories.

NONPRESCRIPTION ANALGESICS

Some women take aspirin or mild analgesics such as acetaminophen (Tylenol, Datril, Tempra, etc.). These analgesics are useful for pain of slight to moderate intensity. They are not addicting. There is some evidence that caffeine in combination with other analgesics increases their effect and reduces the amount of analgesic required, but this is preliminary. Caffeine is a drug and can have adverse effects in certain medical conditions (e.g., fibrocystic breast disease). Ask your doctor which brand of pain reliever he or she recommends for you. Also, read the ingredients listed on the label. If caffeine is present, you may want to avoid taking that pain reliever late in the day, or you may have difficulty sleeping.

Even though mild analgesics are available without a prescription, your doctor's recommendations on a pain reliever considering your personal medical history should be followed. If you are having problems with menstrual pain and have not yet seen a doctor, it is best to consult one to rule out underlying disease as a cause of pain and to treat the cause of the pain rather than just the pain itself. It will also allow your pain to be treated in the most effective manner.

Aspirin

Aspirin relieves pain by working in the brain and throughout the body at sites of chemical action (organs, tissues, joints, etc.). In addition to being a pain reliever, at larger doses aspirin is effective as an inhibitor of the synthesis of prostaglandins. These large doses of aspirin (usually given for arthritis) can be taken only under medical supervision because at this amount there is greater chance of stomach ulceration and adverse effects due to too much aspirin in the blood.

Here are some general guidelines for those taking aspirin on a doctor's recommendation for pain relief. Your doctor will recommend the best form of aspirin for you. Some specially coated aspirin (Ecotrin, Enseals) causes less stomach irritation and ulceration than buffered aspirin (Bufferin or Ascriptin) or than regular aspirin. It takes longer for coated aspirin to work; therefore, it is not the best choice for acute pain.

There may also be incomplete intake into the blood from the stomach. Slow- or sustained-release aspirin offers no advantage over regular aspirin.

Nonacetylated salicylates (Arthropan, Disalcid, Magan, or Trilisate) are related to aspirin and used for pain relief at times. Unlike aspirin, they have no effect on bleeding time, cause less incidence of stomach problems than aspirin, and are preferable for some patients with aspirin sensitivity. They can interact with other drugs, though, just as aspirin does.

Stomach upset caused by aspirin may be reduced by taking it with food or milk or with meals or snacks. Alcohol taken with aspirin can add to stomach irritation, especially if both are taken on a regular basis. Taking aspirin regularly for more than 10 days requires a doctor's supervision.

There are several warning signs that are important; if they occur, call your doctor. Extreme fatigue could be a sign in long-term regular aspirin users of chronic blood loss in the stools leading to anaemia. Ringing in the ears, difficulty hearing, vomiting, diarrhoea, dizziness, confusion, or weakness (lassitude) can be a sign your dose is too high. If you see blood in your stools or black, tarry stools, call your doctor.

If you have ever had an allergic reaction to aspirin or a nonsteroidal anti-inflammatory, nasal polyps, wheezing, asthma, hives, or allergy in response to certain drugs, inform your doctor before taking aspirin.

Aspirin has an effect on platelets, which are blood cells helping your blood to clot when you bleed. You may bleed more easily or for a longer period of time if cut while taking aspirin. You may also bruise more easily or extensively. Even one tablet of aspirin doubles bleeding time for as long as three to four days after taking it. Remember, when you stop taking aspirin regularly, you still may bleed and bruise easily for a while.

Aspirin interacts with many drugs. Inform each doctor, dentist, and pharmacist of every medication you take, even medications bought without a prescription. For example, if you have heartburn and want to take antacids (Mylanta, Maalox, etc.) even in the total amount of five to six ounces each day (about a glassful), you increase the removal of aspirin from your body severalfold. This may decrease its effect as a pain reliever for you by decreasing its time in your body. Some prescription drugs (such as anti-inflammatories and blood thinners, for example) are affected by aspirin in a significant way.

Children are sensitive to aspirin. Keep it out of their reach and in a childproof bottle. If you become pregnant or are nursing, stop taking aspirin immediately and inform your doctor. Aspirin may have harmful effects on your unborn child.

Acetaminophen

Acetaminophen, unlike aspirin, does not cause stomach irritation or affect bleeding time. It may be taken with food or milk. Before buying any medication in a pharmacy, or upon seeing any doctor or dentist, state that you take acetaminophen. Many medications (e.g., Tylenol 3, Empirin 3, and nonprescription cough and cold medicine) contain acetaminophen. Use of too much acetaminophen causes severe liver damage, which is aggravated by use of alcohol with the drug. Alcohol should be avoided when taking acetaminophen. If you are treating your own pain with any product containing acetaminophen, tell your doctor exactly how much you take and how often. If he or she recommends aspirin or acetaminophen to relieve your pain and it is not effective in the amount and at the intervals recommended, call and let your doctor know, rather than increasing the amount you take or the frequency of medicating yourself. You may need a stronger pain reliever, or your disease process may need to be reassessed. This also protects you against taking so much acetaminophen that you may damage your liver. If you plan to become pregnant, become pregnant, or are nursing, call your doctor, as caution is adviced.

NARCOTICS AND RELATED DRUGS

Some of the most commonly prescribed and used pain relievers for endometriosis are narcotics and related drugs. Examples would be codeine (in Empirin 1, 2, 3, 4 and Tylenol 1, 2, 3, 4), oxycodone (e.g., Percodan, Percocet, Tylox), meperidine (Demerol), and morphine. Narcotics are the strongest pain relievers for severe pain.

In discussing narcotics, it is important to realize that addiction (psychological and/or physical dependence) should also be explained. Psychological dependence may result from repeated use of certain drugs. The sign of this is compulsive continued use of a drug for its pleasurable sensations and to blot out psychological pain. It leads to a craving for the drug.

Physical dependence (addiction) is a state of the body in response to continued drug use. The drug is used compulsively, not for the pleasant sensations it produces, but to prevent unpleasant effects that occur when the drug is not taken. For narcotics this would be a flulike syndrome lasting a week or 10 days. The nervous system in the body has adapted to the continuous presence of the drug. Psychological dependence and addiction risk also depend upon use (legitimacy and medical supervision versus street use of drugs), how the drug is obtained (legally or illegally), and the social situation in which it is used (under a physician's supervision and only as directed for a valid medical reason versus street use). Psychological dependence is the most frequent cause of drug dependence and is the most difficult part of drug dependence to treat.

Factors influencing the risk of developing a dependence on narcotics are a history of drug or alcohol abuse in the past, or present abuse of drugs such as alcohol. Physical dependence on narcotics develops after two to four weeks of regular use, even at low doses. Postoperatively, while a woman is hospitalized, there is no concern regarding length of use or development of physical dependence. In fact, it is important at this time not to withhold narcotics needed for pain relief for fear of addiction. Pain is a legitimate reason for use of a narcotic under a physician's guidelines and supervision.

If your doctor prescribes your narcotic to be taken around the clock on a regular basis, take it as recommended. If your doctor recommends taking a certain amount at certain time intervals only when you need it for pain, it is important to follow these directions.

With long-term regular use, more of the drug may be needed to get the same pain relief as when you started the drug. (This is called *tolerance*) You and your doctor will want to watch for this. If you find you are not getting adequate pain relief, do not increase the amount of drug or take it more frequently or take it in any other manner than as your doctor directs. At this point, call your doctor and honestly discuss the fact that your pain relief is not adequate so that your doctor may work with you for effective pain control while minimizing risks to you.

Although narcotics provide pain relief, they also may cause some unpleasant effects. They may cause vomiting in some people. Vomiting and nausea may be reduced by lying down or keeping the head immobile for a while. If you still experience problems with vomiting, medications called *antiemetics* can be given to control this—let your doctor know. Drugs like Empirin 3 and Tylenol 3 are best taken with milk or food to decrease stomach upset.

Narcotics can depress respiration when taken in excessive amounts or when taken with other depressants such as alcohol, tranquilizers, and antihistamines (used in allergies). Alcohol should be avoided while taking narcotics. You will be less alert in activities such as driving, operating tools, etc., while taking narcotics and related drugs. It is best to avoid these situations while taking narcotics.

If you get dizzy while taking a narcotic, get up slowly when going from a lying to sitting to standing position (like getting out of bed). If it is still a problem, call your doctor.

Narcotics have an effect on the endocrine system. They also decrease urine output; commonly after surgery patients have difficulty urinating.

Safe use in pregnancy is not established. Call your doctor if you plan to become pregnant or do become pregnant. Caution should be exercised if you are nursing.

Narcotics affect the eyes. All narcotics except Demerol make the pupil of the eye smaller and constrict it like a pinpoint. This pinpoint pupil caused by most narcotics is an embarrassment. Your vision may also be affected. You may not be able to see as well as before taking the medication, and your eyes may tire more easily as a result. You may not want to get your eyes examined for new glasses or contacts while you are taking narcotics, because a change in vision may be only a temporary effect of the medication.

If your doctor recommends Demerol (usually postoperatively), your pupils will be enlarged. If you have glaucoma, it may raise the pressure in your eye to dangerous levels; tell your doctor before he or she prescribes it. If you wear contact lenses and must take Demerol, you will find your eyes will be drier. As a result, you may be unable to wear contacts as long or may need to use drops (artificial tears) more frequently. It is advisable to take glasses to the hospital instead. Your vision may also become blurred while taking Demerol.

In addition, Demerol can cause dry mouth, increased heart rate, excitement, delirium, and respiratory depression. For dry mouth, use ice chips or sugarless gum so you are not predisposed by sugar to an oral yeast infection.

Narcotics and related drugs release a chemical called *histamine*, which can cause itchiness (which is harmless but irritating), especially around the nose and face, but also anywhere in the body. It is still important to inform your doctor if this occurs, especially with rash, hives, shock, wheezing, or difficulty breathing, as it may also be a sign of a life-threatening allergy.

Because all narcotics cause constipation, a bowel regimen is important with regular use of narcotics. Increase your fluid and fibre intake and get regular exercise if possible. Your doctor may recommend a nonchemical bulk laxative (without stimulants) such as Metamucil on a daily basis, to prevent constipation. It is important to drink a lot of water while taking this, or faecal impaction may occur. If this does not relieve constipation, tell your doctor. He or she may recommend a stool softener to use in addition, such as Surfak.

If you have chronic bronchial problems such as asthma, inform your doctor before taking a narcotic. Narcotics make bronchial airways smaller and can make breathing difficult or aggravate existing lung conditions. If you have difficulty breathing after taking a narcotic, call your doctor.

Narcotics can also cause euphoria (feeling of pleasure) or nervousness or dysphoria (unpleasant mood).

Your doctor may use a combination of prescribed drugs (e.g., Tylenol 3, acetaminophen with codeine; Empirin 3, aspirin with codeine; or Demerol and Vistaril) to get increased pain relief for you. Before taking a narcotic, tell your doctor of any history of drug allergies, liver or kidney disease, alcohol or drug abuse, or of present drug or alcohol abuse.

NONSTEROIDAL ANTI-INFLAMMATORIES (NSAIs)

The drugs of choice for the pain of primary dysmenorrhoea and for some women with endometriosis fall into a class called *nonsteroidal anti-inflammatory agents* (NSAIs) (or *antiprostaglandins*). They are best in preventing pain when taken before pain is severe and as your doctor prescribes for your individual needs. Like aspirin, they work by inhibiting prostaglandins, but they have a much stronger prostaglandin-inhibiting effect than low doses (nonprescription) of aspirin. An imbalance of prostaglandins is the cause of pain, diarrhoea, nausea, and other discomforts of dysmenorrhoea and also may be the cause of similar discomforts in endometriosis.

Of this class, ibuprofen (e.g., Motrin and Rufen) is indicated (by the Food and Drug Administration) for analgesia and dysmenorrhoea. Naproxen (Naprosyn) is FDA-approved for dysmenorrhoea. There are also other anti-inflammatories your doctor may prescribe for pain of endometriosis and dysmenorrhoea: Feldene, Dolobid, Nalfon, Ponstel, Meclomen, Tolectin, Clinoril, Indocin, Oxalid, Tandearil, Butazolidin, Suprol.

Ibuprofen is now available without a prescription at lower than prescription amounts for limited use. Some nonprescription brand names are Advil and Nuprin. These nonprescription products are only for temporary relief of menstrual cramps at lower doses, not for continuous use. If you have persistent dysmenorrhoea, it is wise to see a gynaecologist to look for and treat the cause of the pain and rule out underlying serious disease. He or she may recommend the best pain reliever for you and the amount to be taken.

All of these drugs have high potential to interact with many other prescription and nonprescription drugs. Inform your doctors, dentist, and pharmacist of every drug you take. If you self-medicate after receiving a nonsteroidal anti-inflammatory, inform your pharmacist that you are taking one and ask for advice.

If you have ever had an allergic reaction to aspirin or another anti-inflammatory, tell your doctor before taking this medication, since this may increase your chance of an allergic reaction. Aspirin and anti-inflammatories are chemically related.

Kidney function is important with these drugs. If you have preexisting kidney problems, tell your doctor; close monitoring and dosage adjustment may be necessary. Anti-inflammatories are removed from the body through the kidneys.

Aspirin taken on a regular basis with an anti-inflammatory decreases anti-inflammatory activity and effectiveness by lowering its level in the blood. For most women, one aspirin occasionally for a headache will not significantly interact with an anti-inflammatory, but repeated use may cause problems. It will also increase the likelihood of gastric irritation.

Different brands of antacids can affect naproxen differently. It is best to take antacids only when needed on a short-term basis and to take naproxen and antacids about two hours apart.

All anti-inflammatories, if taken during a pregnancy, may cause difficult and delayed childbirth and can affect your unborn child. If you become pregnant or plan to become pregnant, tell your doctor and stop taking the drug. The drug is not recommended for nursing mothers.

Do not take more drugs or at shorter intervals than your doctor recommends. This could cause long-term damage, especially to the kidneys. Call your doctor if pain is not effectively controlled with the drug or amount prescribed.

If you have problems with intolerable side effects or do not feel you are getting a good response with one anti-inflammatory, inform your doctor. He or she may try another drug in the same category that will benefit you or not cause the same side effects. Individuals vary in response to each of the drugs within this class.

The most common side effect with nonsteroidal anti-inflammatories is stomach intolerance, but it is less with these drugs than with *high* doses of aspirin. Take your anti-inflammatory with meals, milk, or a snack to decrease stomach irritation. Anti-inflammatories may cause diarrhoea or constipation. A bowel regimen similar to the one for narcotics may be necessary, or a change in medication may be warranted. Consult your doctor if these symptoms arise.

Drowsiness, confusion, dizziness, lethargy, and even depression occasionally occur. Report these symptoms to your doctor.

Anti-inflammatories may cause blurred vision or changes in colour vision, or you may even see flashing lights in your visual field. These effects are rare, but your doctor needs to know if they occur. You may not want to have your vision tested for eyeglasses or contact lenses at this time because visual changes may be caused by the drug.

If rash, itchiness, and ear ringing occur, let your doctor know. Water retention (oedema) and weight gain may occur. Loss of appetite has also been reported.

All anti-inflammatories have the same effect on platelets as aspirin. You may bleed more easily and for a longer period of time if cut, and you may bruise more easily and extensively while taking anti-inflammatories.

Feldene occasionally causes increased burning in the sun or a rash in sun-exposed areas (photosensitivity). Talk to your doctor if this occurs; he or she may change your medication or recommend a sunscreen with appropriate chemical protection to prevent this.

Anti-inflammatories may be taken indefinitely as long as toxicity, kidney function, and liver function and disease progress are monitored by a physician. Like other drugs used in the treatment of pain mentioned here, anti-inflammatories do not affect the underlying disease state; they only treat the pain. They are more expensive than aspirin.

Severe liver reactions are rare from anti-inflammatories, less than 1 percent. The early signs are rash, sore throat, fever, easy bruising, or yellow colour in eyes or skin. Call your doctor immediately if you experience any of these symptoms.

Patricia Doyle-Gordon is a woman with endometriosis; she writes drug information articles for several organizations. She received her degree in pharmacy from the University of Wisconsin-Madison in 1981.

3
Hormonal Treatments

DANAZOL AND THE TREATMENT OF ENDOMETRIOSIS
By Mary Lou Ballweg

'*For nine months I was on birth control pills and danazol, which showed no improvement in this condition. All I felt was depressed. Now it has been decided that I should have an operation to excise this extensive disease.*'

Kathy, Sparks, Nevada

'*Since all traces of the disease could not be removed, I was put on danazol. My case was diagnosed as moderate to severe. After six months of medication, I was put into the hospital for a laparoscopy. Small traces of the remaining disease were burned off. A small area remained, and my doctor felt that three more months of danazol were necessary. In April, I went off medication. My period returned 30 days later. Two months later I discovered I was pregnant . . . my husband and I are overjoyed. Our baby is due in April.*'

Marie, Milwaukee, Wisconsin

'*I wonder how a man would react if he was told that he must take a medication that would shrink his penis and make his breasts grow. I have told both doctors that I am willing to try birth control pills but that I absolutely refuse to take danazol. They will not even discuss alternate treatments with me. I belong to an HMO and have exhausted all the possibilities. I am at a loss as to what to do, so I am doing nothing. I don't understand why these doctors insist that I take danazol. I also don't understand their reaction when I refuse their advice. I am not questioning their abilities as doctors, but I believe that the kind of treatment I get should be my choice. Is it possible that most people do what their doctors tell them without bothering to learn about what is happening to them?'*

Paula, Anoka, Minnesota

Danazol (trade name, Danocrine in the U.S.; Cyclomen in Canada), a synthetic testosterone derivative, is the most commonly used hormonal drug for endometriosis today. It is also used in the treatment of fibrocystic breasts (a condition in which normal menstrual cycle breast changes become exaggerated and may cause cyst development and pain) and hereditary angio-oedema. Hereditary angio-oedema is a disorder of the immune system in which abdominal organs, skin, mucous membranes, and the larynx (voice box) swell, due, it is thought, to food or other allergies.

Testosterone is in a group of hormones known as *androgens*, male hormones 'having the capacity to produce masculinity' (Jeffcoate, *Principles of Gynaecology*). Androgens are responsible for the function of the male reproductive system and secondary masculine characteristics such as facial and body hair and deep voice. In women, androgens depress activity of the reproductive tract; women normally produce a very small amount of androgens in their bodies.

Danazol has, according to research studies, three methods of action, although there is still disagreement among researchers as to what is absolutely known about how it works and what is not proven. First, it reportedly suppresses the release from the pituitary gland of FSH, follicle-stimulating hormone, and LH, luteinizing hormone. Second, it reportedly binds to receptor sites normally used by androgens and progesterone produced by the woman. Third, it apparently inhibits the production of hormones by the ovaries.

All of these methods of action disrupt the hormonal cycle and stop ovulation (at least when the drug action is effective). Without the stimulation of ovulation and all the hormonal changes that go with it, the endometrial tissue inside the uterus and outside of it becomes inactive, decreases in size, and wastes away. This effect on the endometrial tissue is of course, what is desired in endometriosis.

Inactivation and decrease in size of the endometrial lesions occurs, according to most studies, in the majority of women with mild and moderate endometriosis. However, the drug is not effective in resolving adhesions or ovarian cysts or in severe endometriosis, although it is sometimes used in these situations before or after surgery to clear small endometrial growths.

The dosage of danazol for endometriosis ranges from 400 mg a day to 800 mg a day. There is a lack of agreement among medical practitioners and researchers as to the best dosages in given situations and whether lower dosages result in fewer side effects. Some practitioners believe the dosage should be adjusted, starting high and going to a lower dosage or starting low and going to a higher dosage, depending on the woman's response.

Although ovulation generally stops while you are on the higher doses of danazol, the *Physicians' Desk Reference* recommends the use of a nonhormonal method of contraception while on the drug. Because of the potency of the drug and the history of very serious harm to the foetus with exposure to hormones, it would be most unwise to become pregnant while on the drug or immediately following treatment. (Ovulation might occur before the first period after going off danazol, so contraception would be wise then, too.)

Information from the manufacturer of danazol states that 'If the patient becomes pregnant while taking Danocrine, she should be apprised of the potential risk to the foetus.' The drug is typically started during your period to help ensure that you are not pregnant.

Another precaution stated in the drug company literature on danazol is that physicians should monitor patients on the drug for liver function by labouratory tests and observation. Liver dysfunction, shown by elevated blood levels of certain enzymes and/or by jaundice, has been reported in patients receiving a daily dosage of 400 mg or more of danazol, according to the drug company literature.

The most common side effects of danazol are weight gain; muscle cramps; water retention and bloating; hot flushes, dry vaginal lining, and other 'menopausal'-type symptoms; depression, irritability, and mood swings; and decreased breast size (the breasts return to their former size after discontinuation of the drug). Smaller numbers report oily skin and acne, fatigue, unwanted facial hair, decreased libido (although a few report increased libido), nausea, vaginal infections, headache, dizziness, insomnia, skin rashes, deepening of the voice, joint lock-up and joint swelling, and pain in the back, neck, and legs. One rare but serious side effect is carpal tunnel syndrome, compression of the median nerve of the wrist, leading to numbness, tingling, loss of sensation, and eventual muscle loss in the area.

Women should be alert for voice deepening, loss of frontal head hair, and enlargement of the clitoris, as these are side effects that may be nonreversible even after the drug is stopped. These latter side effects are rare. Most women report *some* of the above side effects; few experience lots of them. The long-term effects of danazol are not known.

Thousands of reports to the Association over the years indicate that women vary markedly in their reaction to danazol. Some report they never felt better, and others had difficulty with the drug, suffered side effects, or did not find their symptoms relieved. Most typical is the report, in the words of one member of the Association: 'To summarize my experience with Danocrine: it frees me from pain while I am on it, but after I stop taking it the pain returns.'

Description of Danocrine from the *Physicians' Desk Reference, 1986*: 'Danocrine, brand of danazol, is a synthetic androgen derived from ethisterone. Chemically, danazol is 17a-Pregna-2, 4-dien-20-yno (2,3-d)-isoxazol-17-ol. Inactive ingredients: benzyl alcohol, gelatin, lactose, magnesium stearate, parabens, sodium propionate, starch, talc. Capsules 50 mg and 200 mg contain D&C Yellow #10, FD&C Red #3. Capsule 100 mg contains D&C Yellow #10, FD&C Yellow #6.' (The *Physicians' Desk Reference* listed inactive ingredients of drugs for the first time in 1986. Women allergic to the dyes and other ingredients in the gelatin capsule may find removing the drug from the capsule helpful.)

RESEARCH REVIEW ON DANAZOL
By Maria Menna Perper, Ph.D.

Because, as with all hormones, the long-term effects of danazol cannot be known for decades, research findings are important to women with endometriosis and frustrating because they continue to be somewhat contradictory. The studies presented at the fall 1986 American Fertility Society/Canadian Fertility and Andrology Society convention exemplify the contradictions. One found that 'treatment with danazol more than doubles the expected fertility rate in mild endometriosis,' but another study found it ineffective in improving pregnancy rates in minimal endometriosis.

It is clear that more studies are needed. But at the present time, reviewing some of the existent important studies will help women with endometriosis understand more about the drug and, hopefully, assist them in decision making.

'Danazol in the Treatment of Endometriosis' reports on one of the largest early studies of danazol with one of the longest follow-up periods. The investigators analyzed 100 patients who had endometriosis documented by laparoscopy. The women were treated with danazol (800 mg daily) for varying time periods (the average being 17.3 weeks) and were followed up for approximately four years. The pretreatment symptoms were well known to most women with endometriosis: painful periods, 79 percent; pelvic pain, 69 percent; dyspareunia (painful intercourse), 42 percent; and menorrhagia (excessively profuse or prolonged menstruation), 27 percent.

Immediately after completing their course of danazol therapy, and before the 'second look' laparoscopy or laparotomy, the women reported the following pattern of symptoms: painful periods, 19 percent; pelvic pain, 18 percent; dyspareunia, 16 percent; and irregular bleeding, 25 percent. There was a dramatic reduction in the incidence of the symptoms in this group of women. The reduction in the severity of the disease as determined by a repeat laparoscopy or major surgery correlated well with the report of decreased symptoms—94 percent of the women were shown to have improved. A paradoxical finding of the study was that 20 percent of the women with Stage I endometriosis reported no improvement in symptoms while receiving danazol treatment, while 95 percent of the women with Stages II, III, and IV endometriosis reported improvement in symptoms.

Significant side effects were noted in 85 percent of the patients in this study. The major side effects were weight gain, oedema, decrease in breast size, oily skin, hirsutism (excessive facial and body hair), and deepening of the voice. The authors of the article note that 'since most women taking danazol will experience side effects, it is reasonable to review these effects with the patient' before starting the drug. After discontinuing danazol therapy, the average time before resumption of periods was four to five weeks.

A total of 33 percent of the women complained of recurrence of symptoms during the study or were noted to have had recurrent physical findings suggestive of endometriosis. There were 38 pregnancies in 26 of the 56 women desiring pregnancy, for an overall fertility rate of 46 percent. Out of the 38 pregnancies, 29 were full-term, 6 aborted (1 therapeutic and 5 spontaneous), and 3 pregnancies were in the second or third trimester.

The article by Guzick and Rock compares danazol and conservative surgery for the treatment of infertility in 224 women with mild or moderate endometriosis. Women treated with danazol received either 800 mg (72 of 91 of the women), 600 mg (8 of 91), or 400mg (11 of 91) daily and were followed up for 57 months after discontinuation of medication. Women who underwent surgery were followed up for 74 months.

There were no differences in the pregnancy rates in the two groups: 74 percent of the danazol group and 68.3 percent of the surgery group became pregnant within the follow-up periods. These differences are not statistically significant. In the danazol group 74.2 percent of the pregnancies resulted in term deliveries, 9.7 percent ended in spontaneous abortion, and 16.1 percent were undetermined. In the surgery group, 87.8 percent resulted in term deliveries, 1.7 percent were premature, and 10.5 percent resulted in spontaneous abortion.

A preliminary report of the conception rates following danazol plus surgery or surgery alone was presented to the American Fertility Society (April 2–7, 1984) by G. M. Grunert and R. R. Franklin. Forty women with moderate or severe endometriosis (diagnosed by laparoscopy) were divided into two comparable groups. One group was treated with danazol (800 mg daily) for three months and then underwent conservative surgery, while the other group had surgery alone. Of the 31 women with *moderate* endometriosis, 10 of 17 (58.5 percent) in the danazol-plus-surgery group became pregnant, while 3 of 14 (21.4 percent) of the surgery-only group conceived. These differences are statistically significant.

Of the nine patients with *severe* endometriosis, one of four (25 percent) in the danazol-plus-surgery group and two of five (40 percent) in the surgery-only group became pregnant. These differences are not statistically significant. However, the sample size is very small, and a definitive statement cannot be made at this time. It is possible that, with a larger size, the difference would have been significant.

Another report on danazol was presented at the April 1984 American Fertility Society meeting, this one by researchers V. C. Buttram and R. C. Reiter. Their finding was that in mild endometriosis, treatment with danazol alone resulted in conception rates that were only slightly lower than those obtained with conservative surgery alone. However, for women with moderate and severe disease, danazol treatment in the absence of surgery was not found to be effective. The administration of danazol (800 mg/day) for 6 months followed by conservative surgery, however, resulted in pregnancy rates that were 15 percent higher than those that resulted with conservative surgery alone. These authors found that preoperative use of lower doses of danazol was not as effective as administration of 800 mg/day.

A question of great importance for *all* women with endometriosis is the optimal dosage of danazol. Would lower doses, for example 400 mg, be as effective in relieving symptoms, and would the side effects be less severe?

The article 'Management of Pelvic Endometriosis With Low-Dose Danazol' reports on a study of 38 women with minimal, moderate, or severe endometriosis who were treated for 6 months with either 600, 400, 200, or 100 mg/day. The number of women in each group was very small, and, presumably for this reason, statistical analyses were not performed. However, except for very severe disease, there appeared to be no difference in the rate of symptom improvement or resolution of endometriosis at any dose level. The authors felt that the existence of ovarian cysts larger than 2 cm in diametre requires a full dose of danazol (800 mg/day). No discussion of adverse reactions was provided.

Researchers Buttram and Reiter conducted a five-year study comparing the efficacy and safety of danazol 800 mg/day (96 women) and 400 mg/day (107 women) over a period of six months. Interestingly, *there was no difference in the incidence of side effects at the two dosages.* (However, many clinicians *do* note differences in severity of side effects related to dosage.) The resolution of the disease was determined in 110 patients who underwent second-look laparoscopy or major surgery. The observed differences in resolution of the disease were related to extent of original disease rather than dosage of danazol. Endometriosis on the peritoneum (lining of the abdomen) or mild ovarian cysts (less than 1 cm) were resolved to a greater extent than larger ovarian cysts (greater than 1 cm). However, the resolution of the disease did not correlate well with subsequent conception rates.

Obviously, the full story on danazol is not yet in. Published research reports still tend to be somewhat contradictory. Moreover, additional adverse reactions continue to be reported. Besides carpal tunnel syndrome, side effects include in some cases *persistent* lack of periods (28 months) following discontinuation of danazol and, in one unusual case, irreversible voice changes. In this case, a doctor failed to note voice changes as a result of danazol and, as a consequence, did not stop danazol therapy immediately, which should have been done. And, finally, the long-term effects of the drug on women with endometriosis and their offspring are not yet known.

References

1. Barbieri, R. L., Evans, S., and Kistner, R. W. Danazol in the treatment of endometriosis: Analysis of 100 cases with a four-year follow-up. *Fertility and Sterility*, 37:737, 1982.

2. Buttram, V. C., and Reiter, R. C. Treatment of endometriosis with danazol—second interim report. Presented to the American Fertility Society, April 2–7, 1984. *Fertility and Sterility*, 41:21S, 1984.

3. Grunert, G. M., and Franklin, R. R. Preoperative Danocrine therapy as an adjunct to conservative surgery for endometriosis: A preliminary report. Presented to the American Fertility Society, April 2–7, 1984, *Fertility and Sterility*, 41:74S, 1984.

4. Guzick, D. S., and Rock, J. A. A Comparison of danazol and conservative

surgery for the treatment of infertility due to mild or moderate endometriosis. *Fertility and Sterility*, 40:580, 1983.

5. Moore, E. E., Harger, J. H., Rock, J. A., and Archer, D. F. Management or pelvic endometriosis with low-dose danazol. *Fertility and Sterility*, 36: 15, 1981.

6. Peress, M. R. Persistent amenorrhea following discontinuation of danazol therapy. *Fertility and Sterility*, 41:322, 1984.

7. Sikka, A., Kemmann, E., Vrablik, R. M., and Grossman, J. Carpal tunnel syndrome associated with danazol therapy, *Fertility and Sterility*, 147: 102, 1984.

8. Wardle, P. G., Whitehead, M. I., and Mills, R. P. Non-reversible and wide-ranging voice changes after treatment with danazol. *British Medical Journal*, 287:946, 1983.

Maria Menna Perper has a Ph.D. in biochemistry and is adjunct assistant professor of psychiatry at the University of Medicine and Dentistry of New Jersey, Robert Wood Johnson Medical School. She is a consultant on health-related issues. In 1984–85, she served as vice president-research on the board of the U.S.–Canadian Endometriosis Association. She also served as vice president, research and education of the Greater New York Chapter of the Endometriosis Association in 1984 to 1985; president of the Greater New York Chapter from 1985 to 1987; and as president emeritus of the Greater New York Chapter, 1987 to present.

GnRH (LH-RH) ANALOGUE: NEW DRUG, NEW HOPE?
By Suzanne McDonough

Like all people suffering from chronic, puzzling diseases, women with endometriosis have long been hoping for a cure for their illness or at least a safe, effective, and relatively side-effect-free drug to help treat their illness. For some women, danazol has been the drug to fit this bill: it has relieved their symptoms and allowed them to become pregnant. For others, danazol has afforded at best only a temporary respite from the disease, sometimes causing distressing side effects that some women have labeled worse than the symptoms of endometriosis itself. Many women have lamented, 'Isn't there something better?!'

If you have been following the Association newsletter and other endometriosis-related news in the past few years, you may have seen the terms *GnRH analogue, Nafarelin*, and other drug names mentioned as a new treatment for endometriosis. What is this drug? Is it the long-awaited wonder drug? A review of the articles here gives us some clues. But to really understand what GnRH is and whether it may truly help many women with endometriosis, it is necessary to review briefly a little reproductive anatomy and physiology.

As you may know, the pituitary gland is a structure located at the base of the brain that secretes, regulates, and stores a number of different hormones that affect the thyroid, reproductive organs, and many other areas of your body. The hypothalamus, also located in the brain, is attached to the pituitary gland by a 'stalk' and serves as a 'master switch' for controlling the production and release of hormones in the pituitary. Exactly how the hypothalamus and the pituitary gland work together and produce hormones is still not fully understood by medical researchers. However, much progress has been made, especially in recent years. For instance, it was only in 1971 that two researchers isolated and characterized the type of hormone that has given rise to this new drug for endometriosis. This hormone is called *luteinizing hormone-releasing hormone*, or *LH-RH* for short.

Back to the anatomy and physiology lesson: LH or luteinizing hormone and FSH or follicle-stimulating hormone are specific types of hormones produced by a part of the pituitary called the *gonadotrope*. Because they are produced by the gonadotrope, they are often called *gonadotropins*, hormones that have a stimulating effect on the gonads (ovaries and testes). FSH travels from the pituitary by way of the bloodstream to the ovary, where it stimulates the follicles (the sacs where the ova or eggs have been resting). These follicles begin to produce oestrogen, which, among other things, helps the eggs to mature. LH or luteinizing hormone, released after FSH, also travels from the pituitary to the ovary, where it causes the follicles to burst and release the egg. The leftover parts of these follicles (called the *corpus luteum*) now begin to release progesterone.

The hypothalamus comes into the picture as the structure that sends the signal to the pituitary to release FSH and LH. The signal itself is called a hormone and has been given *many* different names and abbreviations, which only makes it more confusing for us! Some of these names have included *LH-RH (luteinizing hormone-releasing hormone), LHFSH releasing factor or releasing hormone*, and *GnRH (gonadotropin-releasing hormone)*. There also is some discussion over whether there is only one hormone that regulates the release of both FSH and LH from the pituitary or whether there are two hormones, one for both FSH and LH. According to Ory (p. 577), the Endocrine Society prefers the term *LH-RH* but also accepts *GnRH*.

The important thing to remember is that LH-RH (or GnRH) is a signal hormone that releases FSH and LH from the pituitary. FSH and LH then travel to the ovaries, setting off a chain of events that cause the ovaries to ovulate and produce oestrogen and progesterone.

Understanding LH and FSH and the hormone that releases them has opened new doors for medical researchers, allowing them to try to develop new drugs to control the release of LH and FSH. Problems with LH and FSH release give rise to a number of other problems and conditions in both women and men, including infertility problems and problems with delayed or precocious (early) puberty.

Because these hormones work to regulate oestrogen and progesterone, researchers were anxious to develop drugs to help treat diseases like endometriosis and cancer, which can be dependent upon these hormones for growth. They are also exploring the possibilities of using these new drugs for both male and female contraception.

The focus of their research has been to develop man-made drugs (analogues) that will resemble the releasing hormone (LH-RH or GnRH). These drugs are sometimes referred to as *agonists* because of their ability to 'bind' to the receptor sites (i.e., on the ovary) where LH and FSH normally 'attach' themselves and set off the chain of events leading to hormone production and ovulation. Researchers have developed a number of these drugs with brand names such as Buserelin (LH-RH ethylamide), Nafarelin, and GnRh-a.

In researching LH-RH, scientists found that it is normally released from the hypothalamus in a pulsatile, or pulsing, manner at different intervals and intensities during the day. To treat infertility and other hormone release-related problems, efforts are made to mimic this type of natural release by having patients use a portable pump administering an LH-RH analogue at regulated doses during the day.

For diseases such as endometriosis, the administration of the drug is termed continuous—high doses of the drug are given usually two to three times a day (often as a nasal spray). At first this causes LH and FSH to increase dramatically, but after a few hours the gonadotrope seems to become overloaded and 'desensitized,' causing it to stop producing LH and FSH. Schriock et al. note that it is possible that the LH-RH analogues may also work directly or indirectly on the ovary to inhibit its sensitization to LH-RH.

Why should drugs such as Buserelin and Nafarelin have any advantage over danazol? To begin with, danazol is a synthetic androgen ('male' hormone). It is thought to work by inhibiting the production of FSH and LH in the pituitary and/or by eliminating the maturation of ovarian follicles leading to a decrease in oestrogen (E2) produced by the ovaries.

Much discussion has occurred among researchers regarding effective dosages for danazol especially related to the levels of oestrogen that will continue to allow endometriosis to grow and proliferate. However, proponents of using LH-RH analogues (Buserelin, Nafarelin, etc.) and the authors of the articles to be reviewed here have shown that these new drugs reduce levels of oestrogen in many cases to levels comparable to those possessed by women who have had their ovaries removed. They also argue that this is accomplished without the androgenic (masculinizing) side effects (hair growth, decreased breast size, etc.) that can occur with danazol.

Since many studies are currently being conducted with many reports now in press, what follows is only a sample of current research on LHRH analogues and endometriosis.

Article 1

The first article, by Meldrum et al., is one of the first studies published on an LH-RH analogue and its effectiveness in treating endometriosis. The analogue studied in this article is termed *GnRH-a*. It was administered to five women with endometriosis (none of whom had taken any hormonal medications for 30 days prior to the study), starting on day 3 of their menstrual cycles. They were given injections of GnRH-a, 100 μg, each morning for 28 days. During the study they were closely monitored by blood samples to measure the amount of oestrogen, FSH, LH, and some other hormones. Samples also were taken before and after completion of the study for comparison.

Five women who had had their ovaries removed (oophorectomized) and were not taking hormonal drugs were matched to the study participants according to age and body weight. They also had blood samples drawn each morning for 28 days. After some initial rises in oestrogen, FSH, and LH during the first part of the study, the authors showed that levels of oestrogen and FSH dropped to low levels comparable to those observed in women who had had their ovaries removed, although LH levels remained high. All subjects reported an episode of vaginal bleeding that corresponded to the drop in oestrogen level.

The authors noted: 'At the end of treatment and in the following cycle, all subjects reported either complete disappearance or improvement of premenstrual pain, dyspareunia, and dyschezia [painful bowel movements]. Resumption of menses was noted 25–31 days following the final dose of GnRH-a . . . Probable ovulation, indicated by the BBT[basal body temperature] rise, occurred between day 11 and 17 following cessation of GnRH-a.' (p. 1082)

Article 2

The next article, by Shaw et al., published in 1983, reports on a study using another LH-RH analogue, Buserelin, to treat endometriosis. The authors began their study with one woman who had 'a particularly severe form of the disease' with a 7 cm endometrioma and numerous other implants of 2 mm throughout her pelvic area. She had chosen not to undergo surgery and had tried danazol without success. She received 400 μg of Buserelin once a day by way of a nasal spray. This treatment started on the second day of her menstrual cycle. She continued to have abdominal pain, and her endometrioma appeared to increase in size. After 13 weeks of treatment, she chose to discontinue the Buserelin. She then had a hysterectomy and removal of her left ovary.

After this discouraging experience, the authors recruited five more women with endometriosis for their study whose cases of endometriosis ranged from mild to severe. All had undergone a laparoscopy/laparotomy to diagnose and classify their endometriosis. With two participants, surgery was performed to remove an ovary and to excise an endometrioma.

The participants' symptoms prior to treatment included abdominal pain (two women), dysmenorrhoea (two), dyspareunia (one), and primary infertility (five). On the second day of their menstrual cycle following diagnosis, the participants received 200 μg of Buserelin intranasally three times a day. Treatment lasted 26–28 weeks with a laparoscopy then performed to assess visually the effects of the treatment. Throughout the study, levels of oestrogen and other hormones were monitored by both blood and urine tests.

Vaginal bleeding occurred in three participants in the first few days of treatment and then stopped, with only one participant having occasional episodes of spotting thereafter. Ovulation was suppressed in all six participants during treatment. Three women showed lower-level suppressed oestrogen secretion, while the other three showed some intermittent surges of oestrogen without a regular pattern.

Four of five participants who completed the study showed complete disappearance of all endometriosismetriotic implants, with one participant still having one 2 mm implant remaining. Menstruation resumed in the five later participants 18–27 days after the treatment was stopped. Three women had normal cycles; two had shortened luteal (postovulatory) phases. One participant conceived two months after treatment ended.

The authors report that symptoms of pain and dyspareunia disappeared during treatment. As far as side effects are concerned, one participant noticed vaginal dryness, which was not severe enough to affect intercourse. No other side effects were reported, but the authors feel that longer-term treatment may lead to hot flushes in some women. (p. 1669)

Article 3

Published in 1984 by the Montreal team led by Dr André Lemay, this article reports on another study of the effects of LH-RH ethylamide (Buserelin) on endometriosis. In this study 10 women, ages 17–34, underwent laparoscopies or laparotomies to determine the extent of their endometriosis.

The severity of their disease ranged from Stage I (minimal, three women) to Stage II (mild, four), Stage III (moderate, one), and Stage IV (severe, two). At the end of these surgeries prior to treatment, adhesions were cut, and two cysts were removed in one participant.

Symptoms prior to treatment included unexplained infertility (four women), abdominal pain (three), progressive dysmenorrhoea (three), and abnormal hysterosalpingogram (x-ray of the uterus and fallopian tubes). One participant had irregular periods.

Treatment with Buserelin was started on days three to six of the women's menstrual cycles. For the first five days of treatment, the drug was given in an injection form of 200 µg every 12 hours. (Evidently, this method of administration for five days served as an initial diagnostic test to record the response of the hormones produced by the pituitary after stimulation with the drug.) After five days the participants took 200 µg of the drug intranasally every eight hours (as did the participants in the Shaw et al. study reviewed above). Treatment continued for 25 to 31 weeks for nine participants, with one participant discontinuing treatment at 12 weeks. Blood and urine tests were performed periodically on all participants throughout treatment to measure hormonal levels. Participants also recorded their basal body temperature daily.

As expected, FSH, LH, and oestrogen levels increased initially in all participants during the first few days of treatment. FSH levels decreased rapidly after this, although LH levels took longer (four weeks) to decrease to levels similar to those normally recorded before ovulation. Oestrogen levels decreased steadily over the first four weeks, reaching below basal levels. For nine participants oestrogen levels continued to decrease to levels similar to those recorded for women who had had their ovaries removed, with some transient elevations in two women (one during an acute episode of asthma). One participant who also had a fibroid tumour had a prolonged bleeding episode beginning at week five. By week 10 her oestrogen levels had steadily increased, and treatment with Buserelin was discontinued.

Other episodes of bleeding occurred in the participants during the first month of treatment, most likely from oestrogen withdrawal. After the first month occasional spotting occurred in three women, corresponding to rises in levels of oestrogen. Some other spotting and post-intercourse bleeding occurred in a few participants, which did not correspond to an increase in oestrogen, however.

Laparoscopies at the end of treatment showed improvement in endometriotic implant size and number for the nine participants completing the study. The authors noted that there was '... almost a complete disappearance of small lesions. In patients one and seven an implant greater than 1 cm could not be found at the second laparoscopy. In two cases occasional residua of previously observed implants could be seen." (p. 867) All participants either had a reduction in the staging of their endometriosis or a reduction in the number of points within their stage (three). (The American Fertility Society classification system gives a certain amount of points for each case of endometriosis based on the number, size, and location of implants and adhesions.) Endometrial biopsies performed in six participants at the second laparoscopy showed atrophic, inactive endometrium in four cases equivalent to the endometrium seen during early menopause.

In the six months following treatment, nine participants who had some form of dysmenorrhoea had disappearance or improvement of this symptom. Five participants who had mild to severe pain between periods had this pain alleviated two to four months into treatment. Three participants had no pain in the six-month follow-up period after treatment, and four participants who had severe dyspareunia had this symptom alleviated during treatment and remained free of it in the six-month follow-up period. One participant had a recurrence of abdominal cramps immediately after stopping treatment.

As far as side effects go, by week 10 all participants experienced significant hot flushes. Two participants had hot flushes end at months four and five. Five women complained of vaginal dryness during treatment. Of the seven women who were sexually active, three participants noticed a constant decreased libido starting at month three of treatment. One other participant had intermittent decreased libido. Four noticed occasional mild breast swelling or tenderness. None complained of nasal irritation from administering the Buserelin. No other problems were reported or found in the labouratory tests performed periodically on all women. Side effects rapidly disappeared after treatment was stopped.

All participants resumed ovulation within 45 days of stopping treatment. Two had short luteal (postovulatory) phases. One continued to have severe menstrual pain during her first period following treatment. Two became pregnant three and five months following treatment. One participant chose abortion; the other, who had been infertile, had a normal pregnancy and delivery.

Article 4

This article, by Schriock et al., published in November 1985, reports on the LH-RH analogue (GnRH analogue), Nafarelin, and its success in treating women with endometriosis.

Eight women, ages 25 to 37, underwent laparoscopies before treatment with Nafarelin. No therapeutic surgical procedures were done. Five participants had been treated with danazol previously, but it had been discontinued at least three months prior to laparoscopy. Three had received no previous treatment. Three of the five who had taken danazol had also previously had conservative surgery for endometriosis.

The laparoscopies found three participants had mild endometriosis, two moderate, two severe, and one extensive. All participants were described as having had 'painful symptoms of endometriosis,' and two had reported rectal bleeding.

The participants began taking Nafarelin during the first three days of their menstrual cycle; 500 μg of Nafarelin were administered intranasally every 12 hours throughout the treatment period. Blood and urine tests monitored hormonal levels and other physiological data periodically throughout the study. Seven participants took Nafarelin for six months. One woman discontinued treatment after two months due to unexplained leukopenia (a reduction in the number of white blood cells), although she had otherwise responded favourably to the treatment with a decrease in symptoms.

All participants had an increase in LH and FSH during day one of treatment. Levels of both hormones fell significantly after two weeks. All stopped ovulating during treatment. Oestrogen increased temporarily in some during the first month of treatment but dropped to menopausal levels accompanied by some withdrawal bleeding by week four of treatment in all participants.

One participant had intermittent increases in oestrogen and one episode of bleeding after the first month, with the highest level of oestrogen recorded during the sixth month. The authors found that this woman had lowered plasma concentrations of Nafarelin when compared with other participants, perhaps caused by problems in absorption or transportation of Nafarelin in her body, by her body metabolizing the Nafarelin at a higher rate than that of the other women, or by a difference in her body's sensitivity to the drug.

The seven women who completed the study were examined by laparoscopy (five) or laparotomy (two). All participants had a decrease in the staging of their disease. Five of seven participants had *no* endometriosismetriotic implants after treatment. These women had had varying severity of the disease, including one woman who had had severe endometriosis. Some adhesions, however, were present in these women following treatment. One participant who had mild endometriosis had a small implant in her cul-de-sac after treatment, and the other who had extensive endometriosis continued to have active disease affecting one fallopian tube and ovary. She had a 6 cm endometrioma that remained throughout treatment, although it decreased slightly in size. The authors noted that this woman's oestrogen levels had been only moderately suppressed during treatment.

According to the authors: 'Most women had significant symptomatic relief by 4 weeks of treatment, and improvement was maximal in all women by 12 weeks of treatment. Rectal bleeding completely resolved in the two patients with this complaint.' (p. 585)

All participants developed 'oestrogen deprivation' symptoms. The major complaint of all participants was hot flushes. In three women these were severe enough to lead to a reduction of the dose by half, to 250 μg. Four women reported vaginal dryness. Five women developed mild transient headaches; two women reported mild, transient depression.

After completing treatment, menstrual periods resumed within a range of 36 to 57 days. All side effects disappeared within one month following treatment. When their periods resumed, six women reported a decrease or absence of dysmenorrhoea. Three to six months after treatment, four women had partial return of dysmenorrhoea, and two women had a complete return.

The authors note: 'The effect of significant hypooestrogenemia (oestrogen deprivation) for six months on bone density in young women (decrease in bone density is associated with osteoporosis) is unknown and is presently under investigation. Recent nonhuman primate studies with intermittent GnRH agonist administration, however, suggest that markedly suppressed E2 (oestrogen) concentrations may not be required for an adequate therapeutic effect in all patients. Moderate suppression of E2 may eliminate many of the symptoms and detrimental effects of marked hypooestrogenemia.' (p. 587)

Two American Fertility Society Papers

Many other studies, including NIH studies and others at medical centres across the country, are now under way. At this writing, however, the results of the more recent studies have yet to be published. Abstracts of papers presented at the American Fertility Society's annual meeting (fall 1985) seem to confirm the findings of the above studies. A brief discussion of two of these follows.

In 'Intranasal Administration of Luteinizing Hormone-Releasing Hormone Agonist for Treatment of Endometriosis and Uterine Leiomyoma,' presented by G. Holtz et al. of the Department of OB/GYN and Medicine at the Medical University of South Carolina, the authors report on the use of yet another type of LH-RH analogue given intranasally to women with endometriosis in a dose of 100 μg three times daily for at least three months. Hormonal levels fell significantly to menopausal levels after a brief initial increase, hot flushes were the only significant side effect, and significant regression of endometriosis implants occurred.

In another abstract entitled 'The Use of Gonadotropin Releasing Hormone Agonist (GnRH-a) in the Treatment of Endometriosis' presented by R. Lyles et al. from the Department of OB/GYN, Baylor College of Medicine, Houston, Texas, the authors report on a study of 10 women with endometriosis treated with 20 to 500 μg of GnRH-a by both injection and nasal spray for an average of 176 days. Suppression of LH and oestrogen was consistent; however, suppression of FSH was not. With only one exception, partial or complete resolution of endometriosis was noted at laparoscopy after treatment. However, findings did not correlate with the degree of oestrogen suppression or with the dosage or method of administration of the drug.

The authors of the above articles seem fairly confident of the safety of using LH-RH analogues as supported by the periodic lab tests during treatment and short-term follow-up after treatment as well as by the studies using similar drugs for other disorders. However, a consent form for participants from an ongoing NIH double-blind study (using an LH-RH analogue, danazol, and a placebo) cautions that enlargement of the pituitary (which they point out often occurs normally in pregnancy) and benign (noncancerous) tumours of the pituitary have been reported in animal studies using doses of an LH-RH analogue 15 times higher than the doses in their study. None of the reviewed studies reported pituitary problems of this sort during the course of treatment.

Another risk that the consent form outlines is possible harm to the foetus if the woman should become pregnant while taking an LH-RH analogue. For this reason they advise using barrier methods of contraception (condom, diaphragm) during treatment. The NIH researchers also note that they have no reason to believe that any harm could occur in a child conceived *after* treatment, but that 'it remains possible that an unforeseen harmful effect of this sort could occur.'

Article 5

Article 5 by David Meldrum, M.D., which appeared under 'Editor's Corner' in the same issue of *Fertility and Sterility* as Article 4, is a useful, interesting summary and analysis of research on LH-RH analogues and endometriosis through 1985. In this article, he briefly reports on a study he co-authored with Steingold et al. entitled 'Treatment of Endometriosis with a Long-Acting GnRH Analogue—A Blinded Evaluation.' In this study of 16 subjects, endometriosis was significantly suppressed by visual observation during surgery. However, biopsies revealed inactive residual disease.

Meldrum feels that the Schriock et al. study may show that LH-RH analogues may be successful without complete suppression of ovarian function. Given less of the drug, '. . . side effects may be limited, and long-term therapy with periodic progestin withdrawal may prove to have a high margin of safety . . . Randomized studies will be required to determine whether GnRH agonist therapy is as effective as or more effective than currently available treatments . . .' (p. 582)

Meldrum notes that in all studies published to date (November 1985), ovarian endometriomas have failed to respond significantly to treatment. He also feels that more investigation into the proper doses and ways of administration should be undertaken. He states that the intranasal method requires several times the amount of drugs as injections, which, however, are less practical. He postulates that biodegradable implants '. . . may prove to be the most consistent and economic mode of administration.' (p. 582)

Meldrum notes: 'GnRH analogue treatment is unlikely to replace surgery for endometriosis, even when the tubes and ovaries are not involved with significant adhesions . . . GnRH agonist therapy is effective, but as with other hormonal treatments, disease is generally suppressed, rather than completely eradicated. The treatment is associated with menopausal side effects, which have limited the acceptability of danazol for some women. It is expected to be considerably less expensive than danazol, thus improving access of all women to effective medical therapy.' (pp. 582, 581)

In the future, we will attempt to report on the latest studies of this promising drug for endometriosis and also print personal accounts from women who have been in tests of these drugs. What is this drug really like from 'our side of the fence'?

GnRH Research

In addition to the researchers and institutions listed in the accompanying article on GnRH-related drugs, many others are studying this drug for treatment of endometriosis, in animal studies as well as with human subjects. If you are interested in being in a test programme, bear in mind that each research group and institution establishes its own criteria for inclusion in studies.

Usually these criteria include a laparoscopy (or major surgery if that's being done anyway) before and after the treatment with the test drug so that the extent of the disease can be seen before the drug was used and after it was used. Criteria related to extent of disease, previous treatment, symptoms, infertility, and others may also be defined for each study.

In addition, the time frames for studies change, so, as with other details related to these studies, you must contact the researchers and institutions to obtain the necessary information if you're interested in being considered for a test study.

Because these drugs are test drugs, no one knows, as pointed out in this article, what the long-term effects might be, how safe and effective the drugs are, the best dosage, etc. Be sure to weigh carefully whether you're really willing to be a guinea pig or not, and if the study is a comparative test of one drug against another and/or against a placebo, weigh the possible delay in treatment or opportunity to try for pregnancy should you be put on the placebo or a comparison drug you've already been on.

Articles Reviewed

1. Meldrum, D. R., Chang, R. J., Lu, J., Vale, W., Rivier, J., and Judd, H. L., Dept. of OB/GYN, UCLA. Medical oophorectomy using a long-acting GnRH agonist—a possible new approach to the treatment of endometriosis. *Journal of Clinical Endocrinology & Metabolism* 54:5 (May 1982): 1081–1083.

2. Shaw, R. W., Fraser, H. M., and Boyle, H., Dept. of OB/GYN, Royal Free Hospital, London. Intranasal treatment with luteinizing hormone-releasing hormone agonist in women with endometriosis. *British Medical Journal* 287:3 (Dec. 1983): 1667–1669.

3. Lemay, A., Maheux, R., Faure, N., Clement, J., and Fazekas, A.T.A., Hôpital Saint-François d'Assisse, Quebec and Hoechst Canada, Montreal. Reversible hypogonadism induced by a luteinizing hormone-releasing hormone (LH-RH) agonist (Buserelin) as a new therapeutic approach (or endometriosis. *Fertility and Sterility* 41:6 (June 1984): 863–871.

4. Schriock, E., Monroe, S. E., Henzl, M., and Jaffe, R. B., Dept. of OB/GYN, Univ. of California-San Francisco. Treatment of endometriosis with a potent agonist of gonadotropin-releasing hormone (Nafarelin). *Fertility and Sterility* 44:5 (Nov. 1985): 583–588.

5. Meldrum, D. R., Dept. of OB/GYN, UCLA. Management of endometriosis with gonadotropin-releasing hormone agonists. *Fertility and Sterility* 44:5 (Nov. 1985): 581–582.

Articles Consulted

1. Cutler, G. B., Hoffman, A. R., Swerdloff, R. S., Santen, R. J., Meldrum, D. R., and Comite, F., Section on Developmental Endocrinology, Nat'l Inst. of Child Health & Human Development, Bethesda, MD; Stanford Univ. Med. Ctr.,

Stanford, CA; UCLA; Yale Women's Center, New Haven, CT. NIH conference: Therapeutic applications of luteinizing hormone-releasing hormone and its analogues. *Annals of Internal Medicine* 102:5 (May 1985): 643–657.

2. Dickey, R. P., Taylor, S. N., and Curole, D. N., The Fertility Institute of New Orleans. Serum oestradiol and danazol. I. Endometriosis response, side effects, administration interval, concurrent spironolactone and dexamethasone. *Fertility and Sterility* 42:5 (Nov. 1984): 709–716.

3. Ory, S. J., Dept. of OB/GYN, Northwestern Univ. Medical School, Chicago. Clinical uses of luteinizing hormone-releasing hormone and gonadotropin-releasing hormone analogues. *Fertility and Sterility* 39:3 (May 1983): 577–591.

4. Yen, S.S.C., Dept. of Reproductive Medicine, School of Medicine, Univ. of California-San Diego, La Jolla. Clinical applications of gonadotropin-releasing hormone and gonadotropin-releasing hormone analogues. *Fertility and Sterility* 39:3 (Mar. 1983): 257–266.

Suzanne McDonough has been coping with endometriosis for a number of years. She is founder and former director of the Ann Arbor Chapter of the U.S.–Canadian Endometriosis Association and has been writing her column 'Research Recap' for the Endometriosis Association newsletter since 1983. Suzanne has her master's degree in social work from the University of Michigan and is a clinical social worker at St. Joseph Mercy Hospital, Ann Arbor, Michigan.

4
Surgical Treatments

'*I underwent surgery for the fifth time in 3¾ years . . . I was in endometriosis Stage IV again. I had no pain . . . bowel, intestines, uterus, peritoneum were involved, both ovaries had large cysts . . . It made me realize how strange this disease is . . . and how important research is! I am truly willing to do all I can do so someone in the future doesn't have to go through what I have . . .*'

Dale, New York

'*I have just recently learned of your Association from a friend of mine. I am quite interested in the work you are doing and being an active participant. In November a year ago I had a hysterectomy with removal of both tubes and my remaining ovary. At that time I was 26 years of age. They were unable to remove all of the endometriosis. As of this writing I am still incapacitated and on welfare . . .*'

Karen, Oregon

'*Four months past my laparotomy I'm still run-down and working at reduced hours, which is getting frustrating, but I've been warned that the six-month mark may do the trick. At least now I can swim, haul groceries, etc. I just need to take a nap regularly! I don't know how women with small children cope—my hat's off to them. Still, postsurgical problems are much preferable to chronic pain and codeine-popping.*'

Debra, Massachusetts

50

'I am 55 now, and for the last 15 years I've had a normal "feeling fine" everyday existence. It's been like a rebirth to health. The surgery not only cured the medical problem but was the final proof that I had not imagined the discomforts all those years, and that was a mental lift.'

Ruth, Racine, Wisconsin

'I am 21 years old. I would like to share my experiences with endometriosis and laser surgery.

'For two years I suffered with many yeast infections and abdominal pain during ovulation time. I went to several gynaecologists. They treated me with many kinds of pills. Nothing seemed to help me. I was even admitted into a hospital for treatment.

'One month later a friend of the family told me about a gynaecologist and infertility specialist who dealt with endometriosis. I went to see him. He then did a laparoscopy and laser surgery. I finally found out that all the problems and pain I was having were caused by endometriosis. I felt great after the surgery. I returned to work a week later.'

Nancy, Rhode Island

OVERVIEW OF SURGERY IN THE TREATMENT OF ENDOMETRIOSIS
By Carolyn Keith, M.S.S.W. and Mary Lou Ballweg

Women with endometriosis, particularly those experiencing severe pain, difficulty becoming pregnant, and other symptoms, may at one time or another face decisions about surgery. Like everything about endometriosis, these decisions are often not easily made. In such a decision, as in any other about your health care, it is important that you inform yourself as thoroughly as possible and consider both the benefits and the risks involved, as well as possible alternatives and your own personal concerns and values. Among these may be the extent of your symptoms, your age, the purpose of the surgery, your individual life situation (such as whether you hope to become pregnant), and, possibly, whether you would need oestrogen replacement afterward.

Types of surgery for endometriosis include diagnostic laparoscopy, operative laparoscopy, conservative surgery, and radical or definitive surgery. Microsurgery (surgery using a microscope) and laser surgery are also being used by some surgeons. (A laser beam is an extremely concentrated beam of light that can be directed precisely to destroy diseased tissue.) Presacral and uterosacral neurectomies are also surgical procedures sometimes used in endometriosis, although there is much debate over their advisability—both involve cutting the nerves that transmit pain to the brain.

A definite diagnosis of endometriosis usually requires a laparoscopy. Generally done on an outpatient basis under general anaesthesia, the procedure involves the surgeon's making a very small incision near the navel and inserting a lighted instrument similar to a periscope, through which he or she can inspect the organs within the abdomen. Sometimes endometrial implants can be cauterized (burned off with a fine electric charge), or adhesions (bands of scar tissue) can be cut away, cysts drained, and implants lasered during the operative laparoscopy in which actual surgery, not just diagnosis, occurs.

Like any surgery, particularly one involving general anaesthesia, some risks are involved. Therefore, a laparoscopy need not be done if you have no symptoms, you are not going to undergo treatment, and you have no ovarian masses (which must be distinguished from cancer). It is important that the surgeon doing your laparoscopy be skilled both in the procedure and in the diagnosis of endometriosis. If fertility is an issue and a hysterosalpingogram is planned, it is recommended that it be done at the same time as the laparoscopy. This avoids the inconvenience and possible discomfort of two separate procedures. (A hysterosalpingogram is an x-ray test in which a dye is injected into the uterus and tubes to determine their condition and whether the tubes are open.)

Conservative surgery means that the surgeon attempts to preserve or improve reproductive capacity while removing endometrial implants and adhesions and correcting any other problems with the reproductive organs. The uterus and at least one ovary and tube are left. As with all current treatments for endometriosis except hysterectomy and removal of the ovaries, recurrences of the disease are very common.

Definitive or radical surgery involves hysterectomy and removal of the ovaries. It is usually not considered unless the symptoms are severe and all other treatments have been tried, including at least one previous conservative surgery. Repeated conservative surgeries in the presence of ongoing, severe disease should probably be avoided as the risks and toll on the body and mind are too great.

Be sure to tell the anaesthesiologist about any allergies or prior anaesthesia-related problems you have had and be sure your medical records are available for the anaesthesiologist to check prior to anaesthesia if you had problems. It's important that you speak up about this as complications and discomfort can be reduced after the surgery by using another anaesthesia than the one that previousiy gave you problems. If you are a person who typically needs less of a drug than the average person—for instance, if that is your experience with commonly used drugs—tell the anaesthesiologist that, also. You might also want to draw attention to the research on mitral valve prolapse and its implications for surgery. (See the article on this heart defect in Section IV of this book.) If you typically have low normal blood pressure, you should also tell this to the anaesthesiologist and attending nurses in the preop and postop rooms or type a note ahead of time since you may be groggy when wheeled to the surgical area of the hospital.

Both conservative and radical surgery are major surgeries involving general anaesthesia, an abdominal incision, possible complications, and a hospital stay of a few days to a week or more. Preparation for both, especially hysterectomy, should be both physical and emotional. *Before* your surgery, arrange for some help when you return home with such tasks as laundry, meals, cleaning. Do not expect or force yourself to be Superwoman; it will slow your recovery and could cause the formation of scar tissue that could give you pain and problems the rest of your life. Especially important are the precautions not to take many flights of stairs daily or do any heavy lifting (over five pounds) the first month or so.

In addition, your preparation for the stress of the surgery itself could include following a nutritious diet and taking vitamin/mineral supplements to build up the body's resources, doing vigorous exercise if possible to strengthen heart and lungs, planning simple recuperation projects, and getting needed items before surgery. Remember that a certain amount of depression is a natural reaction to the shock of surgery. Have projects you enjoy ready to help you cope with possible depression, loneliness, and boredom during recovery.

In deciding whether to undergo hysterectomy and in preparing yourself emotionally for it, you may want to reflect on and talk about such issues as desire for children (even women who do not want future pregnancy often find that the definite ending of reproductive possibilities needs to be faced and perhaps grieved for), fears about surgery, possible changes in sexual response, and alterations in self-image. Does feeling like a complete woman mean having my uterus? What have my menstrual periods meant to me, both positively and negatively? What is the attitude of my husband or partner? Raising these questions here does not mean that they all should be major problems for you. Each of them has been important to some women facing hysterectomy—if they are to you, take the time to talk with your partner, women from the Endometriosis Association in your area, and perhaps a counsellor.

Until recently, women preparing for hysterectomy were advised that the surgery would have no effect on their sexual interest or response, except to improve it where pain and disability had interfered. Women were told that any changes they felt were due entirely to psychological factors. Now, the work of such researchers as Masters and Johnson and others has shown a greater role for the uterus and ovaries in sexuality than was previously assumed. The uterus produces contractions that are a significant part of orgasm for many women. And the ovaries have been identified as having a greater role in producing androgens ('male' hormones involved in sexual response) than previously assumed. Many, if not most, younger women report reduced sexual drive after hysterectomy and removal of ovaries. Age at the time of hysterectomy and removal of the ovaries may be a critical factor. The closer the woman is to natural menopause (now averaging about 50–51 years old), the lower her level of hormones already and the less effect the surgery may have. This important issue and many others make it clear why hysterectomy and removal of the ovaries are not an acceptable 'cure' for most women with endometriosis.

The decision as to whether or not the ovaries are removed at the time of the hysterectomy is a very serious one with long-term consequences. Current statistics indicate 85 percent of women with endometriosis severe enough to warrant hysterectomy will have a recurrence of the disease if their ovaries are not removed. On the other hand, women whose ovaries have been removed usually experience menopause immediately or soon after surgery. This premature (before natural menopause would occur) or surgical menopause (brought on by surgical removal of the ovaries) is usually more severe than natural menopause because it is sudden rather than gradual, as is natural menopause, and because a much younger woman is involved, whose hormones are at a level higher than an older woman's. Also, women who go through menopause much earlier than normal face higher risk of developing osteoporosis, a disease in which the bones become thin and fragile due to their inability to maintain sufficient minerals and protein, and *may* face greater risk of developing other serious diseases, such as heart disease and hardening of the arteries. Some physicians believe recurrence of endometriosis due to retained ovaries is likely to cause fewer problems in the absence of the uterus (at least the symptoms directly associated with the period would be eliminated) than premature menopause may cause. The answers do not yet exist, but in any case, *you* should be involved in the decision.

If the ovaries are removed, another decision will have to be faced, which is whether or not to take oestrogen replacement therapy (ORT). Some doctors recommend that the start of ORT be delayed at *least* three to six months after surgery to allow any remaining endometrial implants to regress, thus minimizing chances of recurrence. (Some members of the Association are waiting up to nine months as a precaution.) Remember that it is nearly impossible to remove every trace of the endometrial growths in advanced disease—a factor that must be considered before hormones are put back into the body. Approximately 5 percent of women taking ORT experience continuation or recurrence of endometriosis.

To quote a knowledgeable authority on this important subject (W. P. Dmowksi, M.D., 'Current Concepts in the Management of Endometriosis,' *Obstetrics and Gynecology Annual 1981*, Vol. 10):

> ... Oestrogen replacement therapy in a young patient, oophorectomized [with her ovaries removed] because of endometriosis, should be used judiciously and should probably not begin until residual foci of endometriosis have had a chance to regress, at least three to six months postoperatively. Hormone replacement should consist of low-dose oestrogen or oestrogen in combination with androgen. The treatment can be discontinued or the dose decreased if symptoms or findings suggesting recurrence of endometriosis appear.

It is not clear which menopausal symptoms are related directly to loss of oestrogen. Research presently links only hot flushes and vaginal drying to diminished oestrogen, but some women who have experienced abrupt changes in mood, development of severe headaches, or other changes are convinced that oestrogen loss is the cause though still unproven. Also, reports to the Association make it clear that ORT does not erase all menopausal symptoms.

While a woman who has had a hysterectomy need not fear cancer of the uterus with ORT, some risks do remain, including a greater chance of gallbladder disease and of blood clotting. Research indicates there is no increased risk of breast cancer with hormone replacement in women who have had their ovaries removed.

There are also risks in *not* taking ORT if your ovaries are removed before the normal age of menopause (and possibly when they are removed after menopause also, but more study is needed). These include increased risk of heart attacks and osteoporosis. A dosage of 0.3 mg/day has been found effective in preventing osteoporosis, in one research study, *if* combined with at least 1,000 mg/day of calcium in the diet or from supplements. This is an important finding for women who have had endometriosis who may benefit from starting at the lowest dosage of oestrogen. Prior studies had found that 0.625 mg/day was necessary to prevent osteoporosis, but the effect of calcium in conjunction with oestrogen had not been studied. Exercise is extremely important after hysterectomy and removal of the ovaries. Treat exercise at this point like a prescription—an absolute necessity. Schedule it into your life as a 'must do'!

Progesterone replacement in women who have had endometriosis has, unfortunately, not been studied. Some women are also replacing the testosterone lost when the ovaries are gone, but studies have not yet been done on this procedure, either. Be aware of any side effects you might experience on hormone replacement therapy. Check them out carefully with your health care provider and other sources of information.

Women unable or unwilling to take ORT are exploring alternatives. Vaginal drying and thinning of the walls, which may result in painful intercourse, higher rates of bladder and vaginal infections, and urinary incontinence may be helped by over-the-counter lubricants such as Lubrin, Astroglide, K-Y Lubricating Jelly, and Transi-Lube; application of fresh yogurt to the vagina; frequent sexual activity; and Kegel exercises. Sometimes oestrogen cream is prescribed; remember that the oestrogen does enter the bloodstream.

Some women work out a combination of vitamins, particularly vitamin E, the Bs, and C, to counteract menopausal symptoms. A holistic health practitioner, chiropractor, or nutrition counsellor might assist you with this. Herbalists have information on ginseng, dong quai, fo tien, and other herbs that some women find helpful.

To prevent osteoporosis, some health care providers recommend a combination of tablets of calcium, potassium, magnesium, and vitamin D in proper proportions, combined with regular, vigorous exercise, which is essential for maintenance of good bones. A diet high in phosphorus diminishes calcium in the body, so cutting down on red meat, which is high in phosphorus, may help. Also along dietary lines, some researchers believe hot flushes may be caused or aggravated by sugar, alcohol, and caffeine.

An excellent resource on menopause generally and on diet, including vitamin supplements, is *Women and the Crisis in Sex Hormones*. (Be cautious of most menopause books as they pertain almost entirely to natural, rather than surgical, menopause.) Important books on hysterectomy are *Coping with a Hysterectomy* and *The Castrated Woman*. See Appendix at back of book for details.

Carolyn Keith, M.S.S.W., is cofounder of the Endometriosis Association, former coordinator of health education at Bread and Roses Women's Health Center, Milwaukee, and now programme developer, policy analyst, and consultant in housing for older adults.

THE LASER AND ENDOMETRIOSIS

'I feel much better after having had my surgery. I had rather severe endometriosis with bowel and bladder involvement. I went

from taking three Motrins a day during my period to taking two Anacin 3s for one day before my period. I feel the lesions growing back on my bladder, but it isn't like before, and I have minimal or no pain having bowel movements before and during my period. And the best is that intercourse isn't painful anymore! I'd say, all in all, it was worth it.'

Linda, Brooklyn, New York

'For the first time in several months I am able to function again. Before this surgery I was frequently unable to go out of the house and had trouble taking care of my son.

'I couldn't believe the speed of my recovery. I was able to leave the hospital and fly home four days after surgery! Within three weeks I was back to work, school, and caring for my two-year-old-son. Dr Nezhat didn't give me any false promises, just some time to enjoy my life again.'

Susan, Clifton, New Jersey

As the number of gynaecologists around the country using the laser as a surgical instrument for endometriosis has begun to grow (although the number using it routinely is still small), questions about the laser have increased. So we asked a few doctors using the laser for endometriosis to write the following articles for us and are pleased to present them here.

The article by Dr Camran Nezhat explains what lasers and laser laparoscopy are; the three types of lasers used; the advantages of lasers, particularly the carbon dioxide laser; the way lasers are used; and the way in which they specifically aid in treating endometriosis. The article by Dr Stein describes the use of the YAG laser for endometriosis, and the article by Dr Keye describes the use of the argon laser in treating endometriosis.

Remember that the laser is new for endometriosis, having been used for the disease for only a few years, and that the number of physicians with extensive experience with it is small. You need to proceed with caution if you are considering laser surgery for endometriosis and take time to check carefully the credentials and experience of the laser surgeon and talk to other members with experience and information on it.

Laser laparoscopy is a relatively new procedure that can be used with significant advantage in the treatment of many patients with endometriosis. In the hands of an expert, the technique can produce symptom remission rates and pregnancy rates similar to those of other available treatment measures (hormonal therapy and conventional laparotomy).

Laser Overview and the Carbon Dioxide Laser
By Camran Nezhat, M.D., F.A.C.O.G.

What Are Lasers?

The word *laser* is an acronym for *l*ight *a*mplification by the *s*timulated *e*mission of *r*adiation. In the simplest terms, a laser is a powerful concentration of energy. Lasers have been used extensively in industrial and medical settings for some time. For example, some lasers can slice across metal rods with edges that never dull; others can carry 80,000 simultaneous telephone calls through glass fibres. Lasers can be used as precise tools in the hands of physicians, permitting significant treatment advances in several areas of medicine (ophthalmology, dermatology, and gynaecology, to name a few).

Currently, three types of laser are used the most in medicine: the CO_2 (carbon dioxide) laser, the argon laser, and the YAG (*y*ttrium-*a*luminium-garnet) laser. The carbon dioxide laser is more versatile than the argon and YAG lasers in that it can perform two functions: it can *cut* tissue when it is focused, and it can *coagulate* tissue when it is defocused. The CO_2 laser also is very precise and does not damage the surrounding tissue. The other two laser types can essentially be used only to coagulate tissue. The following discussion will be restricted to the use of the carbon dioxide laser.

What Is Laser Laparoscopy?

Laser laparoscopy is the combined use of the laser and the laparoscope. Just as lasers are not new in medicine, neither is the use of the laparoscope. As mentioned earlier, the use of the laparoscope (an electrically lighted tube containing optical structures allowing the surgeon to visualize internal organs) is essential to make a definitive diagnosis of endometriosis. The laparoscope, in combination with additional, specialized instruments, is also used for other minor surgical procedures, such as tubal ligation, egg retrieval for *in vitro* fertilization, and (by some surgeons) restricted amounts of cautery of endometrial implants.

Advantages of Laser Surgery and the Laparoscope

The combination of the laser and the laparoscope produces a powerful new technique since each of these two entities has advantages over existing methods. These are the advantages of laser surgery:

1. The laser can be concentrated, and the light energy can be focused to a pinpoint, allowing the vaporization of small endometrial implants without the destruction of surrounding tissue. Moreover, the laser beam can reach sites that would be difficult using the scalpel, cautery, or suturing.

2. The laser beam seals small blood vessels, reducing blood loss. Since there is less bleeding, the surgeon has a clear view of the operative site.

3. The laser beam vaporizes excessive tissue in its path. If bacteria are present, they too are vaporized by the laser (which itself is sterile), possibly resulting in lower infection rates than those resulting from conventional surgery.

4. Laser surgery in the hands of an expert can be done more quickly than conventional laparotomy, so the patient can be under anaesthesia for less time.

5. There is the possibility of less scar formation postoperatively. The patient may have less pain and improved chances of pregnancy.

6. Specific characteristics of the CO_2 laser convey additional advantages:
   - There is no scattering from the laser beam impact line. Therefore, there is no effect on the tissue immediately adjacent to the impact site.
   - With the focused CO_2 laser beam, surgeons are able to vaporize or make an incision as small as 1 mm (about the size of a printed 'c' on this page) without touching the tissue. As mentioned above, the carbon dioxide laser can both cut and coagulate. If the surgeon can cut without touching the tissue, the possibility of infection could be less. (There is also less contact with the operative site by surgical instruments.)
   - The laser can be used for the coagulation of small blood vessels when it is properly defocused. Therefore, there is no need for suturing or electrical coagulation.
   - The energy of the carbon dioxide laser beam is absorbed almost completely at a depth of 1 mm from the tissue. It can therefore be used over vital organs without causing damage to these underlying structures.
   - The carbon dioxide laser does not induce genetic mutations in cells (as do gamma rays or x-rays). There is no need for protection aprons.
   - In tissue the light energy from the CO_2 laser beam is converted into local heat. All cell nuclei are destroyed since the temperature is raised at 100 degrees centigrade (212 degrees Fahrenheit), and

the internal cellular water boils immediately. This heat is restricted to the impact area alone, limiting damage to adjacent sites.

Just as the laser has advantages over other types of surgical manipulation, laparoscopy (in the hands of the trained surgeon) can have significant advantages over laparotomy. Many of these advantages are related to the fact that *laparoscopy* is a *minor* surgical procedure, while *laparotomy* is a *major* surgical procedure. (Laparotomy is major abdominal surgery involving an incision of several inches and a fairly lengthy recovery time.) These are the advantages of laparoscopy:

1. The patient may leave the hospital the same day or the next day, and recovery time is two days to one week. With laparotomy the patient remains in the hospital for five to six days, and recovery time is approximately four weeks. The advantages in terms of impact on the patient, loss of work time, and disruption of family life are obvious.
2. Laparoscopy requires two or three small incisions (one-half inch or less), while laparotomy requires a large incision of several inches. Patients concerned with the cosmetic aspects of surgical procedures would find laparoscopy to be a distinct advantage.

When the laser and the laparoscope are combined in laser laparoscopy, these advantages produce a powerful surgical procedure that, when compared to hormonal therapy or laparotomy, can be a relatively simple and inexpensive technique. This is especially true if laser vaporization of endometrial implants and adhesions is performed at the same time as the original diagnostic laparoscopic procedure. Under these conditions the patient is spared the side effects associated with medical therapy or an extended recovery period resulting from laparotomy. In addition, if fertility is an issue, the patient can attempt to become pregnant shortly after the original diagnosis. This is an advantage that is not possible with medical therapy or laparotomy.

Laser Laparoscopy—The Procedure

During laser laparoscopy, two or three small incisions are made. Sometimes, the laser and the laparoscope are connected, and the energy of the laser is directed through a channel in the laparoscope, called the *operating channel*. Under other circumstances, the energy of the laser is directed through a special laser probe, through a different incision at a second site. Both methods have advantages and disadvantages. When the laser is directed through the operating channel of the laparoscope, the surgeon's line of vision and the laser beam are coincident (at the same place). This allows the surgeon a great deal of precision and control, which is particularly necessary when working near the bowel or ureters.

When the laser probe is used through a second incision, the surgeon does not have quite the same amount of precision and control. However, the laser probe allows smoke (which is generated during the vaporization of tissue) to be dissipated more efficiently. The location and extent of endometrial implants and adhesions determine which of these alternatives the surgeon uses. In addition to these instruments, a special type of forceps (an atraumatic alligator grasping forceps) is introduced through a separate incision to allow manipulation of internal organs and tissues during the procedure.

When we perform laser laparoscopy at the Atlanta Fertility and Endocrinology Center, we include, during the procedure, a video camera, video recorder, and high-resolution video monitor. A view of the operating field (what the surgeon sees through the laparoscope) is projected onto the video monitor and is simultaneously videotaped for future reference. The surgeon views the monitor during the procedure rather than looking through the laparoscope. This is a significant advantage because it allows the surgeon to work in a comfortable upright posture (watching the video monitor) rather than bent over the laparoscope. Fatigue is lessened, and precision is enhanced. The second major advantage is that there is a permanent record of the procedure for verification, insurance, and follow-up purposes. (Patients who have requested their operative reports only to find that they are confusing, incomplete, or in contradiction to what they have been told verbally will immediately appreciate the value of this technique.)

Laser Laparoscopy in Endometriosis

Most patients with endometriosis are concerned with two aspects of the disease: the pain (and other debilitating symptoms) that sometimes accompanies the disease and the infertility that may result. Laser laparoscopy may be used effectively to manage both of these aspects of endometriosis.

Pain. Laser laparoscopy helps to control the pain associated with endometriosis by vaporizing implants (which bleed every month during menstruation) and by vaporizing adhesions (which can cause constant pain throughout the menstrual cycle). Adhesions can cause pain because organs may be attached to each other in an unnatural configuration. When the patient moves—walks or breathes—the internal organs also move, causing the adhesions to stretch. Pain is the result.

In addition, the uterosacral ligament can be dissected effectively during laser laparoscopy. This ligament is a frequent site of endometrial implants; lesions on the uterosacral ligament can be particularly troublesome. We have dissected the uterosacral ligaments, and in about 70 percent of the patients we have had complete relief of the pain.

Infertility. Perhaps the usefulness of laser laparoscopy in the management of infertility associated with endometriosis can best be described by presenting the results of the procedure on 102 infertile patients who had endometriosis as the only cause of infertility. Overall, of the 102 patients, there were 62 pregnancies during the follow-up period of up to 18 months. These included nine spontaneous abortions (miscarriages) and one elective termination of a pregnancy. These pregnancy rates compare extremely favourably with those obtained after other treatment regimens (Danocrine or laparotomy).

During laser laparoscopy, endometrial implants were vaporized from the ovary, pelvic sidewall, cul-de-sac, tubes, uterosacral ligaments, bladder flap, and peritoneum or capsule of endometrioma. Adhesions around the ovaries and the fallopian tubes were cut, and endometriomas up to 7 cm (approximately three inches) in diametre were treated.

The 102 patients in this study ranged in age from 20 to 41 years. The largest group were between 25 and 35. Of the 62 patients who conceived following laser laparoscopy, 12 (24.1 percent) were between 20 and 25 years of age, 20 (32 percent) between 25 and 30, 27 (43 percent) between 30 and 35, and 3 (4.8 percent) between 35 and 41 years of age.

The duration of infertility ranged from 12 to 59 months. Fourteen (13.7 percent) of the patients experienced endometriosis-related infertility for 12–23 months prior to surgery. For 48 (47 percent) the duration of infertility was 24–59 months. Forty patients (39.2 percent) reported infertility for over 59 months.

TOTAL OF 102 PATIENTS WITH ENDOMETRIOSIS

Stage	No. of Patients	No. of Pregnancies	Percent	Spontaneous Abortions	Percent
I Mild	24	18	75.1	4	22
II Moderate	51	32	62.7	4	12.5
III Severe	19	8	42.1	2	25
IV Extensive	8	4	50	0	
Totals	102	62		10	

A particularly important aspect of this study is that patients with all degrees of endometriosis became pregnant following laser laparoscopy. The rates of conception related to the stage of the disease are shown in the table above. (The stage of disease assigned followed staging guidelines of the American Fertility Society.) The results of this study should provide significant hope to women who are infertile because of endometriosis.

Another important factor to be noted in this study is that laser laparoscopy was effective in those patients in which danazol therapy is generally accepted as being ineffective: cases in which there are a significant number of adhesions around the fallopian tubes or the ovaries.

Summary

In summary, laser laparoscopy is a powerful technique for controlling the symptoms associated with endometriosis, including infertility. When performed by an experienced surgeon, the results are at least as good as those obtained with hormonal therapy and/or laparotomy, while being less time-consuming and less traumatic for the patient.

Laser Microsurgery and the YAG Laser
By Daniel S. Stein, M.D., F.A.C.O.G.

Although the thought of lasers brings to mind science fiction—from *Flash Gordon* to *Star Wars*—the theoretical foundation of lasers originated with Albert Einstein in his 1917 treatise *The Quantum Theory of Radiation*. It was not until 1958, however, that two scientists extended Einstein's principles to make the laser a reality.

Unlike sunlight or light from a bulb, laser light is focused in one direction and wavelength. This results in a tightly concentrated, intense energy beam that can be precisely aimed and controlled. Laser surgery is a form of microsurgery but does not merely use 'miniature' surgical instruments for traditional burning, cutting, and suturing. Laser surgery does minimize the bleeding, chance of infection, and scarring of traditional microsurgery.

The first and most common surgical laser is the CO_2 laser. Its precision and ability to vaporize tissue cell by cell, until abnormal tissue is nonexistent, is well known. The fact that the CO_2 laser beam is completely absorbed by even the thinnest layer of water or blood makes it difficult to use for tumours or conditions where operative oozing of blood from the surgical site is likely to occur.

The Nd:YAG laser (neodymium: yttrium-aluminium-garnet laser) is the most recent type of gynaecological surgical laser. With a shorter wavelength and a more deeply penetrating beam, this laser has proven to be highly effective in the treatment of certain tumours and common bleeding disorders. The YAG's tremendous advantage is that it has the ability to penetrate a layer of water or blood and prevent bleeding. This lack of bleeding then allows the CO_2 to vaporize the abnormal tissue in a completely bloodless field. This is perhaps the first opportunity in modern science for 'bloodless' surgery.

There are many advantages to the use of laser surgery for endometriosis. Besides those already mentioned, there is the advantage that the healing from laser surgery for endometriosis is very rapid, since the remaining cells are healthy and can multiply quickly to heal the area removed. Postsurgical discomfort and swelling also are reduced. Perhaps most important, scarring or adhesion formation is dramatically reduced. These advantages enhance the effectiveness of any surgical procedure and are especially advantageous for those women who want to become pregnant at a later date or whose endometriosis is causing severe pain due to internal tissue scarring and adhesions.

Laser surgery for endometriosis may be performed in the office or in the hospital. In our Women's Center, laser surgery can be performed on an outpatient basis via laparoscopy if the disease is minimal and there is little scarring. However, it can be difficult because the rigidity of the instruments does not allow for the curving that may be needed to reach hidden tissue or to go around the sides of organs such as ovaries.

Inpatient surgery is done when there is extensive scarring from the disease. Additionally, the instruments at the hospital are capable of curving around organs to reach hidden diseased tissue. A woman can expect a small, low, bikini incision and four to five days as an inpatient, with a recuperative period of three to four weeks.

Daniel S. Stein, M.D., is the president of the Women's Medical Center of America, Inc. and the director of the Laser Institute and the Florida Fertility Institute. Dr Stein is an associate professor at the University of Florida College of Medicine. He is also a founding member of the Gynecologic Laser Society.

Use of the Argon Laser in the Treatment of Endometriosis
By William R. Keye, M.D., F.A.C.O.G.

It was with a great deal of interest that I read the article on the laser in the March 1983 newsletter of the Endometriosis Association, for it was about that very time that I was forming my own impressions about the use of lasers in the treatment of endometriosis. You see, two years before I had been introduced to lasers by a pioneer in the field, Dr John Dixon, president of the American Society for Lasers in Medicine and Surgery and professor of surgery at the University of Utah. He suggested I explore the use of the argon laser in the treatment of endometriosis, for the blue-green colour of the argon laser is selectively absorbed by the red blood contained in areas of active endometriosis.

Intrigued by his suggestion, I spent over six months creating experimental endometriosis in the rabbit and treating it with the argon laser. Fortunately, these studies demonstrated that the argon laser was selectively absorbed by the endometrial implants and thus spared normal tissue that surrounded the implants of endometriosis. Excited by these observations, I began to use the argon laser when I discovered mild or moderate endometriosis at laparoscopy or laparotomy. In addition to its selective absorption by the reddish-coloured endometriosis, the argon laser was appealing because it could be delivered through a very fine (0.6 mm diameter) flexible strand of quartz or optical fibre. As a result, the argon could be used with a standard laparoscope without the expensive modifications or accessories of other laser equipment. [Editors Note: The price of laser equipment has been coming down in the last couple of years.]

During the past two years, over 75 patients in my practice have been treated for endometriosis with the argon laser. To date no complications have occurred as the result of the use of the laser. In addition, approximately 30 percent of the patients have conceived, and a larger percentage have noted a marked reduction in pain and discomfort. Unfortunately, this experience is too limited and the follow-up too brief to draw any final conclusions regarding the use of the argon laser in the treatment of endometriosis. In spite of these limitations, several preliminary observations are apparent.

First, the argon laser, as well as the CO_2 and Nd:YAG lasers, can be used safely to destroy the superficial implants of mild or moderate endometriosis. Second, the argon laser has the advantages of its selective absorption by endometrial implants and its ability to be delivered through an inexpensive flexible quartz fibre. Third, in many cases endometriosis can be eradicated at the time of laparoscopy, thus avoiding the need for an expensive and painful laparotomy or the delay and side effects of oral contraceptives such as Danocrine, or GnRH.

The argon laser has its limitations, however, and is not the treatment of choice for many women with endometriosis, especially those with severe or extensive endometriosis. In addition, the argon laser is not nearly as useful in destroying the *scar tissue* or *adhesions* of endometriosis as is the more powerful CO_2 laser. Finally, many hospitals do not have an argon laser, thus limiting the availability of this new treatment modality.

In conclusion, it appears that any of the currently popular lasers (argon, CO_2, and Nd:YAG) may be useful and sometimes advantageous in the treatment of endometriosis. However, the woman suffering from endometriosis should not be misled by extravagant claims, for to date our experience with the laser in the treatment of endometriosis is extremely limited. The laser has not yet replaced, and probably will never replace, any of the more conventional therapies of endometriosis. The informed consumer should follow with interest our work with lasers for endometriosis but should not abandon more conventional therapy for laser surgery without a great deal of thought and reason.

William Keye, M.D., is a board-certified reproductive endocrinologist who is also associate professor of Obstetrics and Gynaecology and chief of the Division of Reproductive Endocrinology at the University of Utah Medical Center. He is active in research and patient care in the field of endometriosis and fertility.

TIPS FOR CHOOSING A GOOD LASER LAPAROSCOPY SURGEON
By Dr Camran Nezhat

A patient with endometriosis who is seeking treatment via videolaseroscopy or laser laparoscopy should ask the following questions:

1. How long has the surgeon been performing videolaseroscopy? (There is a difference between videolaseroscopy and laser laparoscopy, as explained in the accompanying article, and the patient must look for a physician experienced in the procedure in which she is interested.)
2. Does the surgeon treat only mild to moderate disease, or is he or she treating more extensive disease?
3. On the average, how many cases does the surgeon do a week?
4. Can the surgeon provide the patient with a copy of the videotape of her surgery?

It takes at least one year of continuous practice of an average two to three cases a week (total 150 cases) before one is comfortable in videolaseroscopic or laser laparoscopic treatment of the disease.

Videolaseroscopy and even laser laparoscopy are brand-new. There is going to be a learning curve until the laser surgeons become more and more experienced, competent, and comfortable in doing the procedure. Unfortunately, a lot of

endometriosis patients will be halfway or not completely
treated because of this learning curve.

5
Fertility and Pregnancy Considerations

By Sandy Hintz and Mary Lou Ballweg

'My doctor is very patient and understanding but seems unable to help much. His solution is a hysterectomy, but I've read that it doesn't necessarily cure it ... My husband would also like a child before surgery, but so far we have been unsuccessful.'

Linda, Fort Worth, Texas

'I am only 22 and will never have children. I am looking at a hysterectomy in the near future.'

Rhonda, Hartland, Wisconsin

'My condition was discovered in December. After six months treatment with danazol (600 mg/day), the condition cleared. (Ovary, bladder, and rectum were involved.) Two months after completing therapy I became pregnant—now have a perfectly healthy baby girl. A true miracle to us. I am uncertain of my future with the disease but will never again "hate my body" for letting me down and causing so much physical and emotional pain. My body functions came through for me, and my outlook on life is vastly improved. I had a normal pregnancy, labour, and delivery—no problems.'

Linda, New York, New York

'In March, when I was still single and 25 years old, I had to have my right ovary and fallopian tube surgically removed due to

endometriosis. *I was told that I had some scarring on my left ovary also, but that the doctor was able to remove the scarring and growths without having to remove that ovary as well. From what I have read on the subject, I must have been in the "minority," because unlike what most women experience, I had no heavy cramping or bleeding during my periods, no pain during intercourse, no pain in the middle of the month, and no other symptoms that would have led me to the doctor. It was during what I thought was going to be a "routine" diaphragm fitting at a local Planned parenthood clinic that the physician who examined me found a "mass." About three weeks later I was in the hospital.*

'Needless to say, endometriosis has affected and continues to affect my life. At the time, I was not married, and all my doctor (surgeon) wanted me to do was to hurry up and get married so I could get pregnant. He, of course, heaped anxiety and frustration on top of a situation that was very emotional for me to begin with. He continued to intimate that I had "chosen a career" (I am a professional) instead of motherhood and that I was now paying the price. The irony of it all is that I was not resisting marriage or motherhood in the least—there was just no one in sight! That irony of the entire situation perhaps bothered me most of all.

'Now, however, things in my life are different from when I had the surgery. I have been happily married for almost two years and have been trying to get pregnant for about the last six months. So far, no little foetus! I am trying not to get anxious or nervous yet, but of course certain concerns remain on my mind. Although I have been pronounced basically "cured" of endometriosis, do you know what kind of effect the disease could have on my fertility at this time, more than six years after my surgery? Are there any statistics on women who have had endometriosis in previous years and then try to become pregnant?'

Andrea, Coconut Creek, Florida

'Even with all the problems endometriosis is causing in my life, I feel that I'm one of the lucky ones. I was fortunate to have had two normal pregnancies resulting in two beautiful daughters before endometriosis invaded my body. At least I've been spared the heartbreak of infertility.'

Lillian, Columbus. Ohio

'Why are so many EA members trying to become pregnant and joyfully having babies when the effects of endometriosis on the

next generation and the possible (likely) hereditary component have not been measured? I realize this is a weighty topic (the issue of genetic counselling and decisions about having children in light of possible hereditary health problems for the children), but I am personally astounded at the idea it is OK to go ahead and have babies as if infertility is the only obstacle. I am personally not going ahead with the old 'Go have a baby, and it will help your endo' advice (which I have been told, as is common) even though I have been told I would likely be able, because I have a great fear of producing a child (boy or girl) with endo-related health problems. I feel a responsibility to address this issue sensibly and objectively, much as I would like to have children, since the data seem so absent on this issue, and there is a long line of gynaecological/allergy/GI problems in the female relatives on my mother's side of the family. How do other women address this issue? Without being critical, I must say it seems from the EA newsletters they may be putting all hesitations aside.'

Michelle, Hillsborough, North Carolina

About 30–40 percent of women with endometriosis are infertile, and endometriosis is the cause of infertility in about 30 percent of *all* infertile women, according to infertility specialists. For women with endometriosis, infertility is more likely to result as the disease progresses, with less infertility in the early stages.

The reasons for infertility in endometriosis are not known. A number of factors probably contribute: damage to the ovaries and fallopian tubes by the disease; adhesions and scar tissue on these and other organs due to the disease and sometimes due to surgery; irregular periods; painful sex resulting in less frequent sexual activity; prostaglandin activity; and perhaps hormonal factors. The more severe the endometriosis, the more likely there will be an infertility problem, although there are women with minimal disease and minimal symptoms who are infertile.

Because infertility often results as the disease progresses, and since endometriosis generally does worsen over time, it may be important for those with the disease, especially those who want to conceive, to be treated as soon as the disease is diagnosed. However, because of the nature of current treatments, which are for the most part temporary (with the disease returning in time after treatment), and because the treatments themselves have risks, women without severe symptoms may choose to take a wait-and-see approach, deciding on no treatment or attempting a pregnancy before treatment.

It is generally recommended that pregnancy not be postponed if it is wanted and the woman and her partner are ready to raise a child. Postponement could greatly reduce the chances of conception in the future.

However, we caution you not to forget that pregnancy is a *life* choice and not to rush into it simply because of fear of not being able to become pregnant later. Ways to 'buy time' include treatments such as birth control pills or danazol to hold the disease in check as you make a decision about childbearing. Talking with women in your local Endometriosis Association chapter or support group or from the member contact list will also help greatly as many of them have faced similar situations. And a counsellor sensitive to women as whole persons, not just 'babymakers,' can help you sort through the emotions and confusion that can arise when you learn you have a disease such as endometriosis.

When treatment is the choice, three types are available through traditional medical professionals—hormonal, surgical, or a combination of the two. (In addition, many women report to the Association that they are trying 'alternative' treatments—nutrition, exercise, acupuncture for pain, chiropractic, homoeopathy, and so on. The Association is compiling results on these and all treatments of endometriosis in its data registry.)

Hormone therapy for endometriosis usually attempts to simulate pregnancy (birth control pills) or menopause (danazol). Progesterone-based drugs are also sometimes used. All aim to stop the process of endometrial buildup and shedding, to bring about relief of endometriosis symptoms, and to dry up endometriosis colonies.

There are cautions in using hormonal treatments for women who want to conceive. If a woman becomes pregnant while on hormonal therapy, the chances for infant abnormalities now or many years from now, as with DES, are very real. Thus, danazol and the birth control pills are prescribed to be started at the time of your period to be sure you are not pregnant. A nonhormonal method of birth control (such as diaphragm, or condoms and foam used together) is recommended while on danazol and progesterone. Reports to the Association indicate ovulation does continue for some women on hormonal treatments, particularly danazol. Because of the great emotional concern around pregnancy for many women with endometriosis and the desire of many for pregnancy, no woman in this situation should take the chance of finding herself pregnant under conditions where termination of the pregnancy might have to be considered or continuation would occur under great emotional stress. Also, it is recommended that pregnancy not be attempted for a couple of months after hormonal therapy to give the body a chance to rid itself of the drug and to readjust hormonally in order to support development of a healthy foetus.

A final caution: progesterone-based drugs, according to *Womancare* (see Appendix), is probably an unwise choice for the woman planning a pregnancy soon after treatment. This is because progesterone-based drugs may suppress ovulation for long periods of time (ranging from months to years) after treatment and thus prevent conception.

Conservative surgery is another alternative open to women who want to bear children. Endometrial implants can be removed by cutting or cauterizing, adhesions removed, a severely damaged ovary and tube removed, and organs restored to their correct positions. Recently, laser surgery is also being used by a limited number of surgeons and is said to conserve fertility better than traditional surgery because less tissue is destroyed and scar tissue does not result. Also, danazol and surgery are being used together—with danazol used before surgery to dry up small growths and after to dry up growths impossible to remove in the surgery.

Surgery may be the choice for a woman who wants to conceive who has large cysts, extensive adhesions, or pelvic anatomy distortions, which hormonal treatment would not be able to affect. Or, if a woman is older and feels she does not have the time to wait for months of hormonal treatment to continue attempting pregnancy, she may choose surgery.

A precaution with surgery is that, although a good surgeon will follow fertility surgery procedures to prevent adhesions, surgery itself can cause adhesions that could further contribute to infertility. Also, it is generally considered impossible to remove some endometrial growths with traditional surgery because of size (they can be microscopic) or location (if attached to the bowel or other vital organ or inaccessible). The latter can be removed with laser surgery or microsurgery in the hands of an expert surgeon, however.

Pregnancy rates following hormonal and surgical treatment of endometriosis are often debated and disputed and should be regarded sceptically until further data exist. Pregnancy rates following treatment with the birth control pill, for instance, range all the way from 5 percent to 73 percent; for surgery, from 38 percent to 87.7 percent; for danazol, from 15 percent to 75 percent.

Whatever the treatment, the extent of the disease and adhesions before the treatment are important factors in the pregnancy rate following treatment. Also, more pregnancies occur soon after treatments—the more time elapses from treatment, the less chance for pregnancy.

If a woman with endometriosis does conceive, will her pregnancy be normal? There is no easy answer to this question because very little research on the pregnancy experiences of women with endometriosis has been carried out. Generally, authorities say yes, with two exceptions: women with endometriosis have a higher rate of miscarriage and a higher rate of ectopic pregnancy (two problems that have been researched and documented), probably because of damage to the tube from the disease. (Ectopic pregnancy is a pregnancy in which the fertilized egg implants outside the uterus, usually in the fallopian tube.) This is a potentially life-threatening situation because as the fertilized egg enlarges it may rupture the tube and cause serious internal bleeding. Danger signs of a possible ectopic pregnancy would be a missed period in a month when conception was possible with slight bleeding 7–14 days after the missed period and mild soreness or pain at first with sharp pain later. Faintness, nausea, and vomiting might also occur, or shock. Help should be sought immediately.

Additional information on the pregnancy experiences of women with endometriosis became available through a study by Yale graduate nursing students Carolyn Ansell and Catherine Gorchoff. At the urging of the Association they studied the complete pregnancy, labour, and postpartum experiences of women with endometriosis. A total of 187 members who had attained 334 pregnancies shared their experiences for the study. Ansell and Gorchoff found the women had multiple discomforts during their pregnancies, particularly nausea and vomiting; a high incidence of dysfunctional labour; high rates of postpartum depression; and a faster return of symptoms in those who did not breastfeed. (Write the Association to obtain more information on this study.)

If a woman with endometriosis conceives, what will happen to her endometriosis? In the past, pregnancy was often said to cure endometriosis, but now it is known that this stubborn disease returns far more often than not. Most reports to the Association indicate the symptoms (pain, etc.) disappear during the pregnancy with recurrence after the pregnancy. The length of remission seems to be related to the severity of the disease, with a severe case recurring more quickly. A way to lengthen the time of remission is by breastfeeding—if ovulation is suppressed by the breastfeeding, the disease will usually stay in remission during that time. The most important factors are getting started right away after the birth and breastfeeding the baby on demand without supplementary formula. Be sure to read materials on breastfeeding or check with La Leche League or a similar group to learn how to breastfeed in the way most likely to stop ovulation. Two good books for breastfeeding and pregnancy in general are *Pregnancy and Childbirth: The Complete Guide for a New Life* by Tracy Hotchner (Avon, 1979) and *Nursing Your Baby* by Karen Pryor (Pocket Books, 1973).

There have been a few reports to the Association of the disease worsening during pregnancy, and medical authorities now believe the relationship between endometriosis and pregnancy is poorly understood.

Early, repeated pregnancies were said in the past to protect against endometriosis, and that is also being questioned as women with such histories are found with endometriosis.

Becoming pregnant once does not assure further pregnancies. In a chapter summarizing medical thinking on endometriosis in the *Obstetrics and Gynecology Annual 1981* it was noted that 'only about 20 percent of patients who had coincidental pregnancy and endometriosis conceived again regardless of whether persistence of the disease was observed.

Finally, good nutrition can play an important role in conceiving, with a high-protein diet and the B vitamins considered especially necessary. A good source for dietary information can be found in *Women and the Crisis in Sex Hormones* (see Appendix).

Sandy Hintz is a Milwaukee writer and literary agent.

6

Alternative Treatments for Endometriosis

By Mary Lou Ballweg

'*I have found learning from childbirth education very helpful now that endometriosis symptoms are back ... pain is lessened by meditative-type relaxation and positive healing imagination thoughts. It has helped me cope with the pain much better.*'

Marian, Houston, Texas

'*Hallo, sisters. I read about you while I was writing a book about women's health issues, and I got very interested. Here in Sweden we are a small number of women who have formed a group, a women's health group, and we are talking about starting a clinic. So far we have been doing courses in different subjects, like self-help, natural birth control, pregnancy and birth, massage, psychotherapy, infections, etc.*

'*But here in Sweden it is difficult for us to get information, alternative information that is not the depressing information you can get from the medical establishment. And one subject like that is endometriosis. Women turn to us to ask for our advice, and I don't really know any alternative cure, [other] than trying to keep the body in good balance.*

'*So with this letter I want to ask you if you know of any home remedies for endometriosis. Have you tried some, and which seem to work? I would be very pleased if you would answer me!*'

Bippan, Järna, Sweden

'*I want to share an experience that I had and am having. Having endometriosis for as long as I have (six years) and going along with the conventional treatments without promising results, I decided to try new approaches and started doing research about herbs and found ginseng or Panax ('Cure-all') Ginseng.*

'*Naturally I was skeptical, but I tried it anyway. After a couple of weeks I felt almost normal, and after four weeks I still felt great.*

'*Unfortunately, after that I had setbacks and started feeling symptoms again, but even now I feel better than before I took the tea. Overall I feel that this herb has an effect on endo.*'

Maria, South Bend, Indiana

'*I am writing this letter to inform you and your society of the success I have had with acupuncture for endometriosis. I have suffered from this disease for 26 years, and had I known about the reduction of oestrogen levels through this process, I would have done it years ago. At first I was skeptical that this treatment would work; however, I have no doubts now. I am functioning drug-free (I had been taking all kinds of pills prescribed by various OB/GYN doctors). Now I get needles from acupuncture once a month and can function pain-free the rest of the month. I take only plain aspirins during my period now.*

'*If your members have not investigated this avenue, please do not rule it out! You only have pain to lose!*'

Ann, Ridgewood, New Jersey

In a country that supposedly cherishes freedom of speech and thought as well as individual choice, especially in personal matters, it has always seemed out of keeping with the American character that even to mention or discuss 'alternative' medical treatments is considered heretical and disloyal to the dominant medical profession. As a member from Texas wrote on her Association questionnaire, '. . . to recommend a chiropractor for *any* reason is stupid. Vitamins and herbs are not going to help endometriosis either.'

Insisting that there is only one way to think about health and disease is like saying there is only one religion. Especially when it comes to a disease as frustrating and stubborn as endometriosis, one cannot blame those afflicted if they try a variety of approaches to regain health. In fact, rather than blame them, as some do, we ought to *encourage* individuals to try different approaches in the hope that somewhere someone will find clues to this disease.

Whatever our own particular brand of health 'religion,' we need to be tolerant and supportive of others' beliefs. It is truly disheartening to hear from some women with endometriosis that some alternative practitioners have been just as arrogant about their practice as some traditional medical professionals have been. When Massachusetts member LaVae Allard, for instance, decided to try danazol again when her ovary started enlarging, it 'made my chiropractor of one and a half years so furious she would not give me any of her time to help me think about my alternatives.'

Most of the alternative therapies discussed here are 'holistic' in approach, meaning an approach to health and healing that considers the body and person as a whole—diet, exercise, mental attitude, and so on are all considered important in allowing the body to function well and remain well. Traditional Western medicine, on the other hand, tends to focus more narrowly on symptoms and disease, more so as specialists have become more prevalent, than on the whole person. And, except for exercise, most of the ideas of holistic health are pooh-poohed by the medical establishment, especially in the area of diet, a subject generally not taught at all or in depth in medical schools.

DIETARY MEASURES

'The question of diet and nutrition is seen as crucial in the holistic approach to health,' says Judith Levy, a member of the British Endometriosis Society who runs a health store. 'The food generally available today does not have the nutritional quality necessary for good health for various reasons,' she says in the British Society's bulletin.

'. . . A lot can be done to help. First, eating habits can be revised to exclude processed and refined foods and food containing additives. Organic vegetables can be eaten if available. At least some raw food should be eaten each day. In parallel with this, food should be supplemented with vitamins and minerals.

Vitamins and Minerals

Another article on natural healing approaches appeared in *Prevention* magazine in August 1979 and has been listed on the Association's recommended reading list (see Appendix) for years. In it, author Diane Karnes describes how her endometriosis began as a lump on her 'backside' about a year after the birth of her child. (It's not clear whether Karnes means her buttocks or vulva area.) Repeated surgeries were ineffective and, in fact, possibly spread the endometriosis, according to the article, from the outside lump to her vagina. Danazol did not work, and Karnes was put on another drug, which she unfortunately never names, making it hard to know what really caused her eventual recovery.

'The doctor told me I probably would have to have more operations in the future. With all my talking to this doctor, before and after the operation, I had to read between the lines of what he said. He never came right out and answered my questions bluntly, but maybe deep down I didn't want him to, either. I would not accept the fact that I had something incurable.'

She asked her doctor: 'Will I or will I not ever be cured of this?' His answer was, 'I don't want to see you cry.' He told her to get pregnant. After toying with the idea, she realized her decision about having a child was made in desperation. 'I just could not have a baby to cure an illness.

'That was when I got totally fed up. I was tired of taking those different kinds of medicine that I knew could harm me in the long run. I was tired of having doctors operating and experimenting on me, only to be told that they didn't know for sure if I could be cured or not. That was when I decided that, if a doctor couldn't cure me, then I would have to do it myself.'

As a result of reading on health and hormones, Karnes decided to increase her B vitamins, increase her protein, and lower her sugar intake. She writes that this regimen did not do much for her endometriosis but it did end the bouts of depression she'd experienced, and she felt like a different person, calm and optimistic.

Then she decided to add vitamin E and selenium (the two work together) to her diet to see if it would help. When she added the selenium, she noticed an almost immediate improvement, and eventually, she writes, her endometriosis was gone. Ailsa Irving of the British Endometriosis Society also reported in one of their newsletters that a supplement named selenium-ACE caused a big improvement in inflammation for her and a few others. We have had mixed reports on vitamin E, with some women improving and some reports of symptoms worsening. Vitamin E is a hormone booster, particularly of oestrogen, according to Barbara Seaman, author of an excellent resource book for women, *Women and the Crisis in Sex Hormones* (see Appendix).

Thus, women with endometriosis might want to be cautious in using it, starting with small doses and carefully observing their reaction to the vitamin. (After one's ovaries are removed, however, vitamin E can be very effective in reducing hot flushes.) The E used should be mixed tocopherols, not just alpha—check the label.

The British Endometriosis Society reports that B vitamin complex, especially vitamin B_6, calcium and magnesium, vitamin C, vitamin E, selenium, and a multivitamin/mineral tablet helped 'countless sufferers counteract the depression and listlessness that so often accompany the illness.'

Vitamin B_6 (taken with the other B vitamins, never alone) also has been suggested by doctors to women on danazol or other hormones, which appear to increase the need for B_6. Many women also use it to reduce PMS symptoms as well as to counteract morning sickness. The dosage of B_6 must be watched, however, as high dosages have caused serious nerve damage.

B_6 encourages the production of progesterone, according to an article by noted nutritionist Dr Carlton Fredericks ('Female Dysfunctions, Hormones, Cancer and Nutrition,' *Let's Live* magazine, January 1984). Some research indicates women with endometriosis have oestrogen and progesterone a bit out of balance part of the month (not enough progesterone for the amount of oestrogen). Dr Fredericks identifies a vicious cycle in women like us:

'The early research that found the vitamin B complex critically important in supporting liver-control of oestrogen activity also identified a vicious cycle. Not only does inadequate intake of these vitamins interfere with the breakdown of female hormone by the liver, but oestrogen itself may cause vitamin B complex deficiency.'

Moreover, there could be an inborn problem in some people in absorbing vitamin B_6. Barbara Seaman, in *Women and the Crisis in Sex Hormones*, states that inborn deficiencies in utilizing B_6 are fairly common, especially in families with histories of diabetes, low blood sugar, or malabsorption syndromes such as coeliac disease. Foods rich in vitamin B_6 are whole wheat, blackstrap molasses, walnuts, peanuts, brown rice, herring and salmon, some fruits (bananas, avocados, grapes, pears), and some vegetables (cabbage, carrots, potatoes).

Another source of information on B complex and endometriosis is the article 'Endometriosis: How Women Can Solve a Painful Puzzle with B Complex Vitamins,' which appeared in the January 1983 issue of *Let's Live*. The article cautions that, while severe endometriosis should not be self-treated, good nutrition and fitness 'can go a long way toward postponing a crisis for many women.'

The article goes on to tell the story of Rita, a young woman under stress, working days and evenings and dieting without regard to nutrition. 'No matter how skinny I was, I still felt fat. I was 113 pounds, but still starved myself on 500 calories a day . . . Exercise was something I never did; I thought fitness meant being thin, which meant starving myself.'

After her abdomen swelled up and she made many frustrating visits to her doctor trying to find out what was wrong, she was diagnosed as having endometriosis.

Finally, I decided to take matters into my own hands ... I quit counting calories, but I did not just load up on junk. I ate more fish and chicken—when I was dieting, I always avoided protein because I thought it was "fattening." I still eat vegetables and grains, but don't eat as many carbohydrates as I used to.

Most important, I discovered exercise. I began doing aerobic dancing and found that the movement eased the pain. I wasn't sure why it worked. My doctors had never recommended it. But exercise kept my adhesions from aching and also improved my overall fitness and ability to handle stress. [The article states exercise keeps adhesions flexible.] I weigh more than when I had my problems, but I am well conditioned and healthy and actually look much better than when I was striving to be fashionably thin.

I never weigh myself now, and eat whatever good foods I like. I keep up my exercise, since I teach dancing now, and don't have to starve myself to maintain a good figure. I get a twinge of pain in my abdomen only when I've been careless about my diet. I'm looking as good now as I'll ever look, and I *know* that good eating and fitness cured me when the doctors couldn't.

'Nutritional measures to manage oestrogen do not work overnight,' the article warns. 'They gradually coax the system back to normality, but the initial body response may seem contradictory. Occasionally, women who eliminate sugar, alcohol, and refined foods, while adding B complex supplements, may at first experience a *worsening* of symptoms. This is because the ovaries are the first to respond to improved nutrition and promptly speed up oestrogen production. In time, the liver catches up and degrades the oestrogen as the ovaries produce it.

Evening Primrose Oil

Evening primrose is a food oil, very similar to safflower oil, made from the evening primrose flower. When you first hear about it, you may be tempted to dismiss it as a kooky idea, but wait—it turns out that evening primrose oil (and safflower oil) is a direct precursor of prostaglandin E_1. (For a discussion of prostaglandins and their links to endometriosis, see the article on this topic in Section V of this book.)

Prostaglandins and their synthesis and their roles in health are complex subjects and new ones to medicine, having been studied intently for only a few years. A researcher who has done a lot of work with evening primrose oil is David F. Horrobin of Nova Scotia, Canada. An article published in *The Journal of Reproductive Medicine* in July 1983 by Horrobin reported substantial relief of PMS symptoms (a frequent complaint of women with endometriosis) with the use of evening primrose oil as well as vitamins and minerals that increase the conversion of essential fatty acids to prostaglandin E_1—magnesium, vitamin B_6, zinc, niacin (one of the B vitamins), and ascorbic acid (vitamin C).

Information about prostaglandins and the imbalances in prostaglandins that appear in women with endometriosis and primary dysmenorrhoea tie in very well with what one would expect, given the prostaglandin precursors (essential fatty acids) in the typical North American diet. Our typical diet, high in saturated animal fats and hydrogenated vegetable fats and low in fish oils and nonhydrogenated vegetable oils, makes us susceptible to the prostaglandin imbalance that recent research has found in women with endometriosis and primary dysmenorrhoea. The materials on essential fatty acids and prostaglandin production say nothing about endometriosis, and, vice versa, the materials on prostaglandin imbalances in women with endometriosis and primary dysmenorrhoea say nothing about the dietary precursors of prostaglandins—it's as if the two groups of researchers live in separate worlds. But it all comes together in our bodies.

We first heard about evening primrose oil from the bulletins of the British Endometriosis Society (in which members would from time to time report relief of their endometriosis symptoms with use of the oil), and it is from England that the best-known primrose oil, Efamol, comes. It is not cheap, but cheaper sources may not work well because of the minimal gamma-linolenic acid, the important ingredient in evening primrose oil. Another note of caution: you may wish to start with a small amount as reactions are possible.

Efamol is generally available in health food stores in capsules. A possible cheaper alternative might be to use safflower oil in cooking and salad dressings, but be sure it is a high-quality, nonhydrogenated, cold-pressed oil (such as Hain's).

Another source of information on evening primrose oil is the 30-page booklet *Introducing Evening Primrose Oil*, a Good Health Guide published by Keats Publishing, 36 Grove St., Box 876, New Canaan, CT 06840. (Write for price and other information.)

Macrobiotic Diet

The macrobiotic diet is a diet that includes whole grain flour products, beans, fresh local vegetables, miso soup, fruit, oil, and small amounts of fish, according to the *East West Journal*, the magazine published by the East West Foundation, which promotes the diet and philosophy. Our first encounter with it specifically related to endometriosis was an article in the *East West Journal*, March 1982, titled 'Tonia's Triumph Over Illness and Infertility.' It is about the experiences of Tonia Gagne, wife of Steve Gagne, director of the East West Foundation.

The article was regarded with serious scepticism by members who saw it because it claimed a 'cure' to Tonia's endometriosis six weeks after pregnancy due to macrobiotic diet. The author of the article showed complete ignorance that women with endometriosis frequently show no traces of endometriosis immediately after pregnancy as well as ignorance about the course of endometriosis and the role of drug treatment Tonia had and fails to mention that Tonia's experiences after giving birth sound like standard postpartum depression and return of endometriosis. The article also has a moralistic tone that implies that, if Tonia had only given up her evil ways and become a macrobiotic practitioner sooner, she would have escaped her endometriosis problems.

However, recently, the *East West Journal* published another account of a woman with endometriosis, Dawn Gilmour, who had a long history of ill health and the usual problems in obtaining a diagnosis that women with endometriosis face as well as a terrible series of events with hospitals and doctors. She had also tried, she says, alternative healing approaches, including acupuncture, homoeopathy, herbs, faith healing, and a vegetarian diet, to no real avail. She had also seen psychiatrists and was classed as a manic-depressive.

'I then met a friend who told me about macrobiotics. I decided to go to London to see Michio Kushi [the president of the East West Foundation]. I felt I could not do any more damage by trying something else. I was so desperate to get well—to feel human again.'

She began following the macrobiotic diet and the recommendations of Kushi.

> I felt a difference within four days. Physically, I knew it was going to take a little time to get well, but the change in my mental attitude was so dramatic, so quick, I could hardly believe it. It was an overwhelming transformation for me, and my husband was thrilled with his 'new wife.'
>
> Nine months later I went back to the Royal Infirmary for another internal examination. No endometriosis was found. My doctor, who had performed my previous surgery, thought that my recovery was unbelievable; he was so happy for me and encouraged me to continue on the macrobiotic

diet as that seemed to be the thing that was changing my condition.

My last checkup was in September of 1981, just before I moved to Boston. I had an internal examination ... Again, the results showed no problems.

Finally, we recently received the following account from a Virginia member:

I had a very severe case of endometriosis about a year and a half ago. I had major surgery and was in pain all the time. The doctor dosed me up on Depo-Provera [an injectable form of progesterone that has been linked to breast tumors] (he lied about the dangers of the drug) and said that there was nothing that could be done to help that did not involve that or other equally dangerous drugs. I became so disillusioned with the medical profession (I went briefly to another, female, doctor who was more sympathetic but basically gave me the same drug line) that I stopped going to doctors altogether. I just took painkillers and tried to keep going. I could hardly even hold a job. It was just awful.

Then she moved and, because she now had access to a good farmer's market, a whole grain bakery, and a food co-op, began to eat a healthier diet.

After a couple of months I started feeling much better ... I still had very heavy periods, however. Later I went to see a nutritionist who told me to check into macrobiotics. At that point I began to get more consciously macrobiotic. I still don't stick to the diet 100 percent ... Nonetheless, I am feeling almost totally normal. The endometriosis gives me very little trouble now ... my periods are lighter. The most gratifying difference is that I feel looser inside. And I don't have any problems with holding a job or anything like that anymore.

It took me about two to three months to register real changes. Since then it has been a growing thing. Sometimes I will go six to eight months, no problems, and then hit a bout of pain the next month. But the overall results have been gratifying.

When I started to notice changes, my diet was far from perfect, but I was getting large quantities of fresh farm vegetables, whole grain bread, legumes and brown rice, apples and cider, some dairy products and eggs (far less than before), and no meat.

A word of caution about changing basic food habits—it sometimes takes months or years to transform a basic diet. It's usually easier to start by cutting out the worst things in your diet and adding new, healthier foods gradually. Finding a good nutritionist can help. And most food co-ops and health food stores have books available to learn more about nutrition.

Fasting/Detoxification

Some people believe toxins are built up in our bodies, especially in our intestines, and that fasting and purgatives to remove them from time to time assist in maintaining health. Clara Valverde, author of the article 'Endometriosis: Healing with the Mind's Eye,' appearing in the Canadian publication *Healthsharing* in spring 1981, writes a bit about it in the article. She warns that there are precautions to be taken, and we hope anyone considering this or any other technique discussed here will do background reading and search for a reliable practitioner.

We'd also like to add that from time to time the very ancient notion that menstruation represents the body ridding itself of poisons crops up. This idea goes back to biblical times and is part of a long history of taboos related to menstruation and the idea that women were impure creatures. Let's not buy into ideas like this that are bound to make us feel less good about ourselves as women. (I always wondered, when I heard this old explanation for menstruation, about what happened to the accumulated poisons in men, since they had no periods to wash out the poisons. Or were men so superior that they had no poisons in their bodies?)

RELAXATION, MEDITATION, BIOFEEDBACK, AND VISUALIZATION

A variety of stress reduction, positive thinking, and self-training courses are available with a variety of names. In one of the British Endometriosis Society's bulletins, a member describes what a form of self-training (they call it *autogenic training*) did for her:

> Your therapist guides you through a set of exercises that warm your limbs, steady your heartbeat, calm your breathing. Assuming a relaxed posture, you talk gently to various parts of your body in turn ... You listen to your body, become

aware of its processes, and feel it shedding its load of unwanted tension and stress.

Everyone has different reactions, and everyone finds her own pace. All you need is patience, commitment, and an open mind. Over the weeks you may begin to trust your body a bit more: to feel that if you don't hustle your body, don't harry it, it will return to a state of calm, harmony, and balance. Is that hard to believe? I found it impossible. So I gave up trying to believe and simply worked through the exercises. The results surprised me.

. . . As I worked through the exercises, I heard my own inner voice, and I was appalled. I had an inner sergeant-major, a red-faced bully bawling in my psyche. "Your heartbeat is calm and regular!" this tyrant stormed. No wonder it wasn't! For the first time I asked myself: Why do I treat myself like this? I wouldn't let anyone else do it; I'd fight. So I'm constantly battling inside: a stiff-necked bellyaching private soldier in a pointless private war. Finding this out was the first step toward changing it.

. . . After four weeks, there was a marvelous lifting of anxiety. I cheered up tremendously. The number of my aches and pains diminished as my muscles unknotted. I was amazed to find that many everyday things that had caused me problems were really quite easy; actually, a number of things weren't as important as I'd once thought. I couldn't explain what had happened, when people asked suspiciously after the origins of my high spirits: but I knew life had altered. There have been ups and downs since, but perhaps life doesn't get to me in the same way . . . If you've had even a week of feeling calm and healthy, you know it can happen again—and it will.

In *biofeedback*, machines measuring body temperature, heartbeat, etc., are used to help you train yourself in stress reduction. Yoga—techniques of relaxation through exercise, breathing, and self-focusing—is used by some for stress reduction and centering too.

Visualization is a technique of using the power of your mind and hope to help self-heal. It involves picturing yourself as a strong, healthy person and attempting to focus on healing the hurt inside rather than focusing on negative thoughts and anger at your body. At the least, it might help some of us feel good about our bodies again.

In its information sheet on alternative medicine, the British Endometriosis Society suggests relaxing and breathing into each part of our body. 'From there we can move on to visualize the weak confused endometriosis cells (lost in the wrong place) and the strong purposeful army of white blood cells ... flooding in with increased blood flow, destroying the endometriosis cells and getting rid of them, soothing pain and tidying up scar tissue. We can visualize our internal organs pink and healthy, freely mobile and hormones balanced, and see ourselves healthy and full of energy, achieving the goals we want.' They suggest doing this 15 minutes at a time three times a day.

The article 'Endometriosis: Healing with the Mind's Eye,' published in a Canadian publication, *Healthsharing*, spring 1981, discusses endometriosis and visualization. Another source on the power of the mind in overcoming illness is *Anatomy of an Illness*, a beautiful book by Norman Cousins, renowned thinker and former editor of *Saturday Review* magazine.

PAIN-CONTROL MEASURES
Acupuncture and Acupressure

Women writing us have reported acupuncture helped relieve pain but, not surprisingly, did not cure the disease. Acupuncture and acupressure involve the use of needles or pressure (using fingers or hands) or electrical current to affect nerves that conduct pain messages.

The British Endometriosis Society reports, in its information sheet on alternative medicine, that it has had mixed reports on acupuncture and endometriosis. 'Some have found it very beneficial; others feel that it possibly aggravated the condition. This may depend on the type of acupuncture. Some people prefer traditional acupuncture and are against electrical techniques.'

Member Linda Kames, a Los Angeles psychologist, treats chronic pelvic pain 'as a psychologist along with an acupuncturist in a dual approach. We have had much success helping women reduce pain and cope with the disease and its consequences more effectively. We are studying the effects of a nontraditional approach to this pain through the University of California-Los Angeles Pain Management Center in collaboration with UCLA's OB/GYN Dept.' Kames has endometriosis herself.

TENS
By Anne Stuart, Albany, New York, area member

TENS is an acronym for a pain-management technique that may have some application for women with endometriosis. TENS—transcutaneous electrical nerve stimulation—involves passing a weak electric current into nerve fibres just beneath the skin. One or more electrodes, often coated with a gel to increase conductivity, are attached to the body at or near the site of pain. These transfer the small electrical charge.

A. L. Russell, an Ontario physician, has written that there are two theories about how TENS actually relieves pain. One is that the procedure increases the release of a natural painkilling substance in the blood and spinal fluid, blocking pain impulses to the brain. The other is that TENS somehow closes a 'gate' between the source of the pain and the pain-control centre in the brain.

A TENS treatment can last anywhere from 20 to 30 minutes to several hours, depending, of course, on the individual patient. TENS units can be ordered from some hospital supply houses, but to get the maximum benefit from the treatment, it's recommended that anyone interested seek advice from professionals skilled in TENS treatment. Many medical centers, hospitals, universities, and rehabilitation facilities have, in recent years, developed 'pain clinics' specializing in controlling discomfort. Some clinics are using TENS to block out pain for reasons ranging from childbirth to accidents, athletic injuries to postsurgical aches.

It's difficult to find information about TENS use for relieving endometriosis pain, but since the procedure is sometimes used on women with premenstrual syndrome (PMS) and other forms of gynaecological distress, it's possible that a clinic may be able to assist a woman with endometriosis.

There are a few cautions about TENS. For instance, TENS should never be used while sleeping or by anyone wearing a pacemaker. But if used properly, a TENS unit is quite safe, and there should be no shock. The only reported side effect is possible skin irritation from the gel used to attach the electrodes.

Anne Stuart, a former daily newspaper reporter, is currently a Boston-based freelance writer. Her work has appeared in *Newsday, Boston Magazine, Prelude*, and other publications. She graduated from Michigan State University and the Columbia University Graduate School of Journalism, and she has had personal experience with endometriosis.

CHIROPRACTIC

Chiropractic is 'a philosophy, art, and science that deals with the proper alignment of the spine,' according to Mary Ann Maris, who writes for a Milwaukee chiropractor. It is based on the belief that disease is caused by interference with nerve function. According to Maris, all the nerves in the body exit through the vertebrae of the spine, so chiropractors use techniques of spinal manipulation to realign the vertebrae when they are out of alignment. A member who has had experience with chiropractic is Elizabeth Cain Nelms of Colorado. She wrote recently in response to our request for experiences related to 'alternative' approaches to healing:

> After nearly losing a marriage due to side effects of danazol, I gave up working with traditional doctors who seemed more intent on paying for their new office toys, e.g., ultrasound, than in helping me. For a year now I have been working with a chiropractor/kinesiologist who told me I had a tipped uterus (and he corrected it) as well as the usual spinal alignment problems. I have had no pain during menstruation several times in the past 12 months. My periods are now normally predictable at 31 days instead of anybody's guess of 30–50 days. I suspect that further reduction in pain could be accomplished by better diet control as this method has helped dramatically with my headaches.

LaVae Allard of Massachusetts went to a second chiropractor after her first one reacted negatively to her decision to go on danazol. 'X-rays were taken when I decided I needed to know exactly what my bone structure looked like in order to eliminate the possibility of a real problem there. Sure enough. My fifth lumbar was out, first degree, but certainly a cause for the pain of the last few years. It was fixed in two treatments but will need attention all my life intermittently when it goes out. I learned the importance of bone alignment and good structure so that all muscles, ligaments, and organs can operate as they should.'

And a North Carolina member wrote that she was going to 'a holistic-type chiropractor' and that a remarkable improvement had taken place rapidly. 'I had little faith it would help at all, but it has helped hugely, and I have new hope for a normal life.'

EXERCISE AND MASSAGE

Exercise can be difficult if not impossible to pursue when endometriosis is active, but it's probably important to try to exercise to the best of your ability during the good times of the month or when the endometriosis is less active. Exercise increases the body's production of endorphins, natural pain-blocking substances.

Even walking has been too painful for some women to bear when their endometriosis was active. Possibly a very gentle massage by a loving friend could help at these times to increase general circulation, promote relaxation, and allow us to experience some pleasure in our bodies.

Exercise that jars or stretches too harshly, such as jogging, could cause more pain by pulling on adhesions and scar tissue. (Some individuals believe exercise helps keep adhesions flexible, however.) For the most benefit, an exercise programme should provide both aerobic activities (meaning it gets the heart and lungs working at good capacity and strengthens and exercises them) and muscle stretching and motion. After removal of the ovaries, exercise is no longer an option (if it ever was!) but an absolute must to help in preventing osteoporosis, a serious bone disease affecting older women and younger women who've had their ovaries removed early.

HOMOEOPATHY

Homoeopathy is defined as 'a system of medical practice that treats a disease especially by the administration of minute doses of a remedy that would in healthy persons produce symptoms of the disease treated.' According to an article in *Health News and Review*, homoeopathy operates by stimulating the immune processes of the body to fight the illness, prompting the body to self-healing.

Homoeopathic doctors are always M.D.s, the article states. 'Homoeopathy is a formal branch of medicine, like any other, but avoids the hazards of drugs and surgery.' In addition to their traditional training, homoeopathic doctors are trained in herbalism and nutrition. Homoeopathic doctors use diluted doses of substances meant to stimulate the immune system, somewhat the way vaccines work, except vaccines are given when a person is well.

'We continue to be very optimistic about the results of homoeopathic treatment as so many seem to be making remarkable headway this way,' writes Ailsa Irving, founder of the British organization, in a letter to the Association. Another member of the group, Carole Boyce, writes in a recent newsletter of the British group about the discussion of 10 women recently at an alternative medicine workshop:

> We first redefined health and therefore disease in homoeopathic terms: as a *process*—a radically different definition from the orthodox, which sees each disease as a separate entity: a *thing*.
>
> We went on to discuss homoeopathic methods, the remedies used, and how their action might be explained (we discovered how clumsy our language is in this culture)—the possibilities of healing, how to contact a reliable practitioner, and how much it might cost (we decided comparatively little). The issue of taking responsibility for our own health was

raised, and the group as a whole seemed convinced that was certainly the way they had moved or were moving. Several had found that giving up their hormone therapies, changing their diet (even in small ways), taking exercise, and changing their attitude toward their illness had already made significant improvements. They no longer felt fearful and helpless about their 'plight,' but were consciously working to improve their overall level of health and therefore, correspondingly, the quality of their lives.

An information sheet on alternative treatment methods published by the British Endometriosis Society also discusses tissue salts, frequently used by homoeopaths, according to the information sheet. 'Tissue salts are not vitamins but are based on Schussler's system of Biochemic Medicine in which he identified 12 salts as being present in the body and being responsible for the body's correct functioning.' We have been unable to obtain much information on tissue salts or homoeopathy. Anyone wishing more information on homoeopathy can write to the Homoeopathic Development Foundation Ltd, 19a Cavendish Square, London W1.

ALTERNATIVE APPROACHES: A SUCCESS STORY

Many alternative treatment practitioners combine a variety of the alternative treatment approaches described in this article. An example of this is the following story from member Mollie Ridout.

'I had typical symptoms—painful periods, pelvic discomfort, etc—for about four years . . . About a year [after laparoscopy], the symptoms became worse, with pelvic discomfort and fluid retention continuing for about 20 to 25 days out of the month and disabling cramps during my period . . . Someone suggested I go to an acupuncturist.

'After conducting a complete physical, the acupuncturist recommended some dietary changes—eliminating, as much as possible, salt, caffeine, sugar, and alcohol from my diet. (All the fun stuff!) As I understood it, these are all substances that affect metabolism levels, thereby increasing stress and indirectly affecting hormone levels. In addition, salt of course affects fluid retention. My doctor [the acupuncturist] describes endometriosis as a by-product of a hormone imbalance, where oestrogen levels rise and progesterone levels are too low to balance them. Treatment is aimed at re-establishing normal hormone production levels by reducing stress, controlling diet, and using acupuncture. She told me that once my hormone imbalance was corrected, it would take about two years for my body to repair the damage caused by the endometriosis and eliminate the symptoms.

'I was supposed to stay on the prescribed diet for a month before she started acupuncture treatments, but in the meantime she did two things. She prescribed 500 mg of vitamin B_6, to be taken for 10 days before each period (along with a lot of other vitamins to prevent any imbalance). [Large, continuing doses of B_6 *should not* be taken without a doctor's supervision; it can cause nerve damage.] This made an immediate, dramatic improvement in the fluid retention problem— except for slight tenderness in my breasts, I haven't had any fluid retention in two years.

'She also put "semipermanent" acupuncture needles in my earlobes. These are very small stainless steel studs with a sharp point (when you get tired of explaining what they are, you can pass them off as punk jewelry). They stayed in my ears for about three weeks before I eventually knocked them out. Their purpose is pain relief, and they were very effective. When my period started a week later, I had no cramps at all, no need for drugs!

'After a month on the diet, she began a series of acupuncture treatments, using "modern" acupuncture, that is, with an electrical current rather than by inserting needles. The current is applied with a probe-like instrument at carefully plotted points on the ears, forehead, scalp, and hands. The treatments lasted for a half-hour, once a week for five weeks. It was mildly uncomfortable, but not as bad as going to the dentist. By the time the treatments ended, I was free of endometriosis symptoms.

'About eight months later, I began to have some pelvic discomfort (but still no cramps!), so I went back and had three follow-up treatments. That was a year ago. I have pretty much eliminated salt, caffeine, and alcohol from my diet, but not sugar. I have begun to learn yoga as a way of reducing stress. And I feel that I am pretty much free of endometriosis symptoms. During the past spring I had mild cramps a few times, but they were definitely within the limits of what I can live with. No pelvic discomfort, no fluid retention. I haven't attempted to get pregnant, so I don't know about that. In general, I feel more comfortable and 'at home' in my body than I have in the past seven years. I also feel like I have a better understanding of what's going on with my body and access to the tools—diet, vitamins, stress management techniques, and perhaps more acupuncture treatments—that I need to take care of myself and feel good. That sense of helplessness (the worst part of endometriosis!) is gone.

'I have talked to many women who have endometriosis, and the one conclusion I have drawn is that the disease is different for different women. And likewise, the treatment that works for one woman may not work for someone else. My own treatment was a long process of trial and error and trying out things I wasn't sure I believed in. I don't think it's the answer for everybody. But maybe hearing about this can get a few other people started on their own way. We all seem to be explorers in unmapped territory.'

Section III. Coping: The Many Challenges

Endometriosis is a chronic disease. For most women this means living with the symptoms of the disease for many years, each new development presenting a new challenge.

This section provides information on how to cope with medical treatments and with the emotional upheaval that is created by having a long-term, often painful illness. There is also a chapter that tells in moving terms what it means to be a teenager with endometriosis.

The Endometriosis Association teaches women how to live with the disease on a daily basis, without losing sight of the final goal: the conquest of endometriosis.

7
Coping with Medical Treatments

'I suffered for many, many years from so many various symptoms of this disease, with no one taking me seriously. It was only last year when I was actually bedridden from constant pain that I finally found a doctor who was able and willing to help. I underwent a laparoscopy and was diagnosed as having endometriosis. My doctor spent much time with me discussing not only the disease, but the various types of treatments there are for it. I am now relatively pain-free, and the quality of my life has improved 1000 percent.

'That is, of course, not the end of the story, for although my physical pain is not as bad as it once was, the mental pain of suffering from this disease remains. I am 32 years old, single, and living alone, have never had a child or been pregnant. I was brought up in a social climate that not only advocated free love, but also stressed freedom of choice. Birth control was readily available, and all of my contemporaries and I just functioned with the assumption that we would get pregnant whenever we wanted to. Now I am faced with the fact that I no longer have a choice. I have to ask myself whether I still would have the choice if any of the (over the years) dozens of doctors I saw since I was a teenager had taken me seriously, taken my symptoms seriously, or had tried to do some research on diseases like this. I wish there were a group in my area with whom I could share this

mental anguish and anger, but, in lieu of that, I continue to look forward to your newsletters as a main source of support.' [Since Jane wrote this letter, she helped to start a chapter in Cincinnati.]

Jane, Cincinnati, Ohio

'I am confused as to what kind, if any, of ongoing treatment I should be undertaking. My ob/gyn suggests nothing—he feels hormone and drug therapy is necessary only when there are problems with infertility. I have completed my family . . . I would hate to find out too late that I could have avoided surgery if I'd had treatment.'

Anne, Idaho

'One of my New Year's resolutions was to find some relief from my severe menstrual cramps and painful intercourse. When I heard of your organization, I immediately wrote to you and received information on endometriosis I didn't even know existed . . . I kept a detailed diary of my symptoms for several months. Over the years the doctors I went to treated my symptoms as everything under the sun but endometriosis. When I finally found a doctor that suggested endometriosis, you can imagine my feelings of relief . . .

'Please tell your readers that there is hope. Our doctors are slowly but surely becoming familiar with and educating themselves on endometriosis. In sisterhood.'

Tammy, Missouri

WHAT WOMEN WITH ENDOMETRIOSIS WANT TO KNOW AND WHAT MEDICAL PEOPLE ARE (NOT) TELLING THEM
By Mary Lou Ballweg

Surprise! Women with endometriosis are not receiving the information they want about endometriosis from health care professionals. Of course we all know this is no surprise. Nearly all of us have suffered the frustration of wanting and needing more information about this disease and not being able to rely on health care professionals to give it.

Linda Kimel, a registered nurse pursuing graduate nursing studies at Northern Illinois University and a member of the Association, decided to try to find out what information women with endometriosis wanted and what information they were given by a nurse or doctor. She designed a simple two-page questionnaire, and the Association mailed it to 200 randomly selected members and nonmembers in a bulk mailing in February 1983. One hundred eleven questionnaires were returned from 26 states, a good return. Twelve of the returned surveys were eliminated from the study because they did not meet criteria for the survey (confirmed diagnosis of endometriosis by physician's direct visualization and the woman had known she had endometriosis for at least three months). Three questionnaires were eliminated from the study because they came from women in Canada, and it was felt possible differences in nursing practice in the two countries might make results less clear. (Since the time this study was done, we've found treatment of women with endometriosis is all too similar in the two countries.) This left 96 women in the sample.

Of the 96 in the sample, at least two-thirds reported wanting information on most of the topics in the questionnaire. Topics included general information on endometriosis such as definition, causes, symptoms, seriousness, treatments; ways to cope with and minimize specific symptoms; and whether groups were available to help cope with the disease. Special interest was shown in information about prognosis (prospect for recovery), infertility, and painful symptoms such as back/abdominal pain, painful periods, and painful sex.

Large percentages of the women did not receive the information they wanted from a nurse or doctor. Some of these findings are understandable—for instance, 52 percent of the women wanted to know how long symptoms last but did not get this information. Because no one could possibly predict this for most sufferers, except to explain that the disease is generally chronic, it's not surprising these women didn't get this information. Also, 71.9 percent of the women wanted to know about groups available to help cope with endometriosis but were not told of any. This is not surprising because in the early eighties most doctors and nurses did not yet know about the Endometriosis Association.

But what is less understandable is that the majority of women experiencing symptoms of endometriosis which they wanted help with did not receive help from a doctor or nurse. Here are some of the findings. (Percentages may not add up to 100 due to rounding.)

- *71% of the women who were experiencing painful sex wanted information about coping with that symptom and did not receive it from a doctor or nurse* (9% who were experiencing painful sex wanted information and did receive it; 20% did not report wanting the information)
- *58% of the women who were experiencing back/abdominal pain wanted information about coping with it and did not receive it from a doctor*

or nurse (19% who were experiencing back/abdominal pain wanted information and did receive it from a doctor or nurse; 22% did not report wanting the information)

- *51% of the women who were experiencing painful periods wanted information about coping with this symptom and did not receive it from a doctor or nurse (32% who were experiencing painful periods wanted information and did receive it from a doctor or nurse; 17% did not report wanting the information)*
- *51% of the women who were experiencing diarrhoea/constipation/painful bowel movements wanted information about minimizing the symptoms and did not receive it from a doctor or nurse (9% who were experiencing these symptoms wanted information and did receive it from a doctor or nurse; 40.5% did not report wanting the information)*
- *52% of the women who were experiencing heavy menstrual flow wanted information about coping with it and did not receive it from a doctor or nurse (9% who were experiencing heavy menstrual flow wanted information and did receive it from a doctor or nurse; 38% did not report wanting the information)*

Similar patterns emerged with other symptoms women were experiencing and wanted information on: bladder irritability, dizziness, nausea/vomiting with periods, and frequent colds/infections. No explanation is offered in the study for those who did not report wanting information on a specific symptom or topic, but a possible explanation is that the individual already knew the information.

A slightly different pattern emerged with the topic of infertility. Here, as with other symptoms, the majority of women wanting information about dealing with the symptom did not receive it from a doctor or nurse—61 percent. However, 12.5 percent of these women did not report experience with infertility. For all other symptoms, most of the women wanting information on ways to cope with a symptom had experience with the symptom.

In addition to the 'information gap' on symptoms, gaps between what women wanted to know and the information they received existed in other areas. For instance, 29 percent of the women reporting experience with medications and wanting information on side effects of medications did not receive the information from a doctor or a nurse. And 35 percent reported wanting information on what to expect during tests and did not receive it. Nineteen percent reported they did not receive information on test results. Sixteen percent reported they did not receive information on surgical results.

Thirty-five percent of the study group reported not receiving information on the seriousness of their endometriosis even though they wanted it. And 23 percent reported not receiving information about the possibility of infertility.

Kimel suggests that further research is needed to determine why such a gap exists between what women want to know about endometriosis and what they are told by medical people. A number of explanations for the gap emerge from Association experience, and we hope follow-up research on them will occur. Among these explanations are:

• *Perhaps doctors don't know all the symptoms of endometriosis and so don't give information about them to women with the disease, and perhaps nurses know little at all about the disease.* Almost no mention is made in medical textbooks of some symptoms we have found prevalent in our data registry and contacts with women with endometriosis, especially fatigue, symptoms usually associated with primary dysmenorrhoea (diarrhea and bowel upsets, nausea/vomiting, dizziness, and others), and pain at times other than during the period. Kimel's study reconfirmed these as symptoms that frequently go with endometriosis. (See table at the end of this article.) The British Endometriosis Society has also taken note of these symptoms accompanying endometriosis. The mean number of symptoms in Kimel's study was 7.1, so many of the women in the survey were experiencing a lot of symptoms.

An additional symptom emerged in this study: bladder irritability. Thirty-five percent of the women checked 'urinary bladder discomfort (Feel like you have to go, painful urination)' as a symptom they had experienced. Low-grade fever was also reported by 22 percent of the women. (Eighteen percent of the women in our first data study reported this symptom concomitant with their other endometriosis symptoms.) Twenty-seven percent of the women in Kimel's survey reported 'frequent colds/infection.' (Twenty-five percent reported 'low resistance to infection' in our first data study.)

As for nurses, Kimel wrote to me recently, 'I suspect [based on the literature review and personal conversations with nurses] that nurses lack knowledge about most aspects of endometriosis.'

However, the explanation that some medical people don't know all the symptoms of endometriosis and so don't give information about them to women with the disease doesn't hold true for the two most common symptoms of the disease, painful periods and painful sex, which are mentioned in all discussions of the disease. Other explanations that might help explain the information gap documented in Kimel's study may be:

• *Perhaps some medical people know the symptoms, or at least some of them, but don't know how to deal with them or believe no effective*

RESEARCH REPORT:
EDUCATIONAL NEEDS OF WOMEN WITH ENDOMETRIOSIS

Numbers* and Percentages
Reporting Symptoms

Symptoms	Number	Percent
Menstrual irregularities/hypermenorrhoea (heavy periods)	65	67.7
Dysmenorrhoea (painful periods)	71	74.0
Pain at other times in menstrual cycle	72	75.0
Lower back pain	69	71.9
Vomiting/nausea during periods	36	37.5
Painful bowel movements/diarrhoea/constipation during menstrual periods	69	71.9
Urinary bladder irritability	34	35.4
Dyspareunia (painful sex)	55	57.3
Dizziness during menstrual period	47	49.0
Low-grade fever	21	21.9
Frequent colds/infection	26	27.1
Fatigue	59	61.5
Infertility	49	51.0
Miscellaneous	14	14.6

Numbers* and Percentages
Reporting Treatments Received

Treatment	Number	Percent
None	3	3.1
Pain medication	54	56.3
Oestrogen/progesterone	58	60.4
Danazol	62	64.6
Hysterectomy	6	6.3
Conservative surgery	58	60.4
Miscellaneous	9	9.4

The mean number of treatments reported by women in the study was 2.6

The mean number of symptoms reported by women in the study was 7.1.

*Number of women = 96

---

way to deal with them exists. For example, the symptoms of primary dysmenorrhoea, with or without endometriosis, can often be lessened with antiprostaglandin, anti-inflammatory drugs such as Motrin, Ponstel, etc. But Dr Penny Budoff, author of *No More Menstrual Cramps and Other Good News* (see Appendix), discovered that many doctors did not know about these effective treatments for symptoms of primary dysmenorrhoea. (Of course, women with endometriosis have to be treated for the endometriosis also.)

If the medical professional does not believe there's an effective way to deal with a particular symptom, perhaps, based on the needs stated by women in this study, he or she should clearly state that. Is it hard for medical professionals to say they don't know something? Perhaps this warrants follow-up study.

• *Perhaps, Kimel suggests in recent correspondence, health care professionals are reluctant to discuss symptoms because they are uncomfortable discussing the topics (painful sex, heavy menstrual bleeding, infertility).*

• *Or, perhaps the medical professional feels specific information about symptoms is not necessary because the treatments proposed should take care of all symptoms.* However, given the chronic nature of the disease and the temporary nature of most treatments, this explanation isn't very satisfactory. Perhaps professionals need to be more aware of the disease as a chronic entity so that they can impart coping information for the long run.

• *Perhaps some medical people underestimate how serious and troublesome endometriosis can be, underestimate the symptoms, and so don't feel it's important to impart much specific information.* I remember well the comment of one well-known gynaecologist involved in teaching and training other gynaecologists. When he was first told that women with endometriosis had started the Association, he said, 'Aren't you women making a mountain out of molehill?' His attitude seems reflected in other doctors by the reactions reported by many women with endometriosis who felt their doctors did not treat their endometriosis as a serious matter. If we in the Association had a dollar for every time we've heard from women that they've been given to understand that their problems are in their heads, we'd have a research fund so big we could study all the hypotheses presented here!

• *Perhaps some medical people underestimate what women with endometriosis want to know about the disease.* Kimel's study clearly shows women with endometriosis want much more information than they are getting.

• *Perhaps some women do not ask or try to ask for the information they want.* Reports to us indicate many women think doctors are too busy or their needs too unimportant. ('I don't want to bother the doctor' is what I've heard often.) They fail to see the doctor as someone they have hired to provide professional services. They fail to see *they* are *paying* for the services of the doctor and that, if the doctor is indeed too busy to help, they have an option of getting another, just as they'd get another repair person for a broken appliance if *one* was too busy.

• *Perhaps some women are trying to ask for information or obtain it, but the medical people aren't listening well or are unwilling to give the information.*

• *Perhaps some medical people don't perceive patient education as a part of their job.*

• *Finally, as Kimel suggests in recent correspondence to me, 'perhaps women do not know whom to ask for the information they want. Are women aware that the nurse is (should be) able to offer "helpful hints" and commonsense solutions to many of the discomforts associated with endometriosis? Nurses spend much time answering clients' questions about technical terms used by doctors.'* Kimel suggests women ask nurses their questions—even if the nurse cannot answer the question, it will make nurses more aware of what women with endometriosis want to know and what nurses need to know.

CHARACTERISTICS OF THE BEST DOCTORS FOR WOMEN WITH ENDOMETRIOSIS
Edited by Association staff

An eagerly awaited, yearly feature in the Endometriosis Association newsletter is the article called 'Best Doctors in Town.' This feature was begun to try to determine what traits make an excellent doctor for women with endometriosis and also to provide a change of pace from the many hundreds of letters received every month expressing frustration with the physician-patient relationship in diagnosis and treatment of endometriosis.

In order to be selected as a 'Best Doctor,' a physician must be medically qualified to treat endometriosis and must be nominated by members of the Endometriosis Association. It is not a popularity contest, but instead a tribute to doctors who exemplify the highest standards of the medical profession. (While the selected doctors are honoured and named in our newsletters, we didn't feel it was appropriate to name them in this book.)

Excerpts from the nominating letters often use the same phrases. There seem to be certain characteristics that are found in all of the 'Best Doctors in Town.' The traits mentioned again and again provide a guide to what to look for when selecting a physician.

We all want a compassionate doctor, and many of our nominees are also described as caring, which seems an active form of compassion. As one letter-writer says:

> He truly became not just my doctor—he became my friend along with his family and office staff. The support I have received from all of them is extremely important. He is a very caring man, who, even though he has four children of his own, knows what it is like to want them . . .

I feel it is important that you know that not only is his medical knowledge vast, but he is an understanding, considerate, and compassionate human being—a true credit to his profession. He is always supportive and never too busy for any of his patients who may call on him. He is truly the example of dedication and deserves the title of 'Best Doc in Town.'

'Very thorough and gentle' is the description given of one of the doctors nominated. Gentleness in speech and medical knowledge are highly prized by women with endometriosis. A rough examination or harsh, thoughtless words can increase the physical and emotional pain of the disease.

Some doctors not only help patients with endometriosis but are also supportive of the work of the Endometriosis Association. Despite busy schedules, these doctors volunteer their time and talents in many ways.

He leads a discussion group for women with endometriosis once a month. This is further evidence of his giving of himself . . .

Another woman writes:

He is a driving force in our support group. We use his office for meetings . . .

A doctor who is good at treating endometriosis will also be a doctor who likes and respects women. One of our members paints a vivid word picture of just such a physician:

He doesn't have any magic treatments . . . but the way he treated me as a human being, the way he put me in charge of my own care and my own body, and the way he respected and comforted me through the difficult times was rare. I remember looking up in the recovery room to a bright light and squinting to see; he put his head between my eyes and the light to shield its glare and to let me know that I was OK.

He is also able to suspend his own value judgments concerning women's life decisions, and he will assist a patient in reaching her goal in the most medically sound manner. Dr ——— can best be described as a humane person and a humanistic physician. By addressing both the mind and the body of a patient he becomes more than a 'healer.' More importantly, he emerges as a compassionate facilitator of women's health. Personally, I feel extremely fortunate to have found an insightful and talented physician such as Dr ———.

Listening to a patient is important, and so is giving adequate information.

> He talked to us, understanding what we had been going through . . .

> She listens to your experiences as a patient and displays genuine concern and compassion.

> My first encounter with Dr ——— was at the suggestion of another member of the Endometriosis Association. After joining the Association I complained about my current doctor's lack of knowledge of and treatment for endometriosis. Throughout the nine months of visits to his office he did little more than ill-advise, question my morality, and collect his fees. Dr ——— is quite different. Within five weeks of my initial visit, I had a laparoscopy and five weeks later started on danazol. Dr ———'s assistance in the decision making was not 'wishy-washy' or high-pressure, and he seemed as genuinely interested in my emotional as my physical health. Appointments began and ended with short discussions in his office—away from the vulnerability one often feels in the examining room, something that I have not encountered with other physicians I have hired.

Some of our 'Best Doctors' seem to be true patient advocates who are not afraid of taking on the whole medical establishment, if needed. They are also not timid about letting patients know that women with endometriosis don't always receive good medical treatment.

> He was appalled at the suggestions of my first doctor (hysterectomy without trying any other treatments first). He let my first doctor know that. He gets extremely angry with the treatment women get from fellow physicians. The women in this country need more physicians to speak up as he does.

The 'Best Doctors' are also tops in medical expertise. One of the physicians nominated is warmly praised for his 'professionalism' and 'skill' in performing laser surgery. Another woman writes:

> He keeps me informed of the latest developments in diagnosis and treatment to help me with the difficult decision making process.

I was definitely diagnosed with severe endometriosis during a laparoscopy in the fall of 1984. There were endometriomas on both my ovaries, abundant scar tissue, and many implants. About one year later it became apparent that I was in desperate need of surgery.

I first became familiar with Dr ——— and laser laparoscopy when he spoke at the New York chapter. At first, I had great concern that severe disease could not be treated with laser laparoscopy. However, after having several conversations with Dr ——— and some of his patients, I realized that he was very successfully treating severe disease with laser laparoscopy. I decided to have the surgery.

After a four-hour operation . . . I was discharged the following day. The next day I already felt wonderful. I was able to be fairly active throughout my recovery and returned to work three weeks after the operation. Presently, I feel better than I have in 18 years! My only recurring symptom so far has been infrequent mild pain from some operative adhesions. However, otherwise I feel normal again—I have energy, a light feeling in my abdomen, and look much healthier as well.

Thanks to Dr ——— and his laser laparoscopy, I am once again living a normal life.

Skill and knowledge are justifiably valued, but sometimes it is also important to know when another opinion might be helpful. This is the case with one of our 'Best Doctors.'

He has expertise to provide almost all needed care but doesn't hesitate to ask for help when it is needed.

The doctors our members recommend are well informed and willing to share much of their knowledge with patients. They talk *with* people, not down to them! There is a real healing partnership between many of the 'Best Doctors' and the women that they treat.

Dr. ——— has let me know that he values a well-informed patient, welcomes questions, and realizes that the responsibility for choices concerning my medical options remain *mine*, not his. He is soft-spoken, friendly, considerate, and helpful, and I am very fortunate to have him as my gynaecologist. He is also self-effacing. During my presurgery visit, when he had finished answering my long list of questions to my satisfaction, I said, 'What more could I ask for?' His reply: 'What *less* could you be satisfied with?' He is my idea of what a doctor should be.

As a physician I have found Dr ———'s medical evaluations to be thoughtful, measured, and thorough (unlike other physicians who made rash judgments, frequently in direct opposition to each other). He has listened carefully and thoughtfully to a list of confusing and bizarre symptoms which have plagued me for some 10 years (and which, according to other physicians, [a] are normal for a woman of my age or [b] require no comment at all other than an amused, quizzical look) and has suggested treatments that have proven to be successful. And unlike physicians who only *say* that the physician-patient relationship is a partnership, Dr ——— actually *believes it and practices it,*

Most of us realize that doctors have busy schedules, especially doctors who have an active obstetrics practice! That's why our members are especially pleased when a physician regularly returns phone calls or is as prompt as possible for appointments.

He is always supportive and never too busy for any of his patients who may call on him.

Another doctor is 'honest, interested and available ... He has returned every call the same day...' The return of a phone call may seem a small thing, but it shows a respect for patients that sometimes seems rare.

I called his office, and to my amazement he spoke to me personally on the telephone. Without ever meeting me before, he suggested that I come in to his office at my earliest convenience.

Dr. ——— gave me tremendous emotional support during my crisis by personally calling me at home to check on my condition.

Endometriosis is not a funny topic, but one of our nominees has what is described as a 'unique sense of humour.' Sharing a light moment, or a happy one, can help ease the burden for both doctor and patient. Sensitivity doesn't necessarily preclude laughter or joy.

One of our members wrote:

He has great perseverance in trying various modes of treatment ... a special sensitivity to the emotional aspects of his patients, and he is very supportive ... He has a sense of humour that can take the edge off trying times.

One letter writer told us about a particularly moving moment spent with her nomination for 'Best Doctor in Town.'

> The day I was in labour he canceled all of his appointments and stayed with my husband and me from 9:00 A.M. until he delivered our baby, near 11:00 P.M. He talked to me through the mild contractions and gave me his hand during the strong ones. The same day we celebrated more than our baby's birth. It was his birthday, too ... if it weren't for his help and care, I don't know if I would have had a baby. He delivered our baby and shared in our gift of life!

Our 'Best Doctors in Town' may sound too good to be true, but we can assure you that they are all real men and women. We hope the day will come when all women with endometriosis will be treated by competent and caring practitioners such as these.

CHOOSING A DOCTOR
By the Twin Cities Chapter (Minneapolis/St. Paul, Minnesota) of the
Endometriosis Association

[Editor's Note: Joyce Hall, president of the Twin Cities chapter, wrote that the group developed this guide to what to look for in a health care professional because of frequent calls for doctor recommendations 'and the members felt uncomfortable recommending someone because of problems in the past. When a member recommended her doctor, and another saw that doctor and didn't like him or her, it was an uncomfortable situation. The problem seemed to be different expectations. For example, one woman needs a very caring doctor, when another doesn't care about bedside manner as long as the doctor is knowledgeable.']

Before you begin the process of picking or changing doctors, take some time to examine your personal philosophy regarding health care. Some questions to ask yourself:

- Am I more comfortable with a female doctor or a male doctor?
- Do I want to know details of my illness and treatment, or do I want the doctor to take care of it for me?
- Do I want to follow a traditional treatment plan, or am I interested in a holistic approach?

During the course of the disease, what you want in treatment and in a doctor will probably change. It is important to occasionally reevaluate your current situation and your personal philosophy to make certain the treatment and the doctor still meet your needs.

Finding a Doctor

Check with other women with endometriosis and women's health groups. (They may maintain a consumer comments file.)

Check with nurses and other health care professionals. (They are often privy to 'inside' information.)

Ask your friends who their doctor is.

Find Out About Office Policy and Procedures

Will the doctor's office hours fit your schedule?

Does he or she have a partner who is familiar with your case and has access to your medical records should an emergency arise?

Does the doctor have a nurse practitioner or a nurse who is allowed to take an active role in patient care?

Will the doctor personally answer and return phone calls?

Is there enough time allowed for appointments so you may discuss your concerns?

Is it policy to have discussions between doctor and patient done with the patient clothed, particularly the initial consultation, rather than during the examination itself?

Evaluate the Doctor

Does the doctor have other patients with your medical problem?

Does he or she seem genuinely concerned about you?

Does he or she take the time to listen to you?

Does he or she seem to believe you?

Is he or she comfortable performing surgery?

Does he or she refer patients out, and if so, to whom?

Are a breast exam and a rectovaginal exam part of his or her usual exam?

Is he or she interested in treating disease or primarily in delivering babies?

Take Control

Assume responsibility for your own health care.

Educate yourself about the menstrual cycle, hormonal changes and fluctuations.

Educate yourself about endometriosis and treatments.

Identify for your doctor major areas of concern in your treatment (e.g., pain control, fertility).

Have your questions written down.

Stick to the facts. Control your emotions when talking to the doctor. Be persistent in demanding good health care.

Inform the doctor if you are using him or her as your primary physician so he or she can schedule annual examinations.

Find a support group.

DOCTOR SATISFACTION: A CHECKLIST
By Dorsie L. Hathaway

- Are you treated with compassion and respect?
- Do you trust this doctor?
- Do you feel that your doctor listens carefully to you and believes you when you report new or unusual symptoms?
- Does your doctor answer all of your questions in terms you understand?
- Do you feel as if your feelings and observations are discounted or disbelieved or are attributed to factors other than endometriosis?
- Are you able to be seen immediately when you have an urgent problem?
- How many days do you have to wait for routine appointments?
- How long do you usually sit in the waiting room when you have arrived promptly?
- How long do you usually wait in the examining room?
- Has this doctor done any surgical procedure on you? If yes, did you feel that you were fully informed of risks and benefits prior to surgery?
- Are you personally satisfied with this physician and your treatment programme?
- Would you recommend this doctor to another woman with endometriosis? Why?
- Are your phone calls returned promptly? By whom?

Dorsie Hathaway founded the Portland (OR) chapter in 1985. She is a feminist, a writer, and a full-time nursing student. She has worked as a hotline counsellor, rape victims' advocate, and first president of the Portland Chapter of the Endometriosis Association. She is a single parent of three children. Her advice for others doing battle with endometriosis is 'Arm yourself with knowledge; make informed decisions about your health care. It is you who will live with the consequences.'

EXPERTS USUALLY ARE RIGHT, RIGHT?
WRONG
By Jo Coudert

'*An interesting note for women on danazol—be sure to tell your eye doctor if you are taking the drug. Better still, try to postpone your refraction until after you're done taking it. I had a frustrating (and expensive!) experience spanning one year with three consultations, finally one with an ophthalmologist who said that the danazol could, indeed, change my prescription temporarily. Now I have glasses I can't wear and am back to my original prescription. Also, severe hormone fluctuations during advanced stages of endometriosis and after hysterectomy may also influence eye correction, but this probably isn't as common.*'

Paula, Northfield, Vermont

'*I have enclosed a copy of the letter sent by the first gynaecologist I saw to my then referring GP.*

'*I'm sure you will appreciate my decision to seek a second opinion. Ten days after my visit to this "quack," I had an examination by a very competent gyn. He diagnosed my condition as endometriosis after a quick, painless internal. A week later he performed a laparoscopy to determine the extent of the endo . . .*

'*I'm thankful that I was aware enough to get a second opinion. The pain (physical and emotional) of endometriosis leaves no room for incompetent doctors such as the first I saw. He's still practicing in Toronto. God help his patients.*'

Bette, Toronto, Ontario

[The following is the doctor's letter referred to by Bette.]

'*On examination, this is a high-strung, anxious young woman in no acute distress or discomfort . . .*

'*I counselled this patient regarding her discomfort and pain, and the differential boils down to two things: either she has a pelvic congestion syndrome that may be related to ungratified sexual encounters, excessive masturbation, or no intercourse at all. The second possibility is that she has a low-grade salpingitis on the left side. Because treatment of the second condition is easier and more straightforward, I've elected to put her on tetracycline medication for two weeks' time.*'

Dr ———, Toronto, Ontario

'*Two years ago a friend had given me a copy of your yellow brochure after she had heard of my problems . . . During the two years since I've seen the brochure I've had many frustrating experiences with doctors and hospitals and laboratories and just dealing with the ever-present problem.'*

Marlene, New York

'The doctor told me he removed the endometriosis, but I am now suffering from the same disease again.

'My doctor says I need to make a decision soon as to how to solve the problem . . . I am 26 years old, have two children, and am very afraid of the idea of a hysterectomy . . . Any advice or information you can give me will be greatly appreciated. I am very confused and scared, plus I am running out of time as far as making a decision.'

Nancy, Missouri

[Editor's Note: We are pleased to be able to reprint the following article from *Woman's Day* magazine due to the kind permission of its author, Jo Coudert. Thank you to member Nina Feldman of Oakland, California, for bringing it to our attention. We felt, like Nina, that the article had a valuable message for women with endometriosis.]

My younger sister just called in tears. The head of the daycare centre where her son Tucker goes once a week had told her, 'If this child got enough love at home, he wouldn't cry when you left him.'

Yes, he would. Tucker has his own reasons for crying, which Carolyn very well knows. She's as tuned in to his needs and wants as a world-class rider is to his mount. But that pronouncement by an expert threw Carolyn into paroxysms of self-doubt. Although fears of becoming too attached to her toddler had caused her to take him to the daycare centre in the first place, she now wondered if she was failing him.

I tried to reassure her. 'He's a fine, secure baby and you know it,' I said. 'The woman at the centre doesn't know what she's talking about.'

'But she has a master's degree in child psychology,' Carolyn wailed. 'She *must* know.'

I reminded my sister of the time she and I found four newborn kittens abandoned in a field. 'Animals that young can't survive without their mother,' the veterinarian told us. But we couldn't bear to let the kittens starve. We bought toy nursing bottles and took turns getting up in the night to feed them. 'The vet was an expert,' I remarked, 'but he happened to be wrong about the kittens.'

'That was different,' Carolyn said.

'All right,' I went on, 'how about that morning in Vermont when the hot light came on in the car? Was that different too?' She remembered as well as I did how quickly we stopped at a garage. 'Don't worry about it,' the mechanic assured us. 'The light will go off as soon as the car gets warmed up.' We knew the car, and we knew the hot light had never lit up on any other cold morning—but the expert had told us it was all right, so we drove on.

It turned out that the radiator was frozen. We almost ruined the car, to say nothing of our weekend. 'It served us right,' I reminded Carolyn, 'because we listened to someone who was supposed to know instead of paying attention to our own sense of the situation. And that's exactly what you're doing with Tucker. You're letting somebody who doesn't know your baby ruin your pleasure in being a good mother just because she's supposed to be an expert. Well, I think that's foolish.'

I was scolding, but I was sympathetic too. The world has become so complicated that we've lost confidence in our own ability to understand and deal with it. But common sense is as useful now as it ever was. No amount of expertise substitutes for an intimate knowledge of a person or a situation. At times you just have to trust your own judgment.

It almost cost me my life to learn that. I was reading a book one day, idly scratching the back of my head, when I noticed that, in one particular spot, the scratching echoed inside my head like fingernails on an empty cardboard carton. I rushed off to my doctor's office the very same day.

He laughed. 'Got a hole in your head, have you?' he teased. 'It's nothing—just one of those little scalp nerves sounding off.' Two years and four doctors later, I was still being told it was nothing. To the fifth doctor, I said, almost in desperation, 'But I live in this body. I *know* something's different.'

'If you won't take my word for it, I'll take an x-ray and prove it to you,'' he challenged.

Well, there it was, of course: the tumour that had made a hole as big as an eye socket in the back of my skull. After the operation, a young resident paused by my bed. 'It's a good thing you're so smart,' he said. 'Most patients die of these tumors because we don't know they're there until it's too late.'

I'm really not so smart. And I'm much too willing to be docile in the face of authority. Is that a particular problem for women? It was for me. I didn't want to make waves. I didn't want the doctors to think I was challenging them or that I was difficult. 'Never, for the sake of peace and quiet, deny your own convictions,' Dag Hammarskjöld, former secretary-general of the United Nations, once said. But that's exactly what I'd done.

Would I have acted the same way if the doctors had not been men? Maybe not. Men's opinions carry more weight. They expect to be listened to more than women do, and they pontificate more. It's hard for us to question such absolute certainty.

When my friend Minna inherited some money, she decided to put it into blue-chip stocks until she was ready to retire. But one evening she listened to an economist state unequivocally that the 1982 recession was about to turn into a full-scale depression, and the Dow Jones Average would drop below 500. Minna sold all her stocks, thinking it was better to take a sizable loss than to risk further erosion of their value. The next week the stock market turned, and the Dow Jones began its climb to record highs well above 1,000.

'He sounded so sure,' Minna complained. 'I thought he must really know.'

Of course he sounded sure. Experts always do. Neville Chamberlain was positive, just before the start of World War II, that there would be 'peace in our time.' Producer Irving Thalberg did not hesitate to advise Louis B. Mayer against buying the rights to *Gone with the Wind* because 'no Civil War picture ever made a nickel.' Even Abraham Lincoln surely believed it when he said in his Gettysburg Address: 'The world will little note, nor long remember, what we say here . . .'

Each of these men proved to be wrong, as those in authority often are. It's time we stopped being intimidated by experts. When it's an area we really know about—our bodies, our families, our houses, our cars — let's listen to what the experts say, then make up our own minds. Our guess is probably as good as theirs—and sometimes a whole lot better.

Ms. Coudert is the author of four books, including the bestselling *Advice from a Failure*, a contributing editor of *Woman's Day*, and a frequent contributor to that magazine and *Reader's Digest*.

NEVER BREAK YOUR FUNNY BONE; OR, UNTOLD GUIDELINES FOR THE HOSPITAL PATIENT
By Gloria Burk

Since I have been admitted to the hospital 14 times, I fancy myself somewhat of an expert on the subject of hospital patient survival. You may be a patient someday and benefit from my experiences by reading the suggestions I have outlined for you. These suggestions will not cure you; they are meant to help you to survive your hospital stay.

The ideas I propose to you are not usually told to you by doctors or nurses. They are important ideas that answer questions like, 'Who waters the plants that I get as gifts?'; 'May I wear underwear?'; 'May I chew gum?'; 'Is mouthwash optional or mandatory?'; 'What are "keepsies" of the things they give me to use?'; and 'Are chocolate-covered cherries considered "bland"?'

From the moment your doctor says to you, 'I'd like to put you in the hospital,' you'll probably start to cower. But be assertive! Ask him or her boldly, 'What's with this "put you in" jazz?' and 'What do you mean, "*the* hospital"? What hospital? You mean there's only one good hospital in this whole town?'

Do not be intimidated by hospital talk, which is spoken by all medical professionals. They like to use unused words like *void* and *ambulatory*. They're also very big on initials that will make little sense to you, like *NPO*, which means 'nothing by mouth.' Shouldn't the abbreviation for that be *NBM?* Of course, then the patient may become confused and think it means 'no bowel movement,' and she would never be released from the hospital! The initials flow freely; there's IV, IVP, EKG (or ECG), EEG, EMG, OR, ICU, CAT, STAT, and the ever popular BM. They have 'cute' names for serious things, like 'hysties' for hysterectomy patients, 'cholies' for gallbladder removal patients, and 'appies' for appendectomies.

If you don't remember anything else you have read here, remember this: one of the most important things you can do in the hospital after you have surgery is pass gas. The nurses and doctors don't care where it comes from, as long as it leaves your body. It's considered almost a religious experience! In fact, if you *don't*, they will give you tray after tray after tray of 'torture' food. What is that, you ask? It is cool, weak tea (no cream); salty, brown, lukewarm broth; little bright-coloured, very sweet rubbery cubes, called *gelatin;* and a cup of warm, red, sweet juice (which I suspect is melted gelatin!). Take my advice and do it this way: alternate between a spoonful of broth and a sip of juice; take a cube of gelatin and wash it down with water, pretending it's a pill; then slowly sip your tea to settle your stomach. If you consume five trays of that in a day and a half, plus three pitchers of water, I guarantee that you will receive a gold star *and* a happy face on your intake and output chart.

But, if you do not pass any gas, you do not get solid, regular food. You don't deserve it. You'll begin to daydream of the taste of meat between your teeth; the feeling of toothpicks and dental floss; the ecstasy of garlic breath. You'll try to recall the sounds of crunching and munching. You'll begin to think of ways to bargain, beg, and promise! After all, one gas bubble could buy you some real oatmeal or a piece of toast (although I must caution you about becoming too excited about hospital toast; it's like eating a warm, moist powder puff).

If your doctor prescribes peace and quiet for you, forget it. Well, in a way you *are* in for R & R—radiology and rashes! Not to mention restlessness and responsibility! You are responsible for important decisions, like:

1. What problem warrants pressing the *nurse* button? Does a broken television qualify? Are you in enough pain for a pill? What about ice for your water?
2. Should you shut your door? You don't want to appear antisocial, but you also don't want some weird visitor leering at you as he saunters by your room.
3. Whose footsteps are coming down the hall? Do they have a syringe or an enema? Or, maybe you'll luck out, and someone will be bringing flowers. Remember the 'hard and fast' rule: if the footsteps are 'hard,' they're those of visitors; if the footsteps are 'fast,' they're those of the nurses. Maintenance men sound like jingling, slow-moving bears, and doctors float in and out like weightless phantoms.

If it is your misfortune to be in for 'tests,' you are in for an unusual experience. If you're like me, the word *test* itself scares you! Childlike feelings arise from deep within you, and many questions come to mind, like, 'Will it hurt?'; 'Will I pass?'; and, 'What will the tests show?' In order to survive hospital tests, the patient must like pretending to read outdated magazines; receiving laxatives and enemas; abstaining from water, food, and sex; receiving all types of injections in all types of places; drinking chalk; wearing drab, open-backed nightgowns; lying on cold, hard tables; holding her breath a lot; losing her dignity; and waiting. Don't say I haven't warned you.

A large portion of your day in the hospital is spent discussing, requesting, and swallowing pills. The only way you can get a pill is if the doctor orders it. You could be taking tranquilizers for 22 years prior to your hospital visit, but when they clamp that plastic bracelet on your wrist, it's 'Good-bye, tranquilizers; hello, cold turkey'! What could a little tranquilizer or drink hurt? Just a little something to calm the old nerves. Forget aspirin or Rolaids, too. But they can give you anything they want!

Before swallowing a pill, ask what it does for (or to) you and how often they will be giving it to you. Keep a three-by-five file card on each pill, including its complete description, side effects, and what it 'does.' You just may want to ask the nurse its actual name, in the event that you might want to discuss it with your doctor or another nurse later. It will be easier for them that way, too. After all, they might not understand your pill descriptions, like 'teeny, pink, bitter dot things' or 'gigantic, squarish, oblong white horse pills.' (A word of caution about sleeping pills: they're OK if you like to get up for the day at 2:00 A.M., which is when they wear off.)

Roommates can make or break your hospital stay. They are usually of the same sex as you; seldom of the same religion or age; and never have the same ailment or doctor. They fall into several categories:

1. The 'Very Ill.' These are the *very* sick ones and could be sad and depressing, but they don't *have* to be. Try talking to them, then listen to them. You'll be surprised at how much better you both will feel. If they are too ill to converse, at least you get to pick all the television programmes you like.
2. The 'Swingers.' They talk fast, sneak cigarettes, and are frightened of all medical things. Your feelings do not matter to them. Their visitors can be pure torture for you! They bring forbidden goodies, like pizza and beer; they laugh loudly and smoke; and they don't leave even after a nurse tells them that visiting hours are over. If you really want to get rid of them, wait for a lull in the conversation, press the nurse's button, and then, when she asks what you need, say, 'May I have something for the terrible nausea I have?' The visitors will leave quickly, and you get a can of cold 7-Up!
3. The 'Boobtube Freaks.' They watch television from dawn to dusk, and you can bet your bedpan they love all the shows that you hate. They have difficulty with their hearing, so the television is nice and loud. Their favourite programs are game shows, and they don't care for 'MASH.' Help!
4. The 'Nice Ones.' They are the people who admit that they are afraid; excuse themselves, if rude; will listen and talk; compromise with the shelves, television, bathroom, lights, and visitors. In other words, they're clones of *you*! If they laugh at your jokes, buy them some candy and get their telephone number, so you can call them in the future.

After a while, you'll be getting your own visitors. They also fall into categories:

1. The 'Significant Others.' These you need and want to see. They are spouse, children, parents, or siblings. They can come in anytime, in your opinion, and they often have the courtesy to tell you when they are visiting.
2. The 'Good Friends.' These are almost as good as family. They come in, let you talk if you want to, and bring something absolutely wonderful like cold oranges or chocolate creams. Their chats are lighthearted and funny, and they don't overstay their welcome.

3. The 'Awkward Ones,' like aunts and bosses. They usually pop in at the wrong time. The conversation is strained and usually includes questions and cute jokes about the food. Their opening line is, 'Well, you *look* good.' They also like talking about the weather and the view from your window. They don't like to discuss your sickness and avoid emotions of any kind. They mean well, though, and they never stay long.

4. Clergy. If you're religious, they are welcome and comforting. You will probably pray with them about trust, faith, and getting well. You will pray to yourself that they don't notice your risqué get well cards, your see-through nightgown, or your rumbling intestines!

5. The 'Sickies,' the lowest form of parasitic visitor. According to them, the hospital that you are in is one of the worst in the city. They *always* go into detail as to why it's the worst. Their conversation is sprinkled with comforting words like *butcher, malpractice, infection, quack,* and *relapse.* They always stay too long, and the only thing they leave you with is a headache.

In conclusion, a few final 'rules':

1. Don't expect to hear sad, sexy, or jazzy music as you hear on television doctor programmes.

2. Plan your visitor list ahead. Do not tell your boring friends about being hospitalized.

3. Don't write notes or directions on your belly prior to surgery.

4. Be wary of adjectives on your menus. Never be surprised at what you find on a food tray. Never eat anything you don't recognize.

5. If and when you are allowed to take a shower, stretch it out as long as you can. It will be one of the few things that will remind you of home.

6. Don't look too good for visitors. You won't get the pity you so richly deserve.

All kidding aside, in my earnest effort to help you, the hospital patient, I sincerely hope that I have put your mind at ease and that you have taken each and every suggestion given to you in the seriousness it was meant to convey. On second thought, *never* put all your kidding aside!

Gloria Burk is a homemaker, a student, and part-time secretary. At one time, she was the correspondence secretary for the Endometriosis Association. She has been married for 24 years to a letter carrier, and they have two adopted teenaged children. Her hobbies include water-

colour painting, creative writing, ceramics, and volunteering. She wrote
this humorous essay while in the hospital recovering from a hysterectomy.

COPING AFTER HYSTERECTOMY AND REMOVAL OF THE OVARIES: THE HORMONE REPLACEMENT DILEMMA

By Mary Lou Ballweg

'*Early in 1984 I had a hysterectomy and my ovaries removed.
At this point in my life, having been through major and minor
surgery, this was the only way to recover from endometriosis. The
surgery was a breeze (two doctors, an ob/gyn, and an internal
surgeon to cut away the amount of endometriosis grown on every
organ in my abdomen). I recuperated in the hospital 10 days and
stayed home for four weeks, taking daily walks for exercise (it
was a cold winter) and getting my strength back.*

'*I look back now and think this was the smartest medical
decision I made; not only after four weeks was I able to return
to work, but every aspect of my life was back to normal . . .*'

Joan, New York, New York

'*In November of 1985 I had a radical hysterectomy due to all of
the areas that were infected, and I started taking hormones. After
a few months the pain was slowly returning. My doctors took me
off the oestrogen and used progestin shots for six months, stating
that the endometriosis was active again. I feel cheated, with
nowhere to turn. For the last 15 years I've been told that a
hysterectomy was the answer since pregnancy never occurred.
And now, one year after the surgery, I'm still in pain. When does
endometriosis ever die? Certainly not with a hysterectomy. Don't
ever think that it's the answer . . .*'

Georgiana, Arlington, Texas

'*I am feeling so well now that I would like to share my experience
with you. As of now I am recuperating from a total hysterectomy.
My surgery was done a week ago, and I have recovered so well
that even my doctor and nurses were amazed.*

'*I have a very kind, understanding, and wonderful doctor,
who has helped me get through these last four years of turmoil.
He was always there when I needed him. Because I was only 32
when we first suspected endometriosis, he wanted me to wait as
long as I could before giving in to surgery. I was on a combination
of natural vitamins and herbs for a year and a half that actually*

took away my pain. After that this did not help anymore. I tried different vitamins and also watched my diet—cutting out a lot of sugars and carbohydrates. This helped to some extent. I never tried birth control pills or danazol because of religious beliefs (Amish) and also the after effects. I finally came to the point where I had only about five days out of a month that I felt good. Sometimes I thought I was surely losing my mind. But because I knew this was caused by an imbalance in hormones, I was able to fight back. There were times when I wanted to give up, but I knew I couldn't. I have a wonderful and understanding husband who helped me so much. As for pain, it was never unbearable— just nagging, sometimes sharp pains that were caused by the ovaries, sometimes a burning feeling under the skin in the lower stomach that was caused by endometriosis just under the tissues, also discomfort in the rectum caused by endometriosis on the uterosacral ligaments ...

'For me this [hysterectomy] was the answer, but it was a very hard decision to make.'

Barbara, Middlefield, Ohio

[Editor's Note: One of the most difficult problems we face at the Endometriosis Association is how to help women who have undergone total hysterectomy (including removal of both ovaries) and still have the symptoms of the disease. The situation is complicated by the medical controversy over the safest treatment procedures in such cases.

The letter that follows illustrates the anguish felt by women who have undergone a hysterectomy and experienced the return of the symptoms of endometriosis. The response of the Endometriosis Association to this sad situation is included.]

'I am 33 years old, mother of two daughters, homemaker; and when health permits, I am employed as a typist/secretary for short- and long-term assignments.

'My endometriosis was finally diagnosed after the birth of our second daughter when she was 14 months old. I have suffered from this disease for many years ... I am especially interested to receive any information from those of you who have had the endometriosis recur [after removal of ovaries] and, if so, to what degree and how it has been treated.

'When my condition was finally diagnosed, the disease had already eaten a hole through my uterus, causing severe, painful internal bleeding. After a hysterectomy and removal of one ovary, I functioned well for a period of 18 months. Then the remaining ovary became diseased, and the endometriosis rampaged throughout the abdominal and pelvic area.

Surgery was performed again to remove the second ovary after hormonal shots and freezing of endometrial cysts in the vaginal area and on the bladder failed.

'Since that time, I have had exploratory surgery. The disease seems to go in and out of remission very sporadically. Pain is intense and causes me to curtail *all* activities for days at a time.

'My physical problem has become a handicap for me in many ways. I have had to give up good-paying jobs because of the physical stress and pain. It has become humiliating and embarrassing to repeatedly tell my employers of my condition and why I am unable to walk long distances, lift, pull, etc., on some work assignments. At times I feel as though I want to pin a sign on my chest that says, "Handicapped—I am a victim of endometriosis."

'It disturbs me that so many doctors show indifference to this disease and the effect it has on the individuals who are afflicted.

'Several of the women with endometriosis who have written to me told me how ignorant, inconsiderate, unfeeling, and callous the doctors were . . . No one on the face of this earth can even begin to imagine the agony of the disease until they have suffered themselves . . . I need all the moral support I can get and want to give any that I can. *If no one else is going to help all the women who suffer from this disease, then we who have it or have had it must help each other.*'   Karol, Tennessee

Karol raises a couple of questions in her correspondence that we'd like to answer here. First, she raised the issue of recurrence of endometriosis after hysterectomy. We have been trying to alert Association members about this problem, and we will all have to try to help more doctors and medical professionals learn of the latest information about this: yes, endometriosis can recur or continue after hysterectomy, if all ovarian tissue is not removed. About 85 percent of women with endometriosis severe enough to undergo hysterectomy are estimated to get it back if all ovarian tissue is not removed.

If the ovaries are removed, an estimated 5 percent will again experience endometriosis if they take oestrogen to prevent menopause. We have been recommending that women consider not taking oestrogen for some months after hysterectomy and removal of the ovaries to allow time for endometrial growths still in the body to regress from hormone starvation (it is sometimes impossible to remove all as they can be microscopic or in locations the surgeon cannot see or cut on). Menopausal symptoms may be experienced—vitamins and minerals recommended in our article 'Overview of Surgery in the Treatment of Endometriosis,' Chapter 4 of this book, and in *Women and the Crisis in Sex Hormones* may help postpone or ease these symptoms.

One might say, 'Well, if oestrogen could cause a recurrence of endometriosis, I'll just never take oestrogen replacement.' Unfortunately, it's not that simple. Women with early removal of the ovaries are at high risk for osteoporosis and perhaps other health problems that appear to be related to lack of estrogen. Osteoporosis is a disease of the bones in which bones become thin and porous and break easily. It is a serious health problem of older women.

The best current thinking is that women who've had ovaries removed because of endometriosis should wait three to six months (and some of us have waited as long as eight to nine months) and then take a *low* dosage of oestrogen daily. A low dosage of oestrogen is 0.3 or 0.625 mg a day. Too often women tell me they're on a low dosage of oestrogen and go on to say they're on 1.25 or 2.5 mg tablets. These are *not* low-dosage tablets. The safest approach for the woman who's had endometriosis is to take a low dosage of oestrogen and be aware that the endometriosis can recur. This doesn't mean we should worry about it coming back— just don't brush off recurrence of symptoms and be sure you go to a very good doctor if symptoms do recur, not one who doesn't know endometriosis can recur after removal of ovaries.

There are also oestrogen replacement tablets that come with some testosterone in them. These tablets might help offset some of the lessened sex drive reported by some women after removal of the ovaries. (Testosterone is the hormone most linked, researchers believe, to sex drive. Some testosterone is produced in the ovaries.)

Karol also raises the question of endometriosis being cancer. Although endometriosis is sometimes called 'benign cancer' because it can spread like a cancer, it is not cancer. Cancer, by definition, is malignant tissue. Endometriosis, by definition, is normal tissue.

It is possible for endometrial tissue to develop into cancer wherever it is, whether inside the uterus or in the endometriosis growths. However, we have not heard many reports of this happening.

Women who are interested in learning more about hysterectomy and how to cope with it should read *Coping with a Hysterectomy* and *The Castrated Woman* (see Appendix).

OSTEOPOROSIS:
WHAT YOU DON'T KNOW CAN HURT YOU
By Carolyn Keith, M.S.S.W.

Osteoporosis is a condition that has received much media attention recently, and the note sounded is generally alarming. It is often described as a 'silent disease,' stealthily leading to hip fractures, deteriorated vertebrae, and broken arms for women in their later years. Osteoporosis has led to 12 times more deaths (due to complications) than cancer of the uterus. About 25 percent of American women are considered to be at risk of developing osteoporosis in their postmenopausal years.

Though this is a condition that generally does not develop until later life, it is important for younger women to understand osteoporosis so that preventive measures can be undertaken. In younger women who have experienced an early, surgical menopause due to removal of the ovaries, there are some indications of a higher rate of osteoporosis than is true of the general female population. (The average age of natural menopause today is 50 to 51 years old.)

With osteoporosis the bones become increasingly fragile and susceptible to breaking. Though we may tend to think of our bones as permanent, sturdy structures, in reality, throughout our lifetime, bone tissue, like other body tissue, is engaged in a continuing process of cell breakdown and replacement. In the case of our bones, calcium and other minerals are lost from the tissue and replaced. With advancing age, particularly after menopause, that process becomes increasingly unbalanced—the rate of mineral loss exceeds the rate of resorption. The bone mass decreases and bones become more fragile. This gradual decline in bone mass appears to begin as early as the mid-30s, to accelerate for five or six years immediately after menopause, and then to continue at a somewhat slower rate thereafter.

Oestrogen plays an important role in the bone-building process, and it is the declining level of oestrogen in the body that is believed to be involved in the development of osteoporosis. It is for this reason that the process is believed to begin earlier for women who have undergone surgical menopause. At least one researcher suggests that the risk rate for women with surgical menopause may be double that of the general population. A three-year study by University of California-San Francisco radiologist Harry Genant of 37 women who had undergone removal of their ovaries found that on average they lost spinal bone mass at the alarming rate of 9 percent a year after the operation. But low-dosage oestrogen stopped the bone loss and even caused some of the women to regain substantial amounts of bone mass.

Not all women, of course, develop osteoporosis. Among factors that may increase the risk are heredity and health practices. Women who are of slight build, fair skin, and northern European ancestry are at higher risk; heavier women, black women, and women of Mediterranean ancestry are at lower risk.

Since oestrogen seems to be a factor in retarding development of osteoporosis, physicians may prescribe oestrogen replacement for women during and following menopause. While women in general may face the dilemma of deciding whether or not to take oestrogen, a woman whose ovaries have been removed because of endometriosis faces a double dilemma regarding prevention of osteoporosis: not only may she be at earlier risk because of curtailment of her natural oestrogen supply, but she may also be reluctant or unable to take oestrogen because of possible return or continued stimulation of endometriosis. Because of this dilemma, some members of the Association undergoing hysterectomy and removal of the ovaries are choosing *not* to take oestrogen for three to nine months to allow any remaining endometriosis implants or traces to regress and *then* taking low-dosage oestrogen tablets.

Thus, whether you are a woman who has undergone surgical menopause or a woman with ovaries who looks to preventive measures to reduce later-life risk of osteoporosis, knowledge of alternatives—*and the commitment to use them*—may be essential. What are some of those options?

Providing the body with sufficient calcium and the means by which to make optimum use of it is the aim of prevention. We women, for a variety of reasons, generally centred on concerns about weight, tend throughout much of our lifetimes to fail to obtain a sufficient amount of calcium. As we grow older this deficiency is compounded further as our bodies make less efficient use of the calcium we do take in.

It is generally recommended that menopausal and postmenopausal women obtain 1,200–1,500 mg of calcium each day (many health advisors now recommend not waiting that long, but starting this increased intake in our mid-30s). To get that much calcium from food would require eating more cottage cheese, milk, etc., than anyone is likely to want.

In addition to dairy products, certain other foods are good sources of calcium, among them tofu; canned salmon, sardines, and mackerel; and oysters. A number of green leafy vegetables also are high in calcium, but they are not ideal sources since they also contain substances that block absorption of calcium.

Thus it is likely to be best to take a calcium supplement (tablet) regularly. Calcium carbonate is the most concentrated form. Others are calcium lactate (avoid this one, however, if you have a milk intolerance) and calcium gluconate. While bonemeal and dolomite also are forms of calcium, they should be avoided since some brands are contaminated with lead. Since a tablet does not contain the full 1,200–1,500 mg, this enables you to take your daily 'quota' spread out a bit during the day, which increases the body's effective use of it. It's a good idea to take one tablet at bedtime, since the loss of calcium is faster during sleep and since calcium is a mild natural relaxant. Another form of calcium supplement used by some women is antacid tablets. (Many antacids tablets contain calcium.)

Vitamin D is necessary in conjunction with calcium for bone building. Sunshine provides some of our vitamin D, but, particularly for those of us who live in northern areas, that is not enough. Either select a combination calcium and vitamin supplement or take 400 IUs of D daily. Also, magnesium needs to be in balance with calcium (about half as much magnesium as calcium) to build bone effectively. In fact, the authors of *Women and the Crisis in Sex Hormones*, an excellent resource book, explain how taking calcium without magnesium could actually be worse for you than not taking calcium at all because an imbalance could result in excretion of calcium.

Another element necessary for effective bone building is regular vigorous exercise of the weight-bearing bones. This places stress on those bones essential for effective remineralization. This exercise could include walking, running, race walking, aerobic dancing, gymnastics, tennis, and/or weightlifting. While swimming is an excellent lifetime exercise with many health benefits, it is not effective for maintaining strong bones since it does not exert the necessary stress.

Everitt Smith, Ph.D., a research physiologist with the University of Wisconsin at Madison who has done an important study comparing the rate of bone change in women taking oestrogen, taking calcium, or taking calcium and exercising vigorously, recommends 50 minutes of such exercise at least three times a week. His findings suggest that a combination of the right exercise, calcium, and vitamin D may be as effective as oestrogen replacement for many women.

Attention to our diets is another important part of a self-care approach to osteoporosis control. Coffee, alcohol, certain medications such as cortisone and laxatives, soft drinks, and red meat can interfere with absorption of calcium by the body. Meat and soft drinks contain a high level of phosphorus, which is a calcium antagonist. 'At 40, at the latest, it's good prevention to cut down on meat . . .' write the Seamans in *Women and the Crisis in Sex Hormones*.

High stress levels have also been found to retard calcium absorption. And smoking apparently is a risk, too—people who smoke have less bone mass and more fractures than those who do not smoke.

Osteoporosis is a complex topic. If you would like further information about risk factors, diagnostic methods, and preventive measures, an excellent book is *Standing Tall: The Informed Woman's Guide to Preventing Osteoporosis* by Morris Notelovitz, M.D., and Marsha Ware. It's paperback and available at many public libraries. Another resource is *Menopause Naturally; Preparing for the Second Half of Life* by Sadja

Greenwood, M.D. *Women and the Crisis in Sex Hormones* by Barbara and Gideon Seaman is a good source of information about vitamin and mineral supplements and diet. (See Appendix.)

8
When Teens Have Endometriosis

'*I read an article concerning the Endometriosis Association in the* Milwaukee Journal *a while back and found it to be very interesting. My doctors have told me there is a chance I might have endometriosis. They told me a little about it but never went into great detail, and I never went back for the test. I am only 15 years old and very worried. I would appreciate it if you could send me some more information. I really dislike seeing my doctors as much as I do, and if I could read up on this subject a little more I think I might consider having the test taken. But if I were to go back to them and have them beating around the bush again, it would surely be a waste of time. I would appreciate any information you can give me.*'

Lisa, Wisconsin

'*I've been diagnosed with endometriosis for approximately one year. My trouble began at age 10, when I had painful cramps and a heavy menstrual flow. By age 12 I had a cystectomy when a large cyst on my right ovary burst. I had been an active competitive swimmer and was set back for a season. A year later I had another laparoscopy, and other cysts were found. Then, until the age of 17, my problems remained minimal. At 17, I decided to go on the pill. Before that, I had been on it for approximately eight months for my cysts, but the pill proved very*' *irritating. I was on the pill for about six months, and then I was off it for two months, only to return to the terrible pains I had daily. I am 20 today, and I've been on the pill ever since.*

'*During my teenage years, I was always plagued with terrible cramps, bloated stomachs, and a very dull pain on my right side from my ovary. I guess I'm writing in need of emotional support. I am a junior at Penn State University, and I am by far not ready for a family. I'm not wanting a hysterectomy, but also I don't want to live with the pain, emotionally and physically, that I live with every day. I can't imagine what it's like not to have pain and depression every day. There are some days when I actually feel like I'm going to lose my mind! My stomach swells so much that I look as though I'm pregnant. I get so mad, depressed, snooty, and mean from the pill, but it is, by far, my only relief at this point. My doctor is a very feeling doctor, and I have all the confidence in the world in him, but I need some emotional help. My boyfriend of three years has been very understanding and supportive. But I'm not ready to settle down; maybe it won't even be with him. So what am I to do? Wear a sign when I date that says, "Don't consider me unless you aren't sure you want children"? This sounds silly, but it needs to be addressed.*'

Amy, Pennsylvania

'*I am 19 years old, and I have had endometriosis since I was 15. I have had three operations to remove the disease; my most recent operation was two weeks ago. I understand fully that, once a person has been diagnosed with this disease, she usually has it for a number of years to come. I would like your Association to send me some information on this disease, the physical and emotional effects, and if there are some self help groups in my area that you are aware of.*'

Krissie, Georgia

'*I remember the first myth I heard about endometriosis. It was the "working woman's disease." It was supposed to affect only women who delayed having children to build careers. How could that be when I had just turned 19 and had been suffering from painful periods since my first one at age 10?*

'*Two surgeries, danazol, and birth control pills later, I am married and 21 years old. Now, my ability to become pregnant is dependent on another surgery to remove adhesions that are holding down my left tube. It's scary and painful to think about the hospital stay, the recovery, and then the possibility of difficulty in conceiving. All of this for a baby, a natural process that so many women take for granted.*

    'The more I learn about the disease, the better I am able to cope with it. At first, I went through "why me?" Then, after I was done feeling sorry for myself I became angry, and anger made me feel like fighting, and fighting made me strong and determined not to let it overrun my life. Of course, I still have my times when I feel very scared and alone. At those times I turn to my belief in God and that He would never give me more than I can handle. Also, I think of other women who know and understand. Nobody, no matter how much they love you, can truly understand unless they have experienced endometriosis firsthand.

    'I have always been afraid to become involved in the Association because I felt I didn't know enough to help anyone. Well, now that I have come to grips with my own situation and have learned more, I would very much like to help. Just point me in the right direction.'

Loretta, Illinois

'I have just finished reading the article in Self *magazine, May issue, titled "Misplaced Menstruation—Endometriosis." I was very glad to read some printed material on this subject. I have a 13-year-old daughter that has just gone through the scope surgery.*

    'Missy and I have had a hard time dealing with the fact that after the surgery the problem was not corrected for good and that it is something she will have to live with for many more years.'

Sharon, Ohio

'From the onset of puberty, I experienced terrible pain each month. As I reached my later teens, the pain and discomfort only increased. I remember those years, the ones that should be filled with good times spent with your friends and in school activities, but instead I have many memories of being ill to the point of not being able to really participate in the good times.'

One who knows, Oregon

Many members of the Association have histories of symptoms indicative of endometriosis going back to their school years. Currently it is the rare girl or young woman who is diagnosed as having endometriosis at an early age. Yet we know that many women actually have symptoms starting with puberty or a few years afterward. As more treatment options for endometriosis are developed, early diagnosis of the condition may mean that some of the misery of the later stages can be avoided.

The subject of teens and endometriosis is a difficult one. Although research has proven that endometriosis appears in teens, many doctors have thought it was rare in teens. As the chart on page 297 shows, 35 to 38 percent of 1,179 women with endometriosis surveyed by the Association, the British Endometriosis Society, and the Australian Endometriosis Association developed the first symptoms in their teen years but were only diagnosed years later. As with any disease not readily diagnosed, it is important to remember that date of diagnosis does not mean date of inception of the disease.

It is a basic tenet of health care that the earlier a disease is diagnosed, the better we are able to control it. Thus, the first step in helping teens with endometriosis has to be helping them obtain diagnosis. And to do that, we must *listen* to their stories and symptoms and be alert to the symptoms as a possible warning sign of endometriosis. That we do at the Association headquarters, where letters from teens come in continuously. We have included some typical letters here.

For the teen who is experiencing pain and problems now, the letters will help her feel she is not alone, and let her know there are other teens who share her plight. For the adults who wish to help girls with these problems, the letters and the article by Debra Cash will pull at your heartstrings and help you understand that, however hard it may be to believe that these symptoms are happening to your daughter or student or friend, it is important to provide the support and real concern you would provide for other serious problems. Symptoms such as the ones described here should not be ignored! Cash describes some of the actions you and the youngster can consider.

Be wary of the myths that make it hard to help teens who have the disease. The major one is that teens don't have the disease—that it is suffered only by 'career women.' The article by Debra Cash and the letters here dispel this myth. The young women who share their sad experiences have had no time for careers, yet they have already endured all of the anguish of this baffling disease.

Then there is the myth that pregnancy prevents, or even cures, endometriosis. Unfortunately, this idea is still transmitted by some physicians, as well as by well-meaning friends and relatives. It is an especially dangerous myth in this era of epidemic teen pregnancy. Pregnancy is not a cure for anything, and it is important for both teens and adults, including health care professionals, to understand this.

Another time-honoured myth is the one that menstrual pains are women's lot in life and that it's cowardly or useless for a girl to complain about them or seek medical help. Ironically, this particular myth is often passed on by older women in the family who have suffered the same problems in the past. Some of these women may have actually had endometriosis, whether diagnosed or undiagnosed.

But, whatever the case, no young woman should suffer today, just because no help was available in the past for her mother, grandmother, or older sister! Teens are welcome to join the Association, as are their parents. We hope someday to have a special teen support programme that will provide the help needed by girls during this sensitive time of life.

FOR TEENS? IT'S MORE THAN 'THE CURSE'
By Debra Cash

All I wanted was to put my cheek against the cool tiles on the bathroom floor. They beckoned like a shifting mirage—gray, white, speckled, gray, white—as I held my stomach and my legs prickled and then went numb. I had been vomiting and then had diarrhoea—I didn't know whether it was safer to crouch next to the toilet bowl or sit. The pain was excruciating, bewildering, twisting in my pelvis and outlining every muscle. Later, my parents found me lying on the floor: they scooped me up and lay me down among cool cotton sheets. Then they congratulated me. I had got my period. In another month, I would be twelve.

The scene continued, year after year. Some months were better, some worse. The pain would keep me home from school; other times it took a fainting spell to get me to call my mother to come pick me up. For a while I took a painkiller that mixed codeine, dexedrine, and caffeine—and it sometimes took three tablets before I could walk upright. Doped, my thinking was diffuse. It was questionable whether I could safely drive a car.

But, year after year, doctors and family and friends—all wishing me well—reiterated that *all women had cramps*. They reassured me of my 'normality.' Maybe I'd grow out of it. A baby would change how I felt. They gave me medications that the girl across the street swore by. But no one I had ever known got as sick as I did.

They impressed on me that I wasn't really sick. For a decade I believed them. Maybe I had a low pain threshold. Maybe I just had a bad self-image. Everyone else was coping. In the meantime, menstrual pain kept me from the Christmas party I had bought a grab-bag gift for, from seeing Baryshnikov dance with Gelsey Kirkland. I was in my twenties—and increasingly ill—when I finally took a hard look at my situation. A Cambridge, Massachusetts, pharmacist confiscated my codeine prescription on the technicality that I had kept it in my purse for over the seven-day limit on narcotics. I found myself sobbing in the aisles of the drugstore at the threat of living through my period without any painkillers. I admitted, then, that month by month, the anticipation of pain was distorting my life.

What I suffer from is endometriosis. It is a real disease, with a real aetiology and a sisterhood of between four and seven million U.S. and Canadian women who have it too. When my uterine lining sloughs off and flows out in the monthly pace promised by the films we saw in a darkened sixth-grade classroom, there is one complication. Other endometrial cells swell and bleed too, but these tissues are implanted on the outside of my uterus, on the ligaments holding it in place. Scar tissue my body has produced in response to these tiny islands of displaced tissue press on my sciatic nerves, sending shooting pains down my legs. Other women have tissue gluing their ovaries to parts of their pelvic cavity. Some have endometrial tissue in their arms—or even brains, although this is very rare. In the apt metaphor of Julia Older, author of the first major text on the disease written for lay readers, displaced endometrial tissue can be compared to barnacles that attach to their surroundings—the outside of the uterus, the pelvic wall, nerves. This barnacle becomes active, inflamed, and painful at 'high tide,' when oestrogen levels are highest. It remains present, but inactive, at 'low tide.' For women with endometriosis, the experience is of having continuing—and often unpredictable—cycles of exacerbation and remission. The pain gets worse for a time and then seems to lessen or even disappear.

'The difference between a little cramping and endometriosis is the difference between night and day,' says Kate Shaughnessy Low, the nurse who is past president of the Boston chapter of the Endometriosis Association. 'We have to get word out to teenagers and their mothers that terrible cramps may not respond to hot water bottles and aspirin. A 15-year-old who faints when she gets cramps rarely takes the initiative of getting herself to the emergency room.'

Until very recently, it was commonly thought that it was very rare for adolescents to suffer from endometriosis. One woman, Jean, remembers being taken to the emergency room at her local hospital when she was 14. Her stomach pains were so compelling that her doctor suspected appendicitis. When the blood tests ruled out that possibility, she was sent home. A dozen years later she is being treated for the disease.

One of the problems is that young women have traditionally been very complacent about their pain. They may ask an older relative if she has 'bad periods,' but their sisters, mothers, and aunts have little information to share. When, in the late 1970s, Drs. John Leventhal and Donald Goldstein at the Children's Hospital Medical Center in Boston conducted a landmark study that eventually surveyed over 200 teenage women suffering from chronic pelvic pain, they found that more than 50 percent had endometriosis. In many communities and medical practices, young women who complain about their periods get referred to psychologists instead of being given the clinical evaluations that would help name their pain.

Jean might have been diagnosed when she was 14, but positive diagnosis can be made only after laparoscopy—exploratory surgery that allows a surgeon to look at a woman's ovaries, uterus, and pelvic cavity. Two tiny incisions are made: one just below the bellybutton, the other right above the pubis. A special fiber-optic magnifying device is inserted. Although it is usually done without an overnight hospital stay, a laparoscopy calls for anaesthesia, and, for women not covered by medical insurance, it is expensive. But even if Jean had undergone the surgery her symptoms called for, her physician might not have seen the telltale blue-black spots of implanted tissue or other clear indications of the disease. Oddly enough, women with very little endometriosis may experience excruciating pain with their periods or when they ovulate, while others, in whom the disease is quite advanced, may not have any symptoms and so not know that they have the disease until they find they cannot get pregnant.

No one knows exactly why endometriosis happens. Perhaps, some researchers suggest, fluids are pushed back into the pelvic cavity (reflux menstruation), and, if conditions are abnormal, cells implant themselves there. Or, alternately, it may take a few years of menstruation for implants to build up enough to be visible or cause any problems. Another suggestion is that endometriosis is a disorder of embryonic development—that endometrial cells that should have been limited to the inside of the uterus are 'misread' and develop elsewhere.

Nonetheless, it is crucial to be diagnosed as early as possible. Thirty to forty percent of women with endometriosis are infertile. According to one physician, Robert Kistner of the Harvard Medical School, if the statistics on infertility excluded factors of male sterility, endometriosis would be the most common cause of infertility in women older than age 25. And while it is not life-threatening, it can be disabling—from one day to two weeks out of every month.

Early diagnosis does not mean that the endometriosis will not progress—but it does increase a doctor's opportunities for monitoring that progress and for a woman to make informed choices about how she wants to manage it. There are no 'best' bets and no guarantees, and therefore treatments vary. For some women, drugs that inhibit the production of chemicals in the prostaglandin family, such as the over-the-counter drugs Advil and Nuprin, are enough to stop their pain at ovulation or menstruation, since women with endometriosis have abnormalities in the production of those compounds. However, these do not address the underlying problems. The most popular treatment is danazol (trade name: Danocrine). It is formulated to suppress a woman's ordinary menstrual cycle so that her oestrogen production falls, putting her into what has been called a 'false menopause.' Theoretically, this allows the endometrial implants to shrink and be reabsorbed by the body.

Birth control pills, taken on a regular schedule or without the usual one-week breaks so that a woman does not menstruate, suppress the natural oestrogen and replace it with lower amounts of synthetic oestrogen. They improve symptoms for some women, although the disease may continue. Pregnancy overloads the endometrial implants with oestrogen, overgrowing the blood supply so that the entire area of implant may die off. Because of this phenomenon, physicians sometimes counsel women to 'have a baby' to 'cure' the disease. Unfortunately, this is a false promise: in many cases, endometriosis recurs. Having a 'therapeutic baby' to cure a disease is not in the best interests of either the young woman or her child.

Options for women with more advanced stages of the disease include laser and conventional surgery to remove implants and, as a last resort, total removal of the uterus and ovaries. Appropriately, very few surgeons would be willing to remove any teenager's uterus and ovaries. One 24-year-old social service worker whose case of endometriosis is quite advanced finds herself asking extra questions of her clients who have had hysterectomies, gathering information before she needs it. As she explains soberly, 'I know I'll have a hysterectomy before I die—it's just something in my life. I just hope I can have children before that time.'

If you suspect you have endometriosis because of painful periods or ovulation, consistently painful sexual intercourse, backaches, painful bowel movements at the time of your period, or excruciatingly tender gynaecological examinations, you must educate yourself. Endometriosis cannot be diagnosed definitively without laparoscopy surgery, but it is very important to undergo this surgery if your symptoms do not respond to conventional treatments. Joining the Endometriosis Association head-quartered in Milwaukee, Wisconsin, will put you in touch with chapters in your area—a resource for medical referrals as well as personal advice and support—and get you an informative newsletter that tracks medical research, alternative treatments, and explains your options. Write to them at P.O. Box 92187, Milwaukee, WI 53202.

Debra Cash is a member of the Association and a journalist who writes on arts and cultural topics for the *Boston Globe* and other publications. Debra originally wrote this article hoping a popular teen magazine would publish it. We felt it would be useful to our teen readers.

[Editor's Note: Readers who are interested in knowing more about teens with endometriosis are invited to turn to Section V. 'Research Recaps,' Chapter 16 for 'Teenagers and Endometriosis.']

9
Coping with the Emotions

'*My connection to endometriosis is through a woman I am very close to. She has suffered with this condition for some time; she is currently 35 years old. I have been involved with her for the past seven months and in this short period of time have become aware of the pain, the discomfort, the mood swings, the lack of information, and the loneliness associated with endometriosis. We were both excited when we found your address.*'

Michael, Iowa

'*I wish I could perform the "lap" myself so I could see the "enemy" for myself! I hate the uncertainty, the lack of control, the interference in my life. I wish I could know now if pregnancy will be possible when I'm ready—if not, I'd have all that "plumbing" removed and get it over with, behind me! I hate the disease; I feel invaded by a sneaky, unstable alien. It's made my body funny-looking—no breasts, a puffy stomach. I'm noticing a thickening of my muscles (probably from the danazol). I bloat up without warning or am in agony just as suddenly. Usually it's just there, a constant nag. It causes sciatica neuritis in my right leg, and I'm concerned about the long-term effect on the nerves, bones, and joints. I also worry that the tendency for abnormal cells might make me susceptible to cancer later.*

'*I can't trust my emotions—I'm too affected by the hormones;*'

135

a near manic-depressive with a normal stretch here and there. The nagging pain affects my mood, my attitude, adversely. In all, I just can't rely on my emotions or my body, and I resent it like hell. I'm afraid to make major decisions, knowing how I'm not "myself." I can't change jobs easily because of my need for insurance coverage (so many have that wonderful preexisting condition exclusion clause), and I have a terrible absenteeism rate. My mood swings affect every part of my life, but especially my marriage. He doesn't understand or empathize with the female body at all. I asked him to read your leaflet, and he simply said, "How depressing." We don't have a very good marriage anyway, and not being able to talk with him about this is very lonely.

'I hate being a "whiner"; I had been healthy all my life, up until I was 18. I'm sure my friends, spouse, and family are sick of hearing about it. I don't like to hear health complaints, but it helps to talk about it; that puts it in better perspective. My friends are very good about it; they encourage me, ask of the progress, and help me deal with the decisions to be made. I always feel better after talking with a dear friend who empathizes.

'Exercise helps, too. I find I feel much better physically and emotionally if I exercise strenuously and regularly. I really have to force myself and must have the discipline from a class. I'm taking aerobic dancing; it helps keep my weight down and keeps my muscles toned and strong, and I blow off a lot of frustration and anger, which really helps keep me "normal." Believe me, after class I hurt so bad that I think I ruptured something, but the next day I feel good, strong, and serene. I walk very much, too, which is good for my mental state, as well as my body. I've noticed a big difference since I began disciplining myself to exercise, as far as my stamina, my attitude, and all . . . it is so easy for the pain, the frustration and the "no end in sight" to get to you. And with the danazol effect, I can get so depressed, so I'm very careful to get plenty of exercise. I try to play as much as possible, doing silly, active things with my friends. I try to do independent things, go visiting relatives in other cities, etc., anything that will boost my esteem, my attitude. Crafts are an excellent outlet also.

'Next to not knowing what is happening to yourself I think the second worst effect of this disease is the mental aspect and how it affects all of the areas of your life. I've learned to guard carefully against self-pity and defeatist attitudes. I know I must have an active outlet for all the explosive emotions that illness *and hormones cause in order to have a positive, realistic attitude. And now I'm working on accepting the disease. My next "lap" will probably give me a good idea of how long I'll be on the danazol; if it's to be indefinitely, I'll have to accept the hormone's effect as simply a part of my personality, my mentality, and everyone else will have to accept that, too. The worst of it [the drug and the disease] is that it seems to make my tolerance level low, it uses up my energy, so that when there are other crises in my life, I'm not as able to deal with them. So I learn to guard myself to force myself to be strong.*

'I should stop my rambling now. I greatly appreciate your desperately needed help, your patient listening. Thank you for your courtesy and empathy. Feel free to use my responses to aid someone else or to give my phone number or name to anyone who might need someone to talk with. Now that I'm accepting what is happening to me, I think I could help someone else do it, too.'

Barbara, Vermont

'What I wish that I could convey more than ever is that I feel that all women should be informed about this disease and made to understand what it can do, what the symptoms are, and how to react to it. My youngest sister feels she can ignore it until it gets to the pain stage. My middle sister was so frightened of getting it that she went right to the doctor to be tested for it. I ignored all my pains until they got too bad to ignore—and I paid for it. But I want to stress that women who must go through hysterectomy need to think positive and beyond the ordeal. It helps in the recovery; it helps emotionally.'

Joni, Zachary, Louisiana

OVERVIEW OF PERSONAL CONCERNS RELATED TO ENDOMETRIOSIS
By Valerie Weber and Mary Lou Ballweg

Women contacting the Association for the first time often mention a feeling of isolation as a result of having endometriosis; that it is difficult to obtain a diagnosis, information on the disease, or support. By sharing the results of the 'Personal Concerns' section of the research questionnaire (distributed since the Association was started), perhaps we can reduce this isolation by discovering that many women with endometriosis have concerns and needs similar to ours. (For more on the questionnaires and our data registry, see Chapters 20 and 21.)

'How would you describe your mood/feelings generally?' (346 respondents)

Seventy-five percent of the women answered that they felt good about themselves and life in general. One woman's response described best what the majority of these women reported: 'With rare exceptions [I feel] outgoing, happy, determined, positive-minded, and assertive.'

The other 25 percent replied negatively to this question. One young woman explained, 'Emotionally I am devastated that this disease has caused my infertility. I am damned mad, upset, and disgusted!' Another answered, 'I sometimes feel inadequate as a woman because I am unable to have children.'

'And when you are experiencing your endometriosis symptoms?' (315 respondents)

Even the most positive of women were depressed, frustrated, and angry during this time; 39 percent had one of these reactions. Another 19 percent felt a combination of these reactions plus others such as anxiety, helplessness, emotional instability, irritability, and fatigue.

These reactions were in response to a number of factors in their lives, such as physical pain; a lack of support from partner, family, friends, or coworkers; insufficient information about the disease and its effects; a lack of responsiveness and support from their doctors; the feeling that all the pain and symptoms were psychosomatic; and the possibility of infertility. 'Physically feeling bad brings me down,' responded one woman. 'I feel frustrated, helpless, and discouraged. I wonder if I'll be able to conceive if I want to.'

Others felt angry and scared. 'I am pissed, sometimes scared, *HURT*, concerned about myself and about seeing others react to my pain.' Another wrote, '[I am] angry and scared because I'm almost 30 and not sure yet if I want children. I'm fearful I may not [be able to conceive] if and when I decide.' Depending on the severity of the symptoms, other reactions ranged from 'Not very different—maybe more tired,' to 'I cannot sit still; I want to climb the walls—my insides feel as though they've been raked by a metal rake. The pain isn't even severe, but somehow I am not able to ignore the pain as I do with my frequent backaches and headaches.'

Some talked about guilt they felt for having the disease. One especially interesting response was the following:

'Until recently, I felt in particular about the endometriosis very, very frustrated and angry. I felt that I was responsible for having it— some psychological quirk made me have endo. I couldn't define what need it was fulfilling, and I felt guilty about the whole thing. Recently I got angry enough to *reject* the guilt and responsibility, and I have felt freed. I let go of all that negativity around the endometriosis and now hardly think about it or the daily Ovral [a birth control pill] or when the next surgery will/should be. I just decided I'm an animal like the plants and animals of our world—they get diseases, are plagued by insects, respond to their environment (wind, rain, drought, freeze, cars, etc.), and that is just life. We as humans, I decided, have so much ego we think we can *control* everything or at least try to. Although I grant some disease is psychologically/environmentally related, I gave up that relationship for my disease and decided I can control only my *response* to what comes, not what comes.'

'With what thoughts/attitudes do you think you can best get through your present situation?'

Here's what some of the women answering this question wrote:

'I try to tell myself, even though I do not have a baby, I do have a wonderful marriage and understanding husband, so I have a lot to be thankful for.'

'Try to make plans for a fulfilling future without children.'

'I have been brought up very fortunately by parents who did not believe a woman's sole function is baby making. So I never had to wrestle with feeling a lack of womanhood as such, only my own sadness over not being able to give birth.'

'I just keep hoping *something will work*. Every so often I'll hear or read of someone who finally got pregnant—even with endo—by one means or another. It keeps my spirits from sagging too far.'

'By trying to get as much information as possible about endometriosis so that I can be satisfied that whatever treatment I undergo is the best thing for me to do.'

'Hope that future research leads to a remedy short of hysterectomy.'

'I try to keep myself occupied so as not to dwell on present goings-on in my body . . . And always knowing that at most in a few days it will all be over with."

'Fear must be controlled. Pain is made worse, and decision making is harder when I am afraid of the disease.'

'Knowing a lot about the disease has helped me accept my situation.'

'Keeping as active as possible, getting out of myself, helping others with similar conditions, some physical exercise, belief in God.'

'Whom do you look to for support: husband, other family members, friends, others?' (357 respondents)

Most women said they would turn for support to anyone who would listen. Seventy-three percent looked to some combination of their partner, family, and friends. In addition, another 6 percent included their doctors as a source of support. Nine percent also received encouragement from support groups such as Resolve (a U.S. organization that assists infertile couples; see 'Resources' in the back of this book) and from therapists. Additional sources of support included other women with endometriosis, God, and the Endometriosis Association. (Most of these questionnaires were completed when the Association was just starting.)

One woman noted that she relied on a number of people: 'I get support from my sense of humour! My husband is supportive—makes me feel sexy! [He] accepts our infertility problem even though he hates it. My doctor has always tried everything for me. I trust him. God listens to my prayers and gives me courage. Our two adopted children bring joy to my life. I've had two psychologists who have helped me in the past. Friends and family let me talk although I don't like to very much.'

However, some women felt that there was little support outside of themselves. 'The biggest problem is looking *very* healthy, and people don't seem to understand pain and sickness unless they can see physical evidence. This is very frustrating and is the cause of a lot of depression and feeling absolutely *desperate*.'

Said another woman: 'One of the most disturbing emotional problems associated with endometriosis is the refusal of other people to recognize that a problem exists. This refusal has seemed to me to be especially true of women. When I was 17 and first began menstruating, I experienced severe pain, such that I couldn't walk, sit, do anything.' And, wrote another, 'I'm most angry at the insensitivity of others concerning endometriosis—and the fact that pains during periods are not taken seriously enough . . .'

Others found that a lack of support from their doctors led them to doubt themselves. A 29-year-old wrote: 'After being told repeatedly there is no physical cause for the pain or infertility, I began to believe I imagined the pain. I was embarrassed and uncomfortable telling doctors about the pain because the result was the same. A pat on the arm, you're fine, relax . . . The pain continued, and five months later I made an appointment with a fertility specialist. Before the appointment I decided if he found no cause for the pains and infertility I'd consult a psychiatrist. He found a polyp, adhesions, and endometriosis. The pain was real. The Danocrine might "cure" the endometriosis, but I still have to deal with the bitterness. I let other doctors make me doubt myself and my sanity. I don't think I'll ever forgive or forget the emotional pain of doubting myself.'

'What is the most fear-provoking aspect about your present medical situation: infertility, pain, unknowns, other (explain)?' (356 respondents)

The *single* largest fear for 21 percent of our respondents was infertility; another 39 percent feared infertility as well as other things, such as pain or unknowns. Others were frightened of surgery, a hysterectomy, or that endometriosis or drugs used for treatment would lead to cancer or other future problems.

'I'm only 25. How long can this go on?' wrote one woman. 'The uneasiness that my body is working against me,' was the answer of another.

'I hate not knowing what causes this; maybe there was something I could have done to prevent it,' another wrote, echoing the fears of others. 'I dislike filling my body with hormones, which cause side effects, and researchers don't know the effects of long-term usage. Surgery for me is an absolute last resort. I don't like doctors pushing pregnancy on me when I don't want children.'

Another responded, 'It bothers me to hear the doctor's attitude that surgery would be just the thing. He emphasized "after all, you are 36." I am not ready for it emotionally. He didn't ask how I felt about it.' Many generally feared the future. A 22-year-old said, 'I know I will need surgery again, and I fear the kind of life I'll have without my own kids and taking oestrogen therapy. Also, I am afraid of what kind of moods I'll have without my ovaries.' From another: 'The fear that it will never end—that I'll have to have surgery over and over and will lose control of my life.'

'What gives you a feeling of strength or contentment when you need it?'
The answers included the following:

'Faith that it will work out and if I can't become pregnant perhaps adopt.'

'Support from friends; reading articles that show I'm not alone.'

'Love from someone close to me and their understanding and trying to help.'

'Me—and the fact that I've pulled through a number of tough situations. Also, I have a lot of confidence in my doctor.'

'Did you have any difficulty making a treatment choice?' (350 respondents)
Forty-seven percent said yes; 53 percent said no. One respondent explained: 'I believe I had the most trouble accepting this is a chronic disease, and subsequently the treatment choices were very difficult for me. It was hard to stay centred in what I believed in and not listen too much to others about what I should do. It was/is hard to see pain as a legitimate enough reason to ask for surgery, radical or conservative, and to see that it is my choice. I think the hardest part in deciding on treatment is picking the lesser of two evils.'

'*Would you have liked: more information, someone to talk over options with you, other?*' **(293 respondents)**

While 29 percent wanted more information, and 14 percent would have liked someone to talk over the options with, 45 percent wanted both. Others would have appreciated both of these, plus more support, honesty, and information from their doctors. 'I think it is especially important to have a doctor or doctors who will take the time to discuss all questions and alternatives, and if that human element is missing, go find another doctor. They are out there—it just takes searching,' recommended one of our respondents.

With all the questions, there were dozens of responses we were unable to reduce to a few words. The lengthy passages spilled out from women trying to explain their experiences with endometriosis. As one woman replied to the question of sources of support, '[My support comes from] believing that good health care and *feeling* people are out there, that pushing family and friends for support is worth it; we all will grow from it.' Amen—we couldn't have said it better.

Valerie Weber is a freelance writer based in Milwaukee who has been especially interested in the area of women's health since working in a women's health collective in the mid-seventies. She has written extensively for health and human service organizations and for a number of magazines, including articles on career development, adolescent pregnancy, and women with migraines. 'I have seen some of the devastating effects of endometriosis in my family and friends and fully support the Endometriosis Association and all aspects of its work,' she says.

March 21, 1987

Open letter to the reader:
I wrote this poem 10 years into my prediagnostic endometriosis journey. Two years and 12 doctors later I found Dr B, who is walking this journey with me.

He helped my husband to understand, who in turn helped me help our families to understand.

The day-to-day pain is gone, and I stand tall and straight. Friends at the endometriosis support group have been great! My life is better than it's ever been, and best of all, *I am not alone*.

If you think you have endometriosis or have already been diagnosed, find *someone who has endo*, someone who understands the scope of what you feel. You will gain strength in knowing you are not alone. You might feel there is nothing left of you to reach out, but you *must*.

If you can't communicate comfortably with your doctor, find another one. There *is* a doctor out there just for you. Find him or her. Let your anger and frustration work constructively for you. Be persistent, but listen well. You *will* find your answers, and you won't be alone. Believe in yourself. There *is* a better life waiting for you.

With all my love and understanding,

MARY

MY PERFECT LIFE

My perfect life.
A car, a job, a TV, money.
Lots of money.
Nothing more that one could want.

My perfect life.
My perfect marriage
With the perfect husband
And the perfect family.
Nothing more that one could want.

My perfect life.
Living, loving, laughing
So much energy, so much talent
Unselfishly giving, happily doing.
Nothing more that one could want.

My perfect life.
A goal is set. A goal is reached.
Time passes, a life is lived.
Nothing more that one could want.

My perfect life.
With screams that go unheard
Cries ignored, pains dismissed
Worries laughed at, and
the one I love doesn't care.
Oh, how it hurts, I want to cry.

Mary L. Bartnik, 3 July 1980

Mary Bartnik is leaving her career in sales and marketing to go back to school to write children's literature. She recently moved to a farm outside Milwaukee where she lives with her husband Tom, a lithographic stripper and teacher, and their two dogs and one cat. They are applying to become foster parents.

THE SINGLE WOMAN AND FERTILITY: LEARNING TO CLOSE DOORS SOFTLY
By Rebecca Mormann

Two years ago the pain, anxiety, and frustration inside me was given a name. It was called *endometriosis*. For 15 years I agonized over my lack of discipline and weakness—because we all know only 'weak' women have menstrual pain.

During high school I learned a poverty mentality that associated prayer with begging. I was raised Catholic—and each month I went through a begging process. Begging for an *exchange* for the pain. Praying that it would not be painful this month. Or begging that I would not bleed through while in class. Crying because I was weak and because taking two aspirin for the cramps like the other girls never worked. It was a secret begging no one knew about.

I am 33 years old, single, and part of a vastly populated generation that is caught somewhere between 'Friday Night Bars,' video dating services, and spending time alone. We all have some sort of grieving process for the loss of our fertility. And my realization of it coincided with an event in a friend's life.

Two years ago during my initial stage of anger and 'why me,' a good friend became pregnant. A friend without endometriosis. She and her husband were overjoyed. The pregnancy was unexpected. They had been married for 13 years and a few months earlier decided to 'consider' starting a family. Nature and failure of birth control produced the baldest and most charming little fellow named Casey. During her pregnancy I had a shower and invited what we call our 'women's group.' Everyone was overjoyed and came bearing cuddly baby gifts. I was never jealous of my friends and their families—but after our party and celebrating Karen's life, I cried. *Why* couldn't my closest friends share in my pain with a similar energy that they used to celebrate Karen's joy?

We all lose our fertility at some point in our lives. And to steal an image from poet Donald Justice: 'We must learn to close softly the doors to rooms we will not be coming back to.' Women with endometriosis may have to learn to close some doors early—and single women with endometriosis may have to learn to close these doors alone.

Rebecca Mormann is a longtime volunteer for the Association. She served as correspondence secretary on the board of the U.S.-Canadian Endometriosis Association from 1985 to 1986, answering thousands of letters, and previously assisted with correspondence and bookkeeping at headquarters.

COPING WITH LIMITATIONS
By Jeanne Fleming, Ph.D.

'The emotional support of knowing other women are coping with this problem would be very helpful to me.'

Lenore, Hyattsville, Maryland

'I'm happy to know you exist . . . I'm 29 years old. When I was about 22, I experienced pain that seemed to come from nowhere and that I now recognize as an all-too-familiar friend. The first pain happened after orgasm. It came, was intense, then disappeared. And it happened only once.

'About two years later, I was awakened in the middle of the night, in a great deal of pain. It felt sort of like cramping, but different. It really hurt. I could tell the pain was somewhere around my uterus. I went to see an obstetrician in Nashville, Tennessee, who thought I must have an infection. He put me on antibiotics. The pains continued, getting worse, not better. He tried a couple of different kinds of antibiotics, and when none worked, he said he didn't know what it could be. If I wanted to find out, he'd have to run some tests. Not long afterward, the pains got so extreme, I had to go to the emergency ward.

'Looking back, I understand that as bad as the pain was, my fear and lack of context for what was happening was even worse. I had just never experienced pain before, and it terrified me.

'My relationship with my disease has been a continuous challenge. At first, I felt guilty and blaming about it. I thought I had brought it on myself somehow by having an abortion. I thought I was being punished. I was very angry with myself about the whole thing. And my mind would create the worst possible scenarios.

'A turning point came when I started to meet and talk with other women who have endometriosis. Shock number one: The

first woman I talked with had had a child. She still had endometriosis and had much, much worse symptoms than I. The second woman I talked with had five children. She also had had a hysterectomy. And she still had symptoms . . . terrible pain! Woman number one was beautiful. The main thing I got from talking with her was, "Look, this is just the way it is. Some people have club feet, other people wear eyeglasses, some people get in car wrecks . . . we have endometriosis."

'It started to become a very matter-of-fact thing. And then I really began to learn what a common thing it is for women, and again, the isolation, feelings of guilt and impending doom lessened. Shock number two; When I finally told my mother about this, she said, "Oh, yes, I used to get terrible pains . . . the same kind." That hastened the healing process for me, learning that. Suddenly I realized the possibility that it was simply hereditary. My mother had it; I have it. What to do? It certainly didn't kill her. And she doesn't have it anymore. Hummmm, I thought, that means it's likely I won't get worse as I age, but better. Whether it's true or not, it's a much healthier, happier, nourishing thought than the opposite. And nice to have a living example of improvement.

'Still, of course, the major upsetting and remaining terror of it all lingers in varying degrees of strength: "Has my ability to have children been impaired?" Asking this question of myself has forced the entire issue of children to the surface for me . . . It wasn't that I postponed having children per se, it was just that I did not find that man that I wanted to settle down with. I wasn't ready yet. I had a wealth of opportunity available to me, and I wanted to experience life in a way that never quite fit over the long, long run for any of the men I was with. On some deep level, it was apparent to me that I wasn't who I was going to be, I was too unformed, and that marriage wouldn't work until later.

'Anyway, now I'm with a man I've been living with for three years, but guess what! He doesn't want to have children. And after asking myself this question, "Do I want children? Has my ability to have children been impaired?" thousands of times, the answer is yes. I want to have children. My dilemma is, I don't feel I have time to wait for my man to come around (if he ever does). And suddenly, as age 30 approaches, I'm finding myself feeling very single-pointed about my desire to mate . . . And then there's the part of me that feels quite happy with the knowledge that if I try and I can't, I can't. And images of adopted children

of all colours and sizes pop into my brain, and I feel quite pleased with the picture.

'What I'm trying to say is that while this disease has brought with it a good deal of physical pain over the years, it has also been the "poke in the ribs" always reminding me to look carefully at my life. At the most fundamental level, it reminds me of my mortality, it encourages me to meditate, it tells me to look carefully at the question of kids, relationship, and my own form as a woman. It tells me when I'm under too much pressure, and it thanks me when I find places and spaces where my whole being can relax.'
Linda, Colorado

People with physical limitations have a special opportunity to learn adaptive coping. However, this can be delayed by denying a physical limitation, denying the extent of the limitation, emphasizing the limitation, or protecting, coddling, or rejecting the person with the limitation. The first step, then, is to understand the kind of limitations present and have a realistic idea of what effect they will have on long-term functioning. When problems cannot be fully diagnosed, or if the diagnoses change, understanding long-range implications will be difficult. The task then is to accept the uncertainty and fluctuation while trying to understand as thoroughly as possible the range of limitation likely to be present. This uncertainty will probably be hard to live with because humans typically function better with set patterns and habits, but it *is* possible to learn to live with the uncertainty.

Part of learning to accept limitations is to understand that none of us measure up to an 'ideal' in our looks, functioning, skills, or potential. All of us are a combination of traits and skills that either help or hinder us in our interaction with the world. Yet some combination of assets is shown as 'ideal' in literature, by the media, and especially in advertising gimmicks. This idea is false. All of us have to learn to cope with being imperfect and to live a fulfilled life in spite of many unfulfilled desires. All of us have potential for making contributions to society, and understanding our individual differences can help us make the most of that potential.

But, if life seems to put us in situations that no one else we know has to handle, such as illness, physical, or mental limitations, the whole family feels some pain and may feel 'tainted' in some way. The pain may be comprised of several different feelings—anger, sadness, denial, and finally acceptance—and is called the *grieving process*. Some may ask, 'But what are we grieving for?' This is a fair question. The family, as a group and as individuals, is grieving the loss of the 'ideal' mentioned above, the loss of 'normal' functioning. These feelings can be handled so people will like themselves better, understand individual and family strengths, and understand how to function optimally in spite of being imperfect.

People who have ongoing medical problems face special opportunities for learning to cope well with uncertainty. Both the person and the family will likely feel out of control of many parts of their lives and may feel that the family's whole life revolves around one person and her problems. This can make the rest of the family feel resentful, left out, jealous, and sad. Unless these feelings are handled so everyone feels more comfortable, pressure is likely to build so that a family has many arguments or cold wars with individuals giving each other 'the cold shoulder.' The goal for the family is to resolve conflicts so people can live more comfortably under the same roof and for all to feel good about themselves, to acknowledge their strengths and weaknesses, to have friends, enjoy life, and achieve at the highest levels they are capable of.

Problems are turned into growth and fulfillment in several steps. First, people have a right to experience grief for having to cope with problems in the first place. 'Why me? Why my family?' are reasonable questions. Feeling sorry for your situation should be the beginning of learning to cope with it. Other people may have little tolerance for such grief, and people may be told, 'Just be glad it's not . . .,' or 'Oh, stop fretting, it's only . . .,' or 'Just be glad you have . . .' If you hear these comments, you may feel misunderstood and angry. People who make those comments often do so out of ignorance, thoughtlessness, and insensitivity. Some of them may actually be cruel, but most likely they do not know what to say that would feel comforting. If you think they can be educated, tell them how you want them to act toward you and your family, but if you think they cannot be educated, then avoid them either physically or emotionally.

So, a second important step is finding nurturing people to help you. They will care how you feel, will listen to you talk about your feelings and situation, will help you feel that they care about you, and will offer genuine support and help. Friendships are full of give and take, and even though you may feel uncomfortable 'taking too much' right now, remember this: the more effectively you are nurtured in your need now, the more quickly you will get the resources to nurture others who need it later.

A third important step is to find good health care. As a consumer, you need to feel good about the care given you.

Fourth, the whole family needs to restructure itself to accommodate uncertainties and to feel good about all the health and 'normality' it has. To do this, acknowledge your feelings about your situation, do all you can to alleviate the problems, and then deliberately focus your attention on your strengths as individuals and as a group rather than focus on the

Fifth, whenever you start to feet out of control, figure out what is making you feel that way. Do what you can to take care of the problem, and again, focus your attention on your strengths and potential. You may have to go through this process several times. Each time will be triggered by something, such as a medical emergency, new diagnosis, new diagnostic tools, new treatment strategies, fluctuations in the disease process, or other changes. A good rule of thumb is: if your feelings are different, something has changed; so use your feelings as guides. As long as there is uncertainty, fluctuations in what the 'patient' can do will occur and will

Accepting limitations may be hard, but it can be a new beginning for learning new coping skills, liking yourself and others for new reasons, functioning better as a family and as individuals, and developing new sensitivities for feelings. Good luck as you grow and adapt.

Dr. Fleming is a clinical psychologist who has done research on the grieving process of infertility. Her work differentiates between grief about an event permanently finished, such as death, and a process that continues (chronic illness or infertility). She has endometriosis and is infertile, so she can also speak from personal experience. She and her co-author are writing a book for the lay public and planning their next research project. Her research is reported in 'The Infertility Process: Coping or Resolution,' *Journal of Social Work and Human Sexuality*, in press. Dr Fleming is married, has one son, and lives in Longview, Washington.

COUNSELLING AND GOOD HEALTH CARE
By Joyce Gabor, M.S. in Ed. Psych.

'Thank you, thank you, thank you!!! The information and the bibliography that were sent to me were a godsend. I'm finally learning what is wrong with me. I had thought I was overreacting, a hypochondriac! Now that I know what I am dealing with, I knew what questions to ask my doctor and what kind of answers to expect (or find a new doctor). I know . . . how to make realistic decisions concerning its treatment.

'With the education you gave me, I was able to ask my doctor intelligent questions, and his response was very favourable. I guess once I showed my need for and understanding of the facts, he laid it all out for me; he didn't try to simplify or generalize. Most doctors must think women either don't want to know or wouldn't understand. I was very pleased with his directness;

though the answers weren't that optimistic, I at least know exactly what's going on in there.'

Barbara, Vermont

[Editor's Note: The information contained in this article was obtained as a part of research done for a master's degree in educational psychology. The article itself is excerpted from the master's thesis. A sampling of 153 questionnaires was used from the Endometriosis Association Data Registry.

When this study of how women look at their doctors was first made in 1981, it contained some revolutionary information. The level of dissatisfaction that women with endometriosis felt over their medical care had not been realized previously. The Endometriosis Association began to implement a policy of education directed to women with the disease and to the medical profession.

Over the years, this policy has resulted in some improvement in the attitudes of physicians toward women with endometriosis, but there is still much work to be done. It is evident that it continues to be important for women with the disease to work together to be assertive about getting good medical care. As a self-help group, the Association uses education and support groups to instill self-advocacy in its members.

The linkage between good medical care and counselling is not, at first, readily apparent. But in the course of doing the research it became evident that women needed to be more assertive in order to get the kind of care they so desperately needed. It was necessary to consider the question of how to help women take responsibility for their health. A variety of counselling models seemed potentially useful in teaching women how to establish real two-way relationships with medical practitioners.]

Counselling of all types can be a useful tool in helping women to be more confident when dealing with the medical profession, as well as in other life situations. Counselling can also be of help in dealing with pain control, infertility, sexual difficulties, and hysterectomy.

Of course, as much caution should be used in selecting a therapist, a support group, or a self-help group as in choosing a medical practitioner. Traditionally psychology has been just as paternalistic and condescending towards women as has physical medicine. For years the two disciplines worked in tandem. The physician who didn't have the knowledge, diagnostic skills, or equipment to diagnose endometriosis would refer the patient to a psychiatrist (also an M.D.) or a psychologist. The premise would be that the troublesome symptoms were mental and not physical.

There is a need for a feminist perspective in therapy, defining feminism as belief in and work toward equality between men and women. A useful strategy for counselling women with endometriosis could be based on the following feminist elements and on the concepts of dependency and passivity. Feminism's contributions to social interactions, attitudes and cultural standards include the following (Heide, 1978):

- an increase in 'desexigration' of health care
- a decrease in sex stereotyping
- a redefinition of power to exclude sex
- demystification of important knowledge; reorientation of all health care

The concepts of dependency and passivity are important keys to counselling the woman with endometriosis. Since she may need to assert herself and pave the way to her own health and well-being, a woman with endometriosis should choose counselling according to her current level of independence and activity.

Choosing a Method

There are three main avenues of counselling available for any person in need. These are also possibilities for women with endometriosis. They are personal counselling or one-to-one counselling, group counselling, and self-help organization involvement. Each discipline has its own criteria for selection and special effects.

Personal Counselling. Criteria: A choice for dependent and passive women who may not be able to make a change without outside professional support and initiative; also for women who are faced with many changes at once.

Goals: To provide a constant support to the client, to provide attention to wide range of problems if necessary, including the development of problem-solving skills and self-confidence.

A Counselling Model. Personal counselling must be done with the idea that the endometriosis client may need to do group work or may need to participate in a self-help group in the future. One counselling philosophy that is adaptive and compatible with possible future work is William Glasser's reality therapy. 'Responsibility, a concept basic to reality therapy, is defined as the ability to fulfill one's needs and to do so in a way that does not deprive others of the ability to fulfill their needs.' (Glasser, 1975, p. 15) By focusing on the present and on behaviour, the therapist guides the client to see herself accurately, to face reality, to fulfill her own needs, without harm. Self-responsibility as a therapy goal can be a path to the best and most personal health care. The goal of reality therapists is to aid a person in growth from her discontent, distrust, and cynicism.

Reality therapy is also a problem-solving model. This is essential to the woman with endometriosis. She may have to prioritize problems in order to deal with each one.

Each step of reality therapy calls for personal and unique input from the client. For a woman who has found no one to understand and coach her, here is an opportunity for her to have a listener and prompter. When dealing with a woman who has had unfortunate experiences, here is a chance to plan and execute fortunate experiences. For a woman with an uphill battle for proper and prompt medical care, here is the assertiveness training field.

Putting this model to work with women with endometriosis looks like this:

1. The counsellor should be a resource for medical and other information. It is recommended as with all listener/counsellors that acceptance and patience be used with the client's personal account.
2. Discuss what medical options may have been tried and eliminate the unnecessary or undesirable ones. Find out the extent and scope of the medical support network the client has.
3. Find out what in her medical treatment does not meet her expectations or needs. Discuss ways of obtaining the missing parts of treatment. Look for relationship stresses due to symptoms, infertility, incapacity.
4. Plans can include providing information for decision making, planning, and practice of assertiveness with medical practitioners.
5. A commitment to the treatment plan could mean a commitment to better health and may be, therefore, a powerful incentive.
6. Not accepting excuses allows the counsellor to support, prompt, and cue the client while not taking responsibility and self-esteem away from the client.
7. Step 6 also allows feedback from the counsellor without the counsellor's assuming the responsibility. By experiencing a failure in this 'sheltered' situation the client may realize that failing is not devastating and that replanning is always an option.
8. This step provides support and structure while reinforcing the continuum of planning and execution of options.

Reality therapy is only one of the types of personal counselling that might be useful for women with endometriosis.

Group Counselling. The woman with endometriosis can best meet some needs within a group structure. These groups include assertiveness training, support groups, and infertility groups such as Resolve. Her partner may also benefit from a support group to deal with relationship changes, chronic illness, and sexual incapacity related to endometriosis. Both partners could be involved in a group along with other couples and work on couple issues such as infertility.

Goals: Can be set by the particular group; can include sharing of experience, individual goal achievement, insight, growth, and change.

Criteria: Women who are able to take responsibility for themselves at times and be somewhat active in meeting their needs, as well as being able to work with others, may benefit from group experience. There is a gradual building of tolerance for both similarities and differences among members. A woman who at one time thought she was alone with a unique set of circumstances will find she is not alone and can learn from others more experienced in coping.

Self-Help Organizations. 'Self-help organizations are vital to the women's health movement. They involve "assertiveness nurturance" based on the discovery and sharing of knowledge and skills so that women and men create their own health destinies.' (Heide, 1978, p.11)

Goals: Self-responsibility of members, teaching and passing information to the community, social change.

Criteria: In order to meet individual and group goals, members must be capable of active participation and the awareness and strength to assure successful problem solving.

The group process includes sharing common problems to help members devise and effect methods of treatment. Self-help groups generate and reflect certain values, 'including the self-confidence and therapeutic value of being expected to help oneself and others and to possess the skills to do so.' (Heide, 1978, p. 11) The basic principle is to teach participants so they may teach others. Along with knowledge, participants gain self-confidence, competence, strength, and health. The self-help model stresses the total person along with the intuitive, experiential, spontaneous, and consumer-type aspects of health care. An empowered consumer diminishes hierarchical control of medical information and power.

The Endometriosis Association has fulfilled the above criteria in its goal of helping individuals and spreading information. Individual members have been taught self-advocacy and have also been encouraged to help others. Societal and medical attitudes have been changed through the work of the organization. The Endometriosis Association provides a model for how women with the condition can work to change the current health care system. Such changes are essential if the needs and expectations of women with endometriosis are to be met.

Summary

In looking at the women and practitioners dealing with endometriosis, we find many discrepancies. The population of afflicted women is large, and the advances and interest in safe treatment have been small and unsuccessful. The health care system is faced with an emotionally charged medical situation and is not trained to handle it well. Women are expecting their doctors to provide the treatment they desire without knowing and asking specifically for what they want. Often social and psychological ideas of women do not accurately fit the present-day woman.

The way out of this vulnerable, no-win situation lies in increased self-health care and medical knowledge. Self-care assumes self-responsibility. Developing the ability to take responsibility can be done, if necessary, in a reality therapy milieu on a personal basis. It can be done in group situations, and it is the core of self-help organizations. As women and men gain greater medical information, make their own treatment choices, and assert their medical rights, they will receive better quality health care. The most important key to better health care is knowledge— knowledge of the human body and of the abilities and limitations of the medical profession.

References

Glasser, William. *Reality Therapy, a New Approach to Psychiatry*. New York: Harper & Row, 1975.

Heide, Wilma Scott. *Feminism: Making a Difference in Our Health, Medical and Psychological Interfaces*. Vol. 1, New York: Plenum Press, 1978.

Joyce Gabor served as a volunteer with the Endometriosis Association for six years. During this time she served as support group facilitator, facilitator trainer, and Crisis Call counsellor. She lives with her husband and two adopted children in rural Wisconsin.

HOW SUPPORT GROUPS HELP WOMEN WITH ENDOMETRIOSIS
By Mary Lou Ballweg

'Keep up the good work—support systems are wonderful!'
Denise, Vancouver, British Columbia

'I am writing for several reasons, the first being to tell you how much it has meant to me to have a support like the Endometriosis Association. So often in the past six years I have needed an external reference point to validate my own experience in coping

with endometriosis, to let me know that I'm not nuts and that my need for information and support is a valid one . . .

'The chapter is active and growing. At every support group, we see new faces, which is exciting. This group has come to mean a lot to me.'
Sarah, Decatur, Georgia

'Your Association has helped me more than anyone—including my doctor. I have had surgery three times in the last 10 months and I feel I really need the support I get in your newsletters.'
Bonnie, Plenty, Saskatchewan, Canada

'Keep up the good work. You have helped me very much emotionally. The Association is a lifesaver.'
Diane, Oklahoma City, Oklahoma

'This is the second letter I have written to you about my case. I became a member of the Association last fall when I was in a surge of surgeries; between September 18 and November 20 I had four surgeries for complications with severe adhesions and recurring endometrial implants. I have been free of complications since the last surgery in November: until recently, that is.

'My last period they thought was a miscarriage because of the mass volume of blood and large clots I passed in a three-hour-period: then bleeding subsided totally! (I've been in the stirrups so much in the past two years I should be given the title "Girl of the West!") I had seven surgeries in a 17-month period, then had 10 months of relative peace, and I am now facing a possible eighth surgery!

'I don't mind saying I'm a strong, gutsy lady. They knock me down, and I take it with a stiff upper lip. I am human, though, and I have had spells of complete distress! I live in a small town in the middle of the desert in New Mexico, my husband is an Air Force fighter pilot, and they assigned him to this lizard's paradise about 19 months ago. I, however, work in Dallas, Texas, soooo . . . (sic) this tough little cookie gets in the car, drives through the desert for two hours into El Paso, and then gets on a company plane and commutes to Dallas: then I go to work as a flight attendant for the same company and put in five to eight more landings before I hit the pillow! I have never been sickly until this endometriosis hit me the spring of '83 when they diagnosed it. I am faced with some real life-altering decisions . . . I am rapidly feeling the moxie leaking from me! The doc says, "Use it or lose it," "Get pregnant now, or it may be never,"same song and dance we all get.

*'The doc is great. He isn't as blunt as I have paraphrased,
but the dear man has seen my insides now for the past five
surgeries and knows me like Rand McNally knows roads . . .*

*'I know life could be worse. I could have only one eye or
leg, and I am very fortunate to have all I do have . . . but those
philosophies do not solve the disease, do not get rid of the pain,
the tears, or the heartache of frustrations that come with the
problem. There are women who have trouble-free lives and get
pregnant without even thinking about it. There are people out
there breeding like rats, and not an ounce of stress like we have,
and it's damn maddening!*

*'There are an amazing amount of flight attendants in my
company who have been suffering from the problems associated
with endometriosis. We have each other when we run into each
other on the airplanes, but schedules change, and so do crews,
and comfort is few and far between. I have been feeling pretty
good for the past ten months, and it has not really been at the
crisis stage until this month. Now I feel lost again and so helpless.
My body is the destiny of our futures . . . my husband's career,
my own career, our parenthood, our far future goals . . .*

*'This whole ordeal is just awful sometimes. If I get pregnant
soon*, if I can get pregnant ever, much less soon, *Mike can't
change careers with a new baby in the house and debts to pay
. . . it would be* dumb! *If I wait until we are both completely
settled into our careers and the same city and all debts are paid,
it may be too late, and all I'll get is a hysterectomy with no
promises I'll never have endometriosis again! This is a real sick
joke Mother Nature has played on women, and why have 100
years passed and the medical society has practically no answers
for us?! . . .*

'Thank you for allowing me to air out my heart: there's
not many around who can understand or spend the time to
listen to me air out my desperations on an emotional soapbox.
I feel better now, and this ought to last me a few months.
Thank you.'   Linda, Holloman AFB, New Mexico

By the time they find the Association, many women with endometriosis are very needy, after years of building symptoms, fear, uncertainty,
confusion, guilt, lowered self-esteem, and having something that often
they can't discuss with others (sometimes not even their mothers!). By
the time they reach the Association, their faith in their bodies is often
gone, and they sometimes feel like failures as women and in general—

perhaps unable to fulfill the traditional roles and often unable to fill nontraditional roles as well. They are dependent on the medical establishment and often feel powerless in that relationship. Feeling a lessened self-confidence about their bodies and themselves, they have often internalized the confusing, guilt-placing myths about endometriosis, adding to the hurt and making it harder to fight back.

It has been a marvellous experience to see the transformations in these women as they learn how to regain some control of their lives (although the disease makes it difficult) and regain a sense of pride in themselves and in other women. Seeing the Association as a group of women like themselves, with the disease, taking action and taking the lead in fighting the disease, is a critical part of this transformation.

Everywhere around the country, the same magic has occurred. A group of diverse women whose lives otherwise would probably never touch, gather in the same room for a support group meeting. Even before the meeting begins, they are talking—professional and nonprofessional women, women of all income levels, racial groups, educational levels, religious backgrounds, sexual preferences, single and coupled. They share the most intimate personal pain and frustration related to the disease with each other because the need to talk about it is so great, and the fear of others not understanding is gone.

Many of these women have never been to a support group before in their lives. They're sometimes surprised how much they can learn from other women. What the group does for them over time includes the following:

1. *Ends the feeling of being alone,* misunderstood, unsupported, in coping with a disease that has been considered shameful, embarrassing, or nonexistent.

2. *Brings the woman and the disease out of the closet.* Once the woman has found she can talk about it with others in the support group, she is more able to discuss it with others in her life.

3. *Rebuilds lost self-esteem.* The support group helps rebuild a sense of self—after all, she can look around the room at the other women with endometriosis and see that they are OK women. No amount of therapy or support (if she is lucky enough to get it) from a husband or anyone else can do quite as much as seeing others like her cope; seeing that they are whole, respectable people, not just a disease.

4. *Teaches coping skills related to the disease.* Tips and ideas are shared that no doctor could possibly impart because he or she does not live with the disease day by day. (In fact, women with endometriosis have found they often cannot even get help with *medical* symptoms from their doctors.)

5. *Helps women come to grips with the denial process related to the disease.* A serious aspect of endometriosis is denial. As a problem that has been unacknowledged, endometriosis has tended to be denied, just as other unnamed problems in our society—spouse battering, for example. When society as a whole fails to recognize a problem, the individual caught up in it frequently denies it too.

In the case of endometriosis, everything in society reinforces that the woman with it should remain 'in the closet.' Hearing other women's histories related to endometriosis has helped many of our members come to grips with the serious ramifications of denying the disease exists or that it will affect them. The support groups have helped many confront the disease directly so the important life decisions wrapped up in this disease (fertility, sexuality, physical incapacitation, ability to earn a living or pursue other interests, ability to enjoy being a woman, feelings about being a woman) have more chance to be made by the woman than determined by the disease or a doctor. This process is particularly important because so many of the women with endometriosis are so young (teens and twenties), that they often come to the disease without the life experiences or skills to help them through it.

6. *Debunks the myths of endometriosis.* In the support group, the woman need only look around the group and listen to see that the myths about endometriosis are just that—myths. She can see that women with endometriosis are from varying races, income classes, occupations, and levels of literacy. And she can hear the stories of symptoms starting years before the woman was in her thirties and forties (supposedly the age of most women with endometriosis), the women who had early pregnancies but still have endometriosis, the numerous women with ongoing disease despite treatments with supposedly high nonrecurrence rates.

7. *Helps women find a good doctor.* Treating endometriosis is difficult. A good doctor is absolutely vital as treatment may vary depending on the location of the endometrial growths, symptoms, issues related to conserving fertility, sexuality, the serious side effects possible with drug therapies, and sometimes, considerations related to bowel and bladder function.

A doctor who is knowledgeable, experienced with numerous cases of endometriosis, and *sensitive* to the woman, able and willing to treat her as an individual and respect her decisions, is hard to find. The amount of misinformation relayed to women with endometriosis and the disrespect with which they are sometimes treated (truly horror stories in many cases) have been an astounding realization for the Association. The realization is hard to accept, but years of letters from throughout the U.S. and Canada relating the same patterns over and over make the conclusions inescapable. Fortunately, there are wonderful doctors, too, who are willing to work with us to find answers for this disease.

8. *Helps empower the woman vis-à-vis medical professionals needed to cope with the disease.* In a world where we are advised to 'comparison shop,' it's amazing that many consumers do not take such precautions for their own bodies. The support group helps her see that others with endometriosis receive better (or worse) care than her own and helps her form a valid basis of comparison. The group can often help her, too, by encouraging her to obtain her medical records, take brochures on the disease and Association in to her doctor, and read literature about the disease and learn all she can about it in order to be armed with the best information possible.

9. *Helps with difficult treatment decisions, times of crises, etc.* Therapists and professional counsellors have a place (if you can afford them), but most don't have the information or experience with endometriosis that the support group/chapter does. In addition, in times of crisis or pain, their help is unavailable if you can't get out of bed or it's after hours. The EA support groups and crisis call helpers (local and trained through headquarters) have time after time assisted women day, night, weekends.

10. *Improves the quality of treatment women with endometriosis are receiving.* The presence of an active support group/chapter infuses accurate information about the disease into the community. Knowing another source exists for hard-to-get information as well as a place to compare notes on treatment creates competitive pressure to improve the information and treatment given women with endometriosis. In Milwaukee, for example, where the Association has had the longest presence, we do not hear the 'horror' stories today that we did when we began.

11. *Improves the climate of support for women with the disease.* A support group or chapter in the community raises awareness of the often serious, chronic nature of the disease. Husbands, families, employers, and others are less likely to say, 'Aren't you making a mountain out of a molehill?' when they know there's an organization devoted to helping those affected by the disease. (One of the subtle ways we try to build this support as well as increase our donations is to say in our fund drive letters, 'Ask your family and others close to you to donate. Give them the enclosed donation cards and brochure to help explain more about this disease that affects you. Even if they don't make a donation, they'll understand better what you're facing.')

12. *Increases frequency of diagnosis.* The presence of a support group or chapter in the community raises the awareness of the disease throughout the community. By becoming more aware of the early warning signs, more women are asking their doctors about them earlier.

13. *Benefits our sisters, daughters, and other female relatives by having a group or chapter in the community*. More and more, documentation of genetic components for this disease is emerging. We have many members with sisters and other female relatives with it. If the women in our groups and chapters can learn how to cope with this disease, they can share their coping skills with sisters, daughters (as they mature), and others. The presence of the group in a community probably also helps the community take other female 'complaints' more seriously too.

Section IV.
New Directions:
Is Endometriosis
What We Think It Is?

When the Endometriosis Association was formed in 1980, it seemed that little new thought on the disease was occurring. We provided women with education on the disease and with coping skills, but we knew those were just necessary Band-aid measures. What are really needed are effective treatment procedures—and a cure!

The mysteries of the immune system might provide an intriguing key to the riddle of endometriosis. The articles on possible connections between endometriosis and candidiasis have provoked tremendous interest and discussion. Two research studies from our data registry have confirmed the importance of these links.

In the last few years, some daring researchers have been expanding the frontiers of our knowledge about endometriosis. One of the most revolutionary of these is Dr David Redwine, and we're pleased to present his ideas here.

Other intriguing discoveries, important for the direction they point in, are the findings of a heart defect in women with endometriosis and the possibility of diagnosing the disease with a blood test in the future.

10
The Endometriosis-Candidiasis Link

ENDOMETRIOSIS AND YEAST:
A NEW CONNECTION
By Laura J. Stevens

Until recently, few researchers considered the yeast *Candida albicans* a common factor in serious health problems. Now a few doctors are recognizing that in many patients this ordinary yeast may be related to all kinds of physical and mental symptoms, including endometriosis.

What clues suggest a connection between endometriosis and Candida? Besides suffering from endometriosis:

1. Do you have a history of yeast infections—oral, skin, vaginal, or intestinal?
2. Did your symptoms start or worsen after taking birth control pills, antibiotics, prednisone or cortisone-type drugs or after repeated pregnancies?
3. Have you ever taken tetracycline for acne? Have you taken repeated rounds of antibiotics for recurrent bladder, ear, or other infections?
4. Do you suffer from:
   • other menstrual difficulties (such as spotting or excessive bleeding) with symptoms increasing right before or at the beginning of your menstrual period?
   • diminished sexual interest?
   • chronic constipation, diarrhoea, rectal itching, spastic colon or mucous colitis?

- urgent or frequent urination?
- chronic nasal congestion or other respiratory symptoms?
- depression, irritability, and other mental symptoms?
- headaches?
- muscle aches?
- multiple allergies?
- an immune disorder such as multiple sclerosis, lupus, rheumatoid arthritis, or Crohn's disease?

5. Are you sensitive to moulds or baker's and brewer's yeast? Do you feel worse on damp, windy days or in mouldy environments?
6. Do you crave sweets, breads, or alcohol? Does eating refined carbohydrates exacerbate your symptoms or cause gas and bloating?
7. Does exposure to gas fumes, perfumes, insecticides, or tobacco cause symptoms?[1]

If you answered yes to several of the questions above, your symptoms, including those caused by your endometriosis, *may* be related to an overgrowth of Candida.

What are yeasts? Yeasts are single-celled organisms belonging to the fungus kingdom. Like their close relatives the moulds, they live all around you. One species, *Candida albicans*, lives in everyone, inhabiting the mouth, oesophagus, intestines, vagina, and skin. As long as your immune system keeps it in balance, it doesn't cause problems.

But, in 1961, allergist Dr C. Orian Truss found that one of his patients, who suffered from runny nose, migraine headaches, depression, and a vaginal yeast infection, repeatedly experienced complete relief from all her symptoms when she received an injection of Candida extract. Several years later Dr Truss tried this therapy with other patients and again achieved success. These patients, too, experienced dramatic relief from a variety of unresolved mental and physical complaints.[2]

Dr. Truss hypothesizes that the immune system keeps the yeast in check without difficulty in a healthy person. But certain factors affecting the body's chemistry can drastically upset the balance. *Pregnancy* is one. *Birth control pills* are another. Treatment with *antibiotics* kills the good intestinal bacteria, allowing the yeast to flourish unchecked. *Immunosuppressant drugs*, such as cortisone, weaken the immune system so that the body is no longer able to control the yeast. As the yeast colonies multiply, the weakened immune system is challenged further. The body may regain control naturally—or the yeast may continue to spread.

At this point the person may experience an obvious yeast infection—vaginal, oral, intestinal, or skin. However, not everyone suffering from a chronic Candida infection shows these overt symptoms.

In other words, a Candida infection can go 'underground.' Although it doesn't show itself in typical yeast infection symptoms, it may generate other problems. As the yeast colonies multiply, they constantly release a variety of yeast toxins into the bloodstream, paralyzing the immune system. A vicious cycle begins: the yeast multiplies and overwhelms the immune system; the weakened immune system can't control the yeast colonies, so they spread.

Dr. Truss and other physicians interested in yeast-related illness have observed that women with endometriosis often respond to anti-Candida measures. The exact mechanism is not understood yet, but Dr Truss has commented, 'I think it is unquestionable that there is a very high association of endometriosis with chronic candidiasis. Naturally we cannot at this time be sure whether the yeast is causing the endometriosis or whether some common factor predisposes to both. My own feeling is that the yeast is the cause of the endometriosis because it is associated with so much evidence of interference with hormone function in both men and women.'[3]

One of Dr Truss's most severe endometriosis cases was that of his assistant, Diane Debuys. A hysterectomy failed to relieve her pain, and she suffered from extremely severe urinary problems. 'By the time I was 30, my life was totally dictated by my pain,' she recalls. 'I feared I had endometriosis on my bladder or my colon.'[4] Worried that she might have to have her bladder removed and/or a colostomy, she consulted Dr Truss in November 1979. Since antiyeast treatment, she has had only minor urinary infections and feels great.

In responding to the short article 'Yeast Infections and Endometriosis' in the January 1984 issue of the Endometriosis Association newsletter, several members wrote of their experiences with endometriosis and yeast infections.

Marcia, Fremont, Michigan, relates her experience with yeast infections, endometriosis, and other symptoms. Marcia's first painful period occurred after a yeast infection in October 1980. Her pain increased each month. A laparoscopy in 1981 indicated minimal endometriosis. Her symptoms worsened. Another doctor performed a second laparoscopy, cauterizing the endometrial tissue and tying her tubes to prevent further tissue backup. [Editor's Note: This idea has been postulated by a few doctors as a way to stop retrograde menstrual flow, something unproven in itself but theorized to be a possible cause of endometriosis. Serious problems following this procedure have recently come to our attention— a whole syndrome of symptoms so severe in some cases after tubal ligation that hysterectomy followed. Anyone with experience or information on this is urged to write us.] Now she suffers from a host of other symptoms:

urinary frequency and urgency, lower back pain, menstrual irregularities, extreme fatigue, vague muscle pains, headaches, nasal congestion, and allergy to chemical fumes.

Her symptoms worsen after mould exposures. She has always consumed foods high in starches and refined sugars. Now she is changing her diet and taking nystatin, an antiyeast medication. Even before reading about 'the yeast connection,' Marcia suspected her problems were yeast-related.

Another EA member, Renee, Alaska, also suspects her endometriosis is yeast-related. Her first yeast infection occurred at age 16. By the time she was 18 she had recurrent, monthly yeast infections, each needing medical attention. By age 19 her periods became more and more painful, eventually leaving her unable to function for one to two days each month.

Suzanne, Ann Arbor, Michigan, believes her endometriosis and other health problems are allergy- and yeast-related. Sugar, wheat, milk, and eggs aggravate her symptoms. Following a low-carbohydrate diet and taking nystatin have greatly improved her symptoms.

Dr. William Crook, author of *The Yeast Connection*, writes about the frustration many women with yeast-related health problems have endured:

> Many women with yeast connected illness are tired, depressed and feel bad all over. They tend to complain of aches and pains in almost every part of their bodies. The typical woman with these symptoms has consulted many different physicians, including gynaecologists, internists, urologists, otolaryngologists and neurologists. And because their complaints continue and no apparent explanation is found, they may be told, 'You'll just have to learn to live with these symptoms.' If they continue to complain, their families, friends and physicians will usually label them as 'hypochondriacs.' And if their symptoms are severe and disabling, their physicians are apt to say, 'I think you should discuss your problems with a psychiatrist.'[5]

Like Dr Truss and other physicians, Dr Crook has found that women with a variety of complaints, including endometriosis, respond dramatically to anti-Candida measures.

What are anti-Candida measures? Dr Truss recommends the following programme in treating a chronic Candida infection.[6]

Steps to Avoid Yeast

1. Reduce exposure to all yeast foods and their relatives in your diet.
2. Begin a low-carbohydrate diet. Yeast colonies cannot live and repro-

duce well on proteins and fats alone; by depriving them of high levels of carbohydrates, you help kill them off. Dr Truss's recommended carbohydrate level for this diet is about 60 to 80 grams per day. In setting up your low-carbohydrate diet, take care to ensure adequate nutrition. Cravings for carbohydrates tend to come and go. (Do the best you can.)

3. Stay away from antibiotics, unless absolutely necessary.
4. If possible, avoid contraceptive hormones. [Editor's Note: Women with endometriosis must, of course, weigh the risks and benefits of oral contraceptives and other drugs for treatment of their endometriosis.]
5. Minimize your exposure to high-mould environments.

Drugs Used to Kill Off Yeast

Two antiyeast prescription drugs are available to reduce Candida colonies in the body. Nystatin (Mycostatin, Nilstat) is the drug most often used since it is effective and has fewer and less serious side effects. It is available in tablets, but the coloured coatings often bother the sensitive person. Your pharmacist or doctor can order pure nystatin powder from the drug company. The other drug used is ketaconazole (Nizoral), which must be carefully monitored.

Strengthening the Immune System

First of all, eat a nutritious diet. Next, your doctor should rule out (or treat) any medical condition, such as thyroid imbalance, that impairs the immune response. If possible, avoid immunosuppressant drugs, such as cortisone or prednisone. Supplementing certain vitamins, minerals, and other nutrients may also be very helpful. Finally, treatment with Candida extract by a physician experienced in its use may strengthen the immune system and help relieve symptoms.

For further details, consult *The Complete Book of Allergy Control* by Jaura J. Stevens.[7] This book will help you detect 'hidden' allergies, discusses how to avoid your allergens, and explores the underlying causes of allergy symptoms (such as Candida). You will find *The Missing Diagnosis* by pioneer Dr C. Orian Truss fascinating and instructive.[8] (It includes copies of his original medical journal articles.) Dr William Crook's *The Yeast Connection* explains yeast-related illnesses in terms you'll understand, with lots of helpful information and tips.[9]

Notes

1. Stevens, Laura J. *The Complete Book of Allergy Control.* Macmillan, 1983.
2. Truss, C. Orian. Tissue Injury by *Candida albicans:* Mental and Neurological Manifestations. *Journal of Orthomolecular Psychiatry (1):* 18–19, 1978.

3. Letter from Dr Truss to Mary Lou Ballweg, President of Endometriosis Association, January 19, 1984.

4. The Story of Chronic Candidiasis. *Inn America*, 1 (3).

5. Crook, William G. *The Yeast Connection.* Jackson, TN: Professional Books, 188–189.

6. Truss, C. Orian. Restoration of Immunologic Competence to *Candida albicans. Journal of Orthomolecular Psychiatry* 9 (4): 289–300, 1980.

7. Stevens, Laura J. *The Complete Book of Allergy Control.* Macmillan, 1983.

8. Truss, C. Orian. *The Missing Diagnosis.* P.O. Box 26508, Birmingham, AL 35226.

9. Crook, William G. *The Yeast Connection.* Future Health, Inc., Box 846, Jackson, TN 38302.

Laura J. Stevens is the author of *How to Feed Your Hyperactive Child, How to Improve Your Child's Behavior Through Diet, The New Way to Sugar-Free Recipes,* and *The Complete Book of Allergy Control.* She has recently coauthored with William S. Crook, M.D., *Solving the puzzle of Your Hard-to-Raise Child.* She is the founder of a self-help support group called Allergy Awareness and has herself suffered for many years from serious allergies, chronic yeast infections, and endometriosis—problems, we are now learning, that are interconnected. Ms. Stevens lives in Lafayette, Indiana, with her husband and two children.

Tips for Avoiding 'Simple' Vaginal Yeast Infections

The accompanying articles discuss the problems associated with systemic yeast infections, meaning yeast, normally found in everyone's body, that has overgrown and colonized into areas of the body beyond its usual areas or has grown out of balance with the good bacteria in our bodies that help keep it in check. Here are some ideas, long known in women's health circles, for avoiding the simpler vaginal yeast infections (for serious yeast problems, an antiyeast regimen such as described in the accompanying articles is probably needed).

- Do not use feminine hygiene sprays or bubble bath. They are irritants.
- Avoid wearing pantyhose and underwear that is not all cotton. Synthetic materials, especially in pantyhose, trap moisture in the crotch area, making it easy for yeast to grow.
- When on antibiotics or oral contraceptives or drugs such as danazol that can predispose you to yeast infections, eat yoghurt that contains lactobacillus. (Be sure the container says it contains this or 'active cultures.') If you don't like yoghurt, you can buy acidophilus tablets.
- Take B vitamins. They are very important to reproductive health and especially essential when on oral contraceptives and hormone drugs.

- Avoid a lot of sugars and starches in your diet. Yeasts love them—
  they create a more alkaline system that is more susceptible to yeast.

How We Learned About the Yeast Connection
By Mary Lou Ballweg

Late in 1983, Gloria Burk of Milwaukee, then on the board as correspondence secretary, brought to our attention something she was a little fearful would be thought farfetched. Another member of her family who has endometriosis had found that, under treatment for systemic (meaning throughout the body) yeast infection, symptoms she thought were due to endometriosis improved. She convinced Gloria to go to the allergist she was seeing, Dr Wayne Konetzki in Waukesha, Wisconsin, because Gloria had many of the same symptoms.

Gloria went, and a careful history of symptoms, drugs taken, and chemical sensitivities was noted. In addition, she found Dr Konetzki tested her for Candida sensitivity using Candida extract as an allergy test. She found that she too reacted allergically and began the antiyeast medications and careful diet, under Dr Ronetzki's instructions. Much to her surprise, her symptoms also improved.

She shared with the rest of the board the materials she had received from Dr Konetzki. 'You've probably heard of "yeast infections." And you may know that the yeast germ (*Candida albicans* or monilia) belongs to the same family of germs as bread mould, mildew, and penicillin . . .

'The yeast germ commonly causes vaginal infections in adult females and white patches in the mouths of babies (called *thrush*) . . . Although doctors have known about these annoying infections for many decades, they've usually considered them to be a nuisance and not dangerous or serious. (Yet women who are troubled by persistent or recurrent vaginitis might feel differently!)

'Like most physicians, until relatively recently we felt that the yeast germ was an annoying "pest." . . . We didn't realize that yeast infections could make a person feel bad all over if that person were allergic or sensitive to that yeast.

'Then, in 1979, we learned of the observations and work of Dr C. Orion Truss of Birmingham, Alabama.'

Dr. Konetzki then described the discovery by Dr Truss that some of his patients, especially women with histories of antibiotic use, birth control pill use, or cortisone use, developed the range of symptoms described in the accompanying article. A common problem of his women patients was endometriosis.

Learning of this, another board member, Marie Hathaway, Jefferson,

Wisconsin (vice president of education and community relations), found some of her problems she thought due to endometriosis also were helped by the antiyeast diet and medication. At the board kickoff weekend in July, some of us marvelled at the complicated diet regimen Marie was following, but as she explained, she feels so miserable when she doesn't follow it that following it has become self-reinforcing.

Since Gloria first brought it to our attention, we have been amazed at the building information on yeast and endometriosis, our growing file of materials, and the number of women with endometriosis and documented yeast problems.

We wrote to some of the physicians involved in this work, including the pioneering Dr Truss. Dr Truss wrote, 'I know that you have been helpful to the many women who have suffered with this condition, often since the onset of their menstrual cycles.' This naturally endeared him to us immediately as so many of us have suffered from symptoms of or related to endometriosis since our periods began but no one seems to want to believe that. 'I think it is unquestionable that there is a very high association of endometriosis with chronic candidiasis. Naturally we cannot at this time be sure whether the yeast is causing the endometriosis or whether some common factor predisposes to both.' Dr Truss then stated his belief that the yeast overgrowth precedes the endometriosis.

Hard to believe—at least until one starts reading the studies, especially the related work of Dr C. R. Mabray, a gynaecologist and researcher at Victoria Women's Clinic, Victoria, Texas. (If you find yourself telling doctors you know about this subject, be sure to refer them to Dr Mabray's work, published in medical journals, as most physicians are unaware of this subject and are perhaps going to regard it with suspicion.) Dr Mabray has documented immune system abnormalities in women with endometriosis, and he and a few other physicians have pioneered allergy management techniques in treating some gynaecologic conditions (see *Clinical Ecology*, fall-winter issue, 1982–83). He writes in one of his studies, reported in *Obstetrics and Gynecology*, May 1982: 'Moreover, the present authors have been impressed that the women in their practice who have premenstrual and/or menstrual difficulties also have a high incidence of allergic syndromes, just as Miller was impressed by the high incidence of premenstrual and menstrual problems in his allergy practice.'

Dr. Mabray wrote Gloria Burk early this year that he had no easy answers regarding endometriosis but believes that endometriosis is most likely a symptom rather than a disease in the sense that there is an underlying cause. (If, for instance, it was due to an immune system problem, then endometriosis might be a symptom of the immune system problems rather than a disease itself.) He wrote, 'Studies that we did several years ago seemed to confirm not only that endometriosis is familial [this was later confirmed by Dr Russell Malinak at Baylor and was published] but also it is associated with a strong personal and family history of allergy.' He wrote that 'the key is that it [endometriosis] is not just an anatomical problem at all' and that he and his associates are working on PMS as their model to help them understand the interaction of immune dysfunction and gynaecologic problems.

Other pertinent research includes recent studies in Japan that isolated the toxin produced by yeast and found that it suppresses immunity. And here in the States, there is research by scattered traditional researchers such as Dr Shawky Badawy, director of the Reproductive Endocrinology Unit at State University of New York in Syracuse. He and others are beginning to find evidence too of immune problems in women with endometriosis (see 'Autoimmune Phenomena in Infertile Patients with Endometriosis,' *Obstetrics and Gynecology*, March 1984).

An informal check of about 300 of the questionnaires in our data registry surprised me because it showed that many of the women did report personal and family histories of allergy and a variety of allergy-related problems. Because our questionnaire does not specifically ask about allergies or related problems (it asks if the woman has other health problems) and because so many people are not aware of these problems or don't pinpoint them, our questionnaires most certainly underreport these problems. There is a bias in traditional medical thinking against allergy problems as a serious matter and, beyond that, even more bias against issues of diet and food allergies being potentially a serious issue. This too contributes to underreporting the problem. (A study by Dr Karen Lamb, Director of the Association Research Registry Program, has now confirmed this 1984 observation. Women with endometriosis who reported family members also affected by the disease were found to have 'strong familial tendencies to allergic manifestations' compared to controls. The study was published in the *American Journal of Preventive Medicine* 1986; 2[6].)

Reading about the yeast 'connection,' one is struck by the similar 'it's in your head' approach so many women with endometriosis report. Dr Konetzki writes, 'Much to their distress, on seeking medical help, many patients [with yeast-related symptoms] would be told, "Your physical examination and laboratory studies show no disease. Your symptoms must be caused by emotional stress." Physicians, relatives and others would often accuse such patients of being "hypochondriacs." As a result, patients with the Candida problem go from doctor to doctor seeking help. Help that often isn't forthcoming.'

Other sources of information on yeast problems besides those already mentioned in this and the other articles in this chapter include Dr Sidney Baker, professor of pediatrics at Yale University and associated with the Gesell Institute of Human Development in New Haven, Connecticut, and the Pottenger Nutrition Foundation of La Mesa, California. Dr Baker wrote me: 'I believe that a large portion of the endometriosis problem is Candida related, and can cite some spectacular results in patients managed in this way.'

The yeast 'connection' is a great example of how our networking among women with endometriosis works. It confirms again how much we can learn if we have the courage to share our experiences and work together.

ENDOMETRIOSIS AND CANDIDIASIS: MORE STARTLING CONNECTIONS
By Mary Lou Ballweg

[Editor's Note: After we published the preceding article, we received requests for more information about the subject. In March 1985, the leading doctors and researchers in the U.S. working in the growing field of fungi and human health met for a national conference in San Francisco and shared research results and clinical experiences. Barbara Reynolds, coorganizer of the Association's San Francisco chapter, was able to attend the Yeast-Human Interaction Conference, and the Association has in its library at headquarters the complete set of audiotapes of the conference. From Barbara's report, the tapes, our growing files on this problem and its links to endometrosis, and members' reports, we've compiled this special article on this important topic. It's important to note here that the speakers at the conference (except for Dr Phyllis Saifer and Dr Richard Mabray) do not specifically discuss endometriosis. Research on candidiasis and related subjects at this time is oriented primarily to understanding the basics of what is going on. But that basic research, plus our information at headquarters from women with endometriosis who also have diagnosed candidiasis, makes possible a whole new theory on the cause of endometriosis. This article is the first ever to propose that new theory.]

The Intriguing World of Fungi

Most people who took high school biology probably remember that the living world is divided into major groupings: animals (ranging from bacteria to human beings) and plants (ranging from algae to trees). What I had not remembered very well from my high school or college courses was fungi (fungus, singular; fungi, plural). The lack of awareness of fungi is pretty common—the focus in science and medicine, at least for disease-causing organisms, has been bacteria and viruses. Now, because of new discoveries about fungi and how they relate to human health, this may change.

Fungi are a group of organisms including yeasts, moulds, mildews, smuts, and rusts. According to a pamphlet from the U.S. Department of Health and Human Services, fungi 'cannot make their own food from sunlight. They steal their nourishment from living plants and animals, from decaying matter that was once alive, and even from substances such as paint and wallpaper paste.' Yeasts are one group of fungi, single-celled organisms that reproduce themselves by budding. This budding has been used by human beings for centuries to make bread rise and to ferment vinegar and alcoholic beverages.

There are over 900 species of yeast, including 60 or 70 species of the Candida variety. (A species is a category of biological grouping made up of related organisms potentially capable of interbreeding.) The different types of yeast have a variety of characteristics, life histories, biologies, and compositions, according to Dr John Rippon, who gave a witty introduction to yeasts at the Yeast-Human Interaction Conference. Dr Rippon is author of *Medical Mycology*, a textbook on fungi; director of the Mycology Service Laboratory; a professor of medicine at the University of Chicago; and consultant on fungi for numerous hospitals.

Quite a number of yeasts are part of our normal flora (the microorganisms that typically live in or on specific parts of our body) on our skin and our mucous membranes. Some of them, including *Candida albicans*, cannot live anywhere but in or on warm-blooded mammals. Most of the time, these organisms and human beings establish equilibrium, at least in a healthy individual. But sometimes, under certain circumstances, some of these organisms 'breach the grounds of the equilibrium and become more than just casual residents of us and can then start to invade and to digest and to eat us up,' said Dr Rippon. 'The ecological function of fungi in the world is to recycle organic material. And as far as these organisms and the other fungi are concerned, we are simply a pile of organic material to be recycled.'

As long as we are healthy and happy, our resident fungi are healthy and happy, said Dr Rippon in his talk. But if we are not healthy and happy, our cohabitant yeasts may decide to recycle us. What tells them *when* we are to be 'recycled'? In the healthy person, the immune system and counter-balancing microorganisms, particularly lactobacillus (the key organism in good yogurt) keep the fungi in balance. In a person with immune system problems, whether genetic or induced by drugs such as chemotherapy, and in a person in whom the counterbalancing microorganisms have been killed off by antibiotics, the fungi can gain the upper hand. (Antibiotics kill off the lactobacillus but not the fungi. Without the lactobacillus normally present in the gut to compete with, the fungi overgrow.)

Not a lot is known about yeasts and human health—at least not in comparison to bacteria and viruses. Although some fungi have been known for decades to cause health problems in human beings (ringworm is an example), most have been thought to be probably harmless cohabitants except in immunosuppressed individuals. This belief developed despite the fact that for the most part little was known about fungi.

A more sophisticated view of fungi is developing with the growing number of mycologists (people who study fungi). An example of a yeast, a normal part of human flora, that was never considered to be harmful to humans is a yeast named *Trichosporon mygeli*. It was first reported to cause disease in 1975 and is now widely recognized as causing disease, mostly in immunosuppressed individuals, according to Dr Rippon.

What *is* known about yeasts is intriguing and offers a hint of a whole new frontier in medicine and understanding of the living world. It is known, for instance, said Dr Rippon, that most fungi have the ability to break down some fatty acids. Fatty acids are the precursors of prostaglandins in our bodies, enzymes that have numerous functions, including stimulating and inhibiting uterine and other smooth muscle contractions, playing a role in lowering blood pressure, controlling inflammation, regulating some hormones, and regulating body temperature. (For more on these enzymes, see the article on prostaglandins in Section V of this book.)

Another thing known about yeasts is that they have some intriguing relationships to substances toxic to human beings. The one best known to all of us, as Dr Baker (director of the Gesell Institute and a Yale University professor) points out in his talk, is alcohol, a product of yeasts. While alcohol, in moderation, has long been enjoyed by human beings, it's also long been known that in larger amounts it is a serious poison with multiple toxic effects on the body. We all know, too, that while some mushrooms (what we call a *mushroom* is the reproductive body, or fruit, of fungi) are enjoyed by humans, apparently without ill effect, others are highly deadly.

Perhaps it's not surprising that fungi should be connected to toxins, considering that the ecological role of fungi is to metabolize decaying matter. *Candida albicans*, which lives in all humans, makes its chief home in the intestines (although it also lives normally in the mouth and vagina). Candida probably has an important role in the intestines, possibly even an indispensable role in removal of waste and toxins from our bodies, but as yet, no one knows. Some researchers also postulate that *Candida albicans* may have a role in hormone regulation.

It is known that *Candida albicans*, specifically, makes toxins in our bodies, possibly only in certain stages of its own life cycle (yeasts move from single cell to branching to budding). Or, possibly, Candida causes problems only when the yeast has multiplied to such large numbers that there is a large quantity of toxins present. A healthy immune system keeps this overgrowth from occurring.

A large number of yeast organisms could certainly cause a 'ferment' of activity in the intestine, an overactivity that certainly has caused much distress to many with candidiasis. Also, too many yeast organisms might mean too much breakdown activity in the gut—more breakdown activity might mean that molecules and toxins not normally broken down could then, in a broken-down free form, get into the bloodstream via the intestinal walls.

Enter the Immune System

As Candida releases toxins, the immune system attempts to react—it must make antibodies for all the toxins. Many patients with candidiasis develop multiple 'allergies' and chemical intolerances. As one who has experienced it, it feels as if one's immune system has gone into a frenzy. My sense of the immune system at this point in candidiasis is that it becomes like a crazed, wound-up toy soldier—shooting wildly in every which direction because enemies are coming at it from every direction due to the enormous numbers of toxins!

The confused, overworked, and weakened immune system starts making antibodies to all kinds of things that aren't really 'enemies' or are enemies that healthy immune systems seem to cope with without obvious problems, although the reaction of candidiasis patients might be a strong warning sign for everyone. Some of the substances candidiasis patients begin reacting strongly to are chemicals of all kinds—perfumes, household cleaners, laundry soaps and products; all types of petrochemical products; cigarette smoke; formaldehyde; and dozens more. These reactions can make candidiasis patients so sick that they sometimes cannot leave their homes because they cannot risk exposure to the things that make them sick. To ignore the symptoms and try to 'tough it out' is foolhardy since continuously antagonizing the immune system in this state only weakens it further.

One strain of Candida that's particularly intriguing is a strain that's been found only in Japan or in people who've visited Japan. This strain manufactures alcohol in the intestines of the person with it from carbohydrates and causes them to become literally drunk from within their own intestines. It's a serious illness, and, of course, those with it were assumed to have been hitting the bottle when they developed symptoms of falling down, becoming incoherent, and so on, until it was found in children.

Hormones and Fungi

It is also known that many fungi have receptors in their cell walls for steroid hormones and that certain species prefer or must have certain hormonal environments in order to grow. Dr Rippon describes a certain fungus, for instance, that grows only on the scrotum and its growth is stimulated by male hormones. And in South America, a fatal disease that affects primarily men is due to a fungus that has been studied by Dr David Feldman, professor of medicine at Stanford University School of Medicine and chief of the Division of Endocrinology. Very low amounts of oestradiol, an oestrogen, completely block the ability of the fungus to invade. Thus, menstruating women, who produce this form of estrogen, are resistant to this fungus. Men and nonmenstruating women and girls do not have the protective effect of this oestrogen and therefore are susceptible to this particular fungus. (The nonmenstruating women and girls are not as susceptible to the fungus as men.)

Candida albicans has steroid hormone receptors in its cell membranes, too, but prefers women, it seems, although it causes serious problems in some men, too, particularly following a lot of antibiotics. According to Dr Rippon, some of the oestrogens are known to stimulate the growth of Candida and some are known to inhibit its growth, but he did not specify which in each case, something of obvious interest to women with endometriosis who also have candidiasis. (It might be possible, for instance, to choose a particular type of birth control pill or oestrogen replacement hormone after removal of the ovaries that would be better for us given this information.)

Candida albicans also binds corticoids (adrenal gland hormones) and progestins, according to researcher Feldman. What Dr Feldman and his colleagues have found is the capability for bidirectional binding of the hormones of mammals (currently his lab is working with rats) and yeast 'hormones.' Meaning: the rat hormones bind to the Candida, and the Candida 'hormones' or ligands bind to the rat's hormone receptor sites. (The word *hormone* has traditionally been defined as a substance produced by an endocrine gland and carried in the bloodstream to another organ in which the hormone stimulates some action. Because yeasts are *one-*

celled organisms, some people say the word *ligand* should be used instead of hormone because the notion of the substance travelling from one organ to another doesn't seem to apply, although the function does.)

Thus far, some yeast ligands have been found to be identical to human hormones, and the fact that they can bind in a mammal's hormone receptor sites shows that, as far as the mammal is concerned, they're identical! Even more astounding is that Feldman's research so far has found that the Candida ligand is actually *better* at competing for the mammal's receptor sites than the rat's own hormones! An article in *Science* magazine, August 1984 ('Steroid Hormone Systems Found in Yeast') describes another of Feldman's recent findings: 'Feldman is particularly intrigued by their most recent finding. When he and his associates . . . looked at Saccharomyces, the common baker's and brewer's yeast, they found that it has receptors that bind oestrogens, although it does not have glucocorticoid receptors (as does Candida). Very recently, they found that it actually produces the human female sex hormone 17B-oestradiol . . . "The startling thing is that it is identical to the human hormone."' Remember that Saccharomyces is *not* Candida but a different yeast that does not favour the human environment, apparently, as Candida does. But the ability to produce hormone identical to a human hormone is highly significant and could be expected to be found in other fungi.

It's hard to imagine research with more potential implications for endometriosis than this if indeed the amazing correlation between endometriosis and *Candida albicans* continues. For example, if indeed *Candida albicans*, in candidiasis, can bind the progesterone needed by *us*, it means the progesterone is not available for use by our bodies. The most common hormonal problem found in women with endometriosis is a slight luteal phase defect—not enough progesterone. But even when the findings are normal, to continue in this vein a bit further—that is, normal amounts of progesterone circulating in the blood—it doesn't mean that hormone is available for use if it's bound up. (Work by other researchers, not mycologists, is beginning to suggest that oestrogens enhance antibody response and also inhibit suppressor T-cell activity, findings that would mean perpetuation of a vicious cycle once it was set off by Candida or some other mechanism.)

WAYS CANDIDA ALBICANS CAN MAKE US SICK

- Production of toxin (established)
- Formation of prostaglandins and leukotriens (established)

- Autoimmune processes, antibodies to one's own hormones (established)
- Taking receptor sites meant for one's own hormones (strong evidence)
- Numerous metabolic disturbances of fatty acids and proteins (ongoing studies of Dr C. Orian Truss)
- Stimulate release of histamines that can suppress immune response (established)
- Cause asthma in some people (established)
- Mitral valve prolapse (established but not understood)
- Tetany (Neuromuscular excitability)

The Autoimmune Process

At the same time, an even more insidious process may be occurring related to autoimmune processes. In fighting invasion by Candida, the immune system must make antibodies, molecules that combine with an invader or substance that provokes the body and, after combining with it, destroy it. Antibodies are made to fit the substance that provoked the body *precisely*, like a lock and key, and can only combine with a substance that 'fits' it. If one of the antibodies must fight the Candida ligand that is so similar to the body's own hormones that it's able to take the place on the receptor site for the body's hormone, then the antibody made to fight the ligand will also be an antibody that fits, like the lock and key, the body's own hormone! So the antibody made to fit the ligand will also combine with the body's own hormone and destroy it! And, of course, the reproductive system cannot work correctly if the hormones needed to regulate it are being destroyed.

Does this seem farfetched? It's already been proven (although it's such a revolutionary concept—not the autoimmune process itself, which has been found in other diseases, but that it could be triggered by a fungus and a fungus 'ligand'—that it will probably take many more research studies and much discussion to be widely known and accepted in the medical community). The first research reporting this amazing Candida link was the study 'Antiovarian and Antilymphocyte Antibodies in Patients with Chronic Vaginal Candidiasis,' by S. Mathur et al. in *The Journal of Reproductive Immunology 2*, 1980. (An earlier report, published in 1973, in *The American Journal of Medicine*, discussed related autoimmune processes, but the *Candida albicans* link came later. That report, 'Autoimmune Thyroiditis, Adrenalitis and Oophoritis,' was published in Volume 54 of that journal.) Dr Ed Winger, director of Immunodiagnostic Laboratories and faculty member of the School of Public Health, University of California-Berkeley, described the work in his lab, a study done at the University of South Carolina, and the autoimmune process in his talk at the Yeast-Human Interaction Conference.

In the South Carolina study, researchers found that women with chronic vaginal candidiasis not only had immune reactivity against Candida itself but also that these antibodies reacted against the women's ovaries and possibly against helper T-cells (immune system cells that are a necessary part of keeping organisms such as Candida under control). And 75 percent of the women in the study had some form of ovarian dysfunction.

The antibodies to Candida and ovaries dropped during treatment for candidiasis—meaning the treatment was working. When treatment was stopped, the problem returned, and antibodies to ovaries and to *Candida albicans* rose again. The same response pattern occurred with the helper T-cells.

It was also shown in the study that one could absorb out the antibody to Candida, and the reactivity to ovaries and T-cells was then markedly diminished. 'This classic immunologic technique demonstrated these were one and the same antibodies,' said Dr Winger in his talk.

Another important research study of women with chronic Candida vaginitis was conducted by Dr Steven Witkin, research professor in the Department of Obstetrics and Gynecology at Cornell University Medical College. Dr Witkin studied 65 women with recurrent vaginitis due to *Candida albicans. Recurrent* was defined as at least three separate episodes within the previous 12 months. What Dr Witkin found was that not only did the Candida block macrophages (immune cells that gobble up invaders) from functioning in these women—that is, in the presence of Candida, the cells were *unable* to eat the Candida—but also that in the presence of very specific doses of ibuprofen (a prostaglandin inhibitor, brand name Motrin), the cells became able to eat the Candida!

Dr. Witkin proved that the patients did not have a lymphocyte defect but a macrophage defect. In the presence of normal macrophages, the patients' lymphocytes became able to respond normally to Candida. In the presence of patient macrophages, normal lymphocytes were now *not* able to respond to Candida.

Then, to test if prostaglandins were involved in suppressing a normal response, Witkin repeated the experiment and added ibuprofen, and the patients' macrophages were now able to support normal lymphocyte responses to Candida. He also tested another prostaglandin inhibitor, which also worked but not as well as the ibuprofen. The ibuprofen was effective only over a very narrow range, he noted—too much or too little did not work.

Dr. Witkin believes some women have a macrophage regulatory

defect and that in response to Candida, their macrophages produce excessive prostaglandins that then block the ability of their lymphocytes to respond to Candida. Because of this regulatory dysfunction, these women are highly susceptible to repeated infections.

Autoimmune Endocrinopathy

Immune system regulatory dysfunction is at the heart of the insidious process occurring in a group of diseases called *autoimmune endocrinopathies*. Dr Phyllis Saifer, secretary of the Academy of Environmental Medicine and an allergist, includes endometriosis in her discussion of related endocrinopathies she sees in patients with candidiasis. For a further understanding of this process, let's review some basics of the endocrine system with Dr Winger as he described it in San Francisco:

1. Basically, we have an endocrine gland (ovary, thyroid, pancreas, etc.).
2. Hormone is secreted by that gland.
3. Receptors, located a distance from that gland, are capable of binding low concentrations of that hormone.
4. The bound hormone then turns on the target cell by some intercellular mechanism that is linked either to the receptor on the cell surface or to some intercellular ligand.

What happens in autoimmune polyendocrinopathies is that antibodies attack the receptor sites *and* the hormones or ligands meant for those receptors. (Don't let these big words frighten you. If you take them apart by syllables, they're not so monolithic. For example: auto = self; immune = attacking, defending against, 'allergic' to; autoimmune = self-attacking; disease in which part of the body (immune system) attacks another part of the body; poly = many; endocrine = the glands and parts of the endocrine system; pathy, pathies = disease, pathology; polyendocrino-pathy = disease of many parts of the endocrine system; autoimmune polyendocrinopathy = disease in which many parts of the endocrine system are attacked by the body's own immune system.)

In diabetes, for example, Dr Winger explains, antibodies form against the receptors for insulin and against the hormone insulin. In myasthenia gravis, a disease in which the muscles progressively weaken, antibodies bind to the acetylcholine receptor, remove the receptor from the cell surface after the antibody binds with it, and never recycles it to the surface of the cell. As the number of receptors on the cell surface diminishes, there are eventually not enough available to bind with acetylcholine and stimulate the muscle, leading progressively to the muscle weakness characteristic of myasthenia gravis. A similar process may be occurring in endometriosis.

The mechanisms behind autoimmune endocrinopathy are not new discoveries. What is new is:

1. The possibility of a fungus as a triggering agent for autoimmune endocrinopathy
2. The link of candidiasis to autoimmune endocrinopathy
3. Putting endometriosis in the category of autoimmune polyendocrinopathy

Candida albicans is the culprit being linked to the autoimmune endocrinopathies discussed at the Yeast-Human Interaction Conference. But other fungi are also being implicated in serious immune-hormonal dysregulation diseases.

ARE THE ENDOCRINE SYSTEM AND THE IMMUNE SYSTEM REALLY ONE SYSTEM?

'Both clinical and experimental evidence support the hypothesis that gonadal steroids regulate immune function. This conclusion is based on the following observations:

'(i) a sexual dimorphism exists in the immune response [Editor's note: two types of immune response depending on the sex of the person];

'(ii) the immune response is altered by gonadectomy and sex steroid hormone replacement [gonadectomy: removal of the gonads—ovaries or testicles];

'(iii) the immune response is altered during pregnancy when the amount of sex steriod hormone is increased; and

'(iv) the organs responsible for the immune response contain specific receptors for gonadal steroids [gonadal steroids: steroid hormones of the gonads, that is, oestrogen and progesterone from ovaries; testosterone from testicles].'

From 'Interactions Between the Gonadal Steroids and the Immune System,' *Science Magazine*, January 1985

An Early Warning System

If all of this seems overwhelming from a lay point of view, remember that it's overwhelming to medical people, too. As Dr Ken Gerdes (private practice, environmental diseases) said at the Yeast-Human Interaction Conference, 'This meeting I finally recognized what this all was—it was a plot to get me back in medical school! . . . These people in general are trying to convince me that if I want to do a competent job at this business

I have to learn nutritional biochemistry, ENT (ear-nose-throat), gyn, psychology, gastrology, endocrinology—you know, I'm really beginning to feel overwhelmed! I don't see anyplace where I have to go back and learn orthopedic surgery, and that really helps,' he added humorously. 'If you learn all the ins and outs about Candida and all the ramifications, you know an awful lot about medicine.'

As one of the speakers at the Yeast-Human Interaction Conference, a veterinarian who treats candidiasis in animals, says: 'Candida likes us—it's just trying to tell us something.' What it may be trying to tell us is that modern drugs, diet, and other aspects of twentieth-century life have 'breached the grounds of equilibrium,' to use Dr Rippon's words, between human beings and organisms with which we share space on this earth. And women with endometriosis seem somehow to be in the middle of it. We are perhaps the 'miner's canaries' of the twentieth century. (Before mines were equipped with poison detectors, miners would lower a canary into the mines. If the canary came back up OK, the miners knew it was safe to enter the mine. If the canary came back up dead, the miners knew poisonous gases existed in the mine and it was not safe to enter.) Just as Candida may be trying to tell us something, women with endometriosis (our bodies) may be the messengers telling us all to beware: our modern life may not be healthy for us.

'Most people are prone to view *Candida albicans* as a parasite,' says the veterinarian quoted above. 'They see us as the innocent victims of a malicious, opportunistic organism ... In reality we are not innocent victims of disease ... Every symptom is a signal, an important message that something in our healthstyle needs to be altered ... *As an important part of this early warning system*, Candida albicans *is an invaluable symbiont*. It gives us signals when drugs, foods, and other forms of distress have weakened our own defences. It is our smoke detector, our burglar alarm, our seat belt buzzer. *The signals may be annoying, but the early warning enables us to avoid disaster.*'

Autoimmune Studies and Endometriosis

Autoimmune phenomena have been explored a bit in relation to endometriosis by a few researchers. Briefly, here's what's been studied in relation to this:

- Dr. W. P. Dmowski, who is with Rush Medical College in Chicago, found deficient cellular immunity in five monkeys with spontaneous endometriosis (meaning they developed endometriosis on their own, not lab-induced) as compared to five monkeys without endometriosis. The lymphocyte response of those with endometriosis was *signifi-*

cantly less. The deficiency was pinpointed to be occurring at the *cellular* level. As Dmowski wrote: 'These data suggest that endometrial cells translocated from their normal location may implant only in women with specific alteration in cell-mediated immunity.' (Cell-mediated immunity is the part of the immune system that operates at the cell level, including T-cells and macrophages. It is at the cellular level that some immune defect seems to occur in candidiasis also.)

• Dr. John Weed and Dr George Schneider, New Orleans, have studied an autoimmune response in endometriosis related to the infertility that sometimes occurs with endometriosis. Unfortunately, they have been unable to continue these studies, according to Dr Schneider in a recent letter to me.

• Dr. Shawky Badawy and his associates at the Reproductive Endocrinology Unit, Upstate Medical Center, Syracuse, New York, have also studied autoimmune phenomena related to infertility and endometriosis. 'The preliminary presented data suggest an autoimmune phenomenon in patients with endometriosis,' they report.

• Very important work has been done by Dr Richard Mabray, a gynaecologist in private practice at the Victoria Women's Clinic in Victoria, Texas. Dr Mabray documented significant immunoglobulin abnormalities in women with endometriosis and has also developed intriguing treatment techniques based on desensitizing the immune system to oestrogen and progesterone using allergy management techniques. We hope to report his work in detail at some future time.

• Researchers in the Soviet Union, Poland, and other Communist countries appear to have made significant breakthroughs in this area. Judging from the short English summaries with the articles, and from a translation of one article, they show T-cell and B-cell and immunoglobulin abnormalties in women with endometriosis as well as immune response abnormalities.

• An important study by the group at Rush Medical College in Chicago found peripheral blood monocytes altered in women with endometriosis and that something systemic—meaning involving the body as a whole rather than just local (in the abdomen)—seems to be going on. Another study found evidence that interleukin-1, a protein produced by macrophages, might be a key culprit in endometriosis. Another study confirmed earlier findings of increased macrophages in the peritoneal fluid (the fluid surrounding the organs in the abdomen) of women with endometriosis. But yet another study was unable to confirm the findings of an earlier study of significantly higher macrophage numbers in women with endometriosis.

• Peritoneal fluid studies—one found that this fluid from women with mild endometriosis inhibited fertilization in mice. Another found no difference in effect of peritoneal fluid from patients with endometriosis or unexplained infertility as compared to fertile women on production of progesterone. The same research group, in another study, found that interleukin-1 stimulates progesterone production.

• The familial and personal tendency toward allergic manifestations in women with endometriosis was confirmed by one of the Association's own studies. Called 'Endometriosis: A Comparison of Associated Disease Histories,' it was published in the *American Journal of Preventive Medicine*, 2 (6), 1986. The study also found 'Vaginal yeast infections, a history of mononucleosis, eczema, hayfever, and food sensitivities were reported to occur much more frequently for these women [women with endometriosis].'

11
Endometriosis:
Looking at the Rubik's Cube
from Another Side

THE INTRIGUING NEW IDEAS OF
DR. DAVID REDWINE
Introduction by Mary Lou Ballweg;
Article by Sue Deutsch and Mary Lou Ballweg

[Editor's Note: There's an old saying, 'nothing new on the face of the earth,' and, unfortunately, for years it had been true of thought on the causes and development of endometriosis. But, in recent years, some new thought on how endometriosis comes about has emerged through the work of a few researchers and the Endometriosis Association. One of these researchers is Dr David Redwine, a young gynaecologist with strong professional and personal interest in the disease.

I've often said that endometriosis is probably going to be solved in the way one solves a Rubik's cube. Remember those cube puzzles that were popular a couple of years ago? You had to line up all the little squares to match, and to do it you had to concentrate hard and keep moving the pieces around over and over. Each new movement would necessitate additional changes and undo some of the previous turns. You had to keep turning the cube around and around, constantly looking at it from different sides.

Endometriosis seems to me to be a disease that has been looked at almost entirely from one side only—as a reproductive hormonal disease.

And researchers have built on that assumption. (Since we really don't know what causes it or even, when you come right down to it, *what* it really is, what we think we know about it is really only assumption.)

But suppose one turns the cube to look at other sides—suppose, just for the sake of possibilities, that it turned out not to be basically a reproductive disease. What if, for example, it is an immunologic disease that has reproductive problems as its most visible 'symptom'? Or suppose our basic understanding of hormones was flawed, and we've blinded ourselves to something by our definitions—after all, hormones have been understood to any degree for only a few decades. Or suppose, instead of a disease of any particular system, it was instead a metabolic disease— a biochemical process gone amok?

It's human nature to hang on tenaciously to what we think we 'know.' But, in a case like endometriosis, where so little is *really* known, it's dangerous to hang on to old ideas to the exclusion of new. We dare not laugh at new ideas, though at first glance they may seem outrageous, because we truly do not know where the answers will come from. We need to remember always the lesson of past ages—in the Middle Ages, for instance, it was outright heresy to suggest that there might be any cause for disease other than God's will. And later, when Louis Pasteur proposed that 'invisible enemies' might be causing disease, he was considered crazy. After discovering the bacteria that cause several diseases and also the method of vaccinating with inoculations to protect against these diseases, he became a hero. (But before that, the doctors of his time would not listen to him since he was not a physician and because his ideas were so revolutionary.)

One of the greatest values of an organization like the Endometriosis Association is that it can focus on a disease such as endometriosis from all angles. It need not be limited by professional proprietorship or the 'party line.' Because it is new ideas that will lead to answers for us, we need to *encourage* new ideas and provide a forum for them. Therefore, in that vein, we are proud to present a truly new way of looking at endometriosis—the intriguing and revolutionary ideas of Dr David Redwine.]

Endometriosis is not a progressive disease. The *amount* of endometriosis remains the same from the teenage years on, although it changes in appearance. The disease has a number of visual appearances besides those traditionally recognized. The disease is probably congenital. The current classification systems for the disease reflect a bias that endometriosis in some locations is more serious than others and as such do not adequately reflect the severity or extent of the disease. Surgeons miss much endometriosis due to techniques inadequate for the nature of the disease.

These few simple sentences represent the most revolutionary theory on endometriosis to be presented in the last several decades. The theory is the product of research carried on by Dr David Redwine, chairman of the Department of Obstetrics and Gynecology, St. Charles Medical Center in Bend, Oregon, and fellow of the American College of Obstetrics and Gynecology.

In the 1920s, a scientific researcher named Dr John Sampson coined the term *endometriosis*. He believed the condition described by this term was caused by retrograde menstruation. This means that the endometrial tissue from the uterus backs up and out the fallopian tubes and enters the abdominal cavity.

There are many questions about Sampson's theory today. Some research suggests that all women have retrograde bleeding. However, Sampson's theory has not been completely discarded. Other researchers are looking for the cause for endometriosis within the immune system or in the area of hormonal imbalance; but there is still no definite answer to the puzzle.

Dr. Redwine's theory is based on seven years of research and keen observation of patients, listening carefully to them, and questioning past assumptions about the disease. Simply put, his theory is that endometriosis is a congenital condition, which means that it existed at birth. (Others have proposed a possible congenital theory before; but Redwine has provided a greatly expanded explanation for the process that may be occurring.) As time passes, the endometrial growths change colour until they appear as the 'classic' dark implants. These are sometimes described as chocolate-colored or like powderburns in appearance. They are easily identifiable and were first described in detail by Dr Sampson.

The endometrial lesions that are darker in colour are usually the ones identified and removed by surgeons, says Redwine. The colour is due to 'fibrosis and hemorrhage adjacent to endometriosis.' But what he has observed in women with endometriosis is disease not only of the appearance described by Sampson but also other colors and appearances.

Among the patients he studied, 82 (57 percent) had black lesions, and 91 (64 percent) had lesions of other colors. Fifty-two had black lesions only (36 percent), while 60 had lesions of other colors only (42 percent). This is a total of 112 patients. Thirty-one patients had lesions of both colours for a total of 143 patients in this study. The following table shows the evolution of the appearance of the lesions over time.

EVOLUTION OF APPEARANCE OF ENDOMETRIOSIS WITH AGE

Visual Appearance	N	Mean Age
Clear papules only	6	21.5
Clear and others	20	23.7
Red only	18	26.2
Atypical only	60	28.2
Black and others	82	31.0
Black only	52	32.5

As the table shows, Dr Redwine's research suggests that endometriosis starts out in the form of clear lesions. This is usually present in younger patients. He describes it as typically looking like 'flecks of tapioca in tapioca pudding.' In the mid-twenties, a mixture of different colours of lesions is often seen. Some of the colours noted are white, grey/blue, yellow, and red. By the late twenties, black lesions become more prominent, and they predominate into the thirties and thereafter.

Other doctors believe that when black lesions are found after surgery has already taken place, it means that endometriosis has returned. Dr Redwine believes it means that not all previous lesions have been identified and removed. What others see is just a change in colour in lesions that have already been in existence.

Dr. Redwine's descriptions of the various visual manifestations of endometriosis are intriguing and illustrate the intense study of them he has made. He has also documented the varying visual appearances photographically.

'White implants were of two types: macular [characterized by macules, a patch of skin altered in colour but usually not elevated] and papular [characterized by papules, elevations of the skin]. White macular plaques [a localized abnormal patch on a body part or surface], usually stellate [resembling a star] in shape, between 0.5 millimeters [a millimetre equals 0.04 inches] and one centimetre [0.39 inches] in greatest dimension were seen microscopically to be due to peritoneal scarring or smooth muscle overlying active implants . . . This type of implant is frequently termed "burned out" disease, but the typical endometrial tissue underlying this scarring belies this terminology . . .

'Red implants are of two types: macular and papular. These have a hemorrhagic [pertaining to bleeding from the blood vessels] appearance, and the papular type is the type of implant most commonly found in peritoneal pockets. The macular type may be very small and miliary [made up of many small projections or lesions], resembling petechiae [minute hermorrhagic spots], or more broadly spreading.

'Yellow implants are akin to white macular implants, consisting of fibrosis [a condition marked by increase of tissues resembling fibers in the spaces between the organs] or smooth muscle associated with endometriotic implants.

'Clear implants may appear singly or in clusters. A typical implant may be 0.5 mm to 2 mm across. This type of implant can most accurately be described as looking like flecks of tapioca in tapioca pudding. One patient had a broad, slightly shaggy coat of clear material resembling marmalade on the uterine fundus [the large upper end of the uterus] which was endometriosis. Microscopically clear papules appear as empty glands with sparse stroma [tissue that forms the framework of an organ; in endometriosis, the foundation of a chocolate cyst or endometrioma, the part that bleeds].

'Grey and blue implants owe their colour to erythrocytes [red blood cells] in the glandular [relating to glands, gland cells, or their products] space, with the colour attenuated by thickness of overlying peritoneum.

'All types of implants are associated with causation of pain, and their surgical removal usually results in total pain relief. *That such tiny implants can cause pain should come as no surprise when one thinks of how small a grain of sand under an eyelid can bring a person to agony with pain and inflammation.*'

Dr. Redwine's opinion is that in accordance with the results of his study the 'embryonic rest theory' best explains the development of endometriosis. This theory holds that endometriosis starts through a developmental defect of differentiation or migration of the Müllerian ducts (ducts in the embryo that develop into ovaries, uterus and vagina). What happens is that bits of endometrium that were supposed to be within the uterus do not accomplish their migration. They just remain in the pelvis as the development of the organs is completed. Then, as hormones are produced, the bits of stray tissue develop and cause all the problems we know as endometriosis. (Redwine also found stray tissue derived from Müllerian ducts besides endometriosis in some of his patients, lending more weight to this theory. Also, when he presented his ideas to the Milwaukee chapter early in 1986, he showed a slide of endometrial tissue found in the pelvis during an autopsy of an infant girl, also lending support to this theory).

If this theory is correct, it would be expected that endometriosis will sometimes coexist with other defects of the Müllerian ducts. Also, the Rokitansky-Kuster-Hauser syndrome, whereby the Müllerian structures fail to form a normal cervix, uterus, and fallopian tubes may be viewed as a developmental defect of Müllerian duct formation, and endometriosis has been reported in this condition. In another study, 6 out of 15 patients with endometriosis had abnormalities of the genital tract that were interpreted by the researcher as promoting retrograde menstruation and resultant endometriosis. The other defects in the formation of the uterus or the hymen have also been found alongside endometriosis.

An alternative conclusion can be drawn, and it is the conclusion that Dr Redwine reaches. That is that endometriosis is fairly common in cases of abnormal Müllerian duct formation because it is, in itself, a developmental abnormality of Müllerian duct formation. He concludes that the more severe the abnormality anatomically, the more likely it is that endometriosis will coexist.

The distribution of endometriosis Redwine finds is, in fact, a pattern one would expect to find if indeed stray tissue was left in the pelvis after development of the embryo. Using a pelvic mapping technique in which he divided the pelvis into 16 separate areas, Redwine identified all areas of noncontiguous disease in his patients.

Dr. Redwine found the most common areas of involvement with endometriosis were cul-de-sac, right broad ligament, right uterosacral ligament, left uterosacral ligament, left broad ligament, bladder, then the left ovary, fundus of the uterus, sigmoid colon, and then right ovary. Traditional gynaecology materials have stated that the most common areas of involvement were ovaries, diffuse scattered pelvic areas, uterine surface, tubal surface, cul-de-sac, rectovaginal septum and sigmoid colon, uterosacral ligaments and other sites (*Te Linde Operative Gynecology*, Mattingly, 1977 edition).

The reason for this, says Redwine, is that in the past researchers were placing too much emphasis on infertility as the most critical symptom of endometriosis, ignoring other symptoms or minimizing their seriousness and looking only or primarily at the ovaries and tubes, critical in fertility issues, as indicators of the disease and the fertility status of the patients.

Because of the focus on fertility and the somewhat mechanical view of the body that assume that, if fertility were interfered with by the disease, it was due to mechanical interference with ovulation, fertilization, etc. (rather than a view based on hormonal, immunological, or other biochemical outlook), the classification system developed by the American Fertility Society (AFS) went astray in actually measuring the disease, says Redwine. The AFS system assigns points to assess the severity of the disease so that, theoretically, the more points, the more serious the disease. But the system is heavily weighted toward endometriosis involving the uterus, fallopian tubes, and ovaries and/or extensive pelvic adhesions, says Redwine.

When the points scored with the AFS system were plotted against the number of sites in the pelvis involved with the disease in his patients, Redwine found that the words '*mild, moderate, severe,* and *extensive* provide little useful clinical discrimination by themselves among patients with the disease.'

Ninety-five patients (82.6 percent) were classified as having mild disease, and of this group 43 percent had three or more areas of the pelvis involved. Thirteen patients (11.3 percent) were classified as having moderate disease, and of this group 69 percent had five or more pelvic areas involved. Of six patients (5.2 percent) with severe disease, 66 percent had only one or two areas of the pelvis involved, and of three patients with extensive disease, one had only one area of the pelvis involved.

Several patients with widespread peritoneal involvement with endometriosis only scored three points on the AFS point system. Many times the conservative surgery required for the removal of the disease from the bladder, posterior leaves of the broad ligaments, uterosacral ligaments, cul-de-sac, and sigmoid would require three hours of meticulous dissection by Dr Redwine during surgery. He comments that this is a 'surprising reflection of only three points worth of disease.'

Further evidence that infertility may be less frequent a symptom in endometriosis than previous reports seem to indicate is the frequency of symptoms found by Redwine in his study group. In a series of 132 consecutive patients, for instance, he found the most prevalent symptoms to be chronic pelvic pain (72 percent), painful periods (45 percent), painful sex (39 percent), and infertility (29 percent). If only 29 percent of these patients had infertility as a symptom, why do other physicians have higher percentages of their patient groups with infertility? The answer could be that these physicians are not diagnosing endometriosis much in the group without infertility as a symptom. This could be one explanation for the massive underdiagnosis of endometriosis. (All experts on endometriosis agree that only a tiny percentage of women with the disease are currently diagnosed. The Association has noted over the years in our research data registry and in thousands of contacts with women with endometriosis that diagnosis was difficult to obtain for many, obtained only after seeing quite a number of doctors, and diagnosis followed symptom development by 10 or more years in many cases.)

Dr. Redwine clearly places much emphasis in his research studies on listening studiously to symptoms. He describes pain associated with endometriosis in some of his patients in a compelling description rarely found in medical reports:

'The most common symptom was gradually worsening nonmenstrual pelvic pain, usually described by the patient as sharp, stinging, burning or knife-like. This type of pain is not like menstrual cramps at all and occurred in 64 percent of all patients. Many patients would grip their fist and twist their wrist as if plunging a knife into themselves or toward the questioner. Many patients had been told by their previous physician that they had ovulation pain ...

'A few patients who had come to think of this pain as normal for a woman to bear did not mention pain initially as a symptom: these patients volunteered after excision of their endometriosis that they had never known what it was like to feel so good. The inability of physicians to explain their pain had caused feelings of anger and despair in many symptomatic patients, with resultant deterioration of family and social relationships.'

In addition to missing endometriosis because of lack of awareness of all the symptoms and their relative importance, as well as being unaware of the varying visual manifestations, Dr Redwine believes many surgeons performing laparoscopy and surgery miss the disease because of lack of thorough laparoscopic techniques. Redwine's techniques include magnification of the peritoneal surface, near-contact visualization of the peritoneum and pelvic organs with the laparoscope, and examination of *every* visual abnormality. 'During laparoscopic investigation of pelvic pain, peritoneum that initially appears normal during panoramic viewing will in the majority of cases yield evidence of atypical implants of endometriosis if the tip of the laparoscope is advanced to within a centimetre or less of the peritoneal surface.'

Redwine notes that, by performing laparoscopy with only one incision, much endometriosis can be missed because of the bowel obscuring the area between the vagina and rectum and other problems. With a second incision, another surgical tool can be used to move bowel and cervix out of the way. Also, he notes that the bloody fluid found in the pelvis of many women with endometriosis must be suctioned out to allow visualization of areas immersed in the fluid.

The research done by Dr Redwine has immediate practical application. If his theory of the origin of endometriosis is correct, then complete, initial surgical removal of the endometrial lesions should potentially remove all disease forever from a woman's pelvis. Of course, the physician has to recognize all of the disease in order to remove it. This means accepting Dr Redwine's description of the changing appearance of the lesions.

Dr. Redwine believes that one-half of all patients desiring conservative surgery can have the endometrial lesions removed using laparoscopy. The other half will require more extensive surgical procedures. In his patients, Redwine finds that persistent endometriosis after he has performed surgery is rare. Dr Redwine encountered only two cases of recurring endometriosis in the study group after he performed conservative surgery.

He believes he overlooked areas of endometriosis in the two patients because they were surgeries done early in his research before he refined his diagnostic and surgical techniques. He has followed his cases for up to seven years, but recognizes that additional follow-up study is needed and has arranged for it. We look forward to the results.

12
A Heart Defect in Endometriosis: Another Clue to a Bigger Picture

By Mary Lou Ballweg

From the beginning of the Association, we have been aware that women with endometriosis often report low normal blood pressure (as well as low body temperature). Also, we've consistently heard reports of mild heart conditions that seemed surprising, given that we all have believed we're dealing with a reproductive disease, that heart conditions generally affect men more often than women, and that, when they do affect women, they affect them at a much older age than most of our members. So what did this mean? We just didn't know.

Recently, a surprising research finding has come to our attention that may provide some answers as to why women with endometriosis report these conditions. But it also raises more questions than it answers. The surprise finding is that the Omega Fertility Institute of New Orleans, a fertility centre that is best known for its pioneering work in developing the laser for gynaecological surgery, has discovered that *all* of its patients with endometriosis checked for a heart defect called *mitral valve prolapse* have it.

Now, before you start feeling fearful, you need to know that Dr Janos Voros of the Institute believes that 95 percent of the time the defect is a benign condition causing no problems. Specifically, mitral valve prolapse is a defect in which a valve on the left side of the heart flaps up instead of closing tightly, allowing some blood to backflow.

Very little is known about mitral valve prolapse, how frequently it occurs (except that it is more common in women than men and children), or exactly what it means for the health of the person with it. Like endometriosis itself, it reportedly can cause no symptoms at all or a range of symptoms from mild to severe.

When symptoms occur, they include chest pain, palpitations, fatigue, and difficult breathing. Impressions from members so far indicate these symptoms, when experienced, are sporadic and relatively mild. Other symptoms can include dizziness when changing positions (as from lying in bed to standing up), panic attacks, and, though rarely, fainting. (When the last occurs, it can be a sign of more serious problems with the mitral valve prolapse.)

Mitral valve prolapse is diagnosed by careful listening with a stethoscope to the activity of the heart and by echocardiogram. The defect may run in families. According to an article by Dr David W. Synder on mitral valve prolapse that appeared in the April 1985 issue of *Postgraduate Medicine*, the defect is often found in conjunction with skeletal abnormalities of the thorax (the part of the body between the neck and the abdomen). These abnormalities include scoliosis (curvature of the spine), straight-back syndrome, and pectus excavatum (depressed or hollowed-in chest).

The article notes that it is also often accompanied by low body weight, elevated levels of catecholamines (substances involved in dilation and constriction of blood vessels), and hyperthyroidism. The elevated catecholamines may explain the low normal blood pressure in women with endometriosis if, indeed, mitral valve prolapse is common in endometriosis. 'Certainly, relatively low blood pressure is common among individuals with mitral valve prolapse,' wrote Dr Synder in response to a letter from the Association, which asked if mitral valve prolapse might explain the low blood pressure we hear about in women with endometriosis.

Dr. Synder also noted in his letter, however, that 'an increased incidence of mitral valve prolapse has been reported in association with a host of disease states.' He did not elaborate. The association with hyperthyroidism may be of particular interest to women with endometriosis because of growing awareness of the frequency of thyroid problems in women with endometriosis.

Dr. Synder notes in his article that there is debate about the importance of mitral valve prolapse but that 'without question, those patients with a redundant and deformed mitral valve do face some increased cardiovascular risk.' He also notes that the more serious complications of mitral valve prolapse are more often found in men with the defect.

The American Heart Association currently does *not* recommend preventive treatment in those without symptoms, according to Synder's article, and at least one heart drug has caused deaths when given to those with the defect. For those with persistent murmur, there is debate over preventive use of antibiotics to prevent endocarditis, inflammation of the lining of the heart caused by bacteria.

Dr. Voros, the physician at Omega Institute who has publicized the mitral valve finding in women with endometriosis, has suggested preventive use of antibiotics at the time of surgery because this is what has been suggested for mitral valve prolapse patients in the past. However, during a conversation with the author, Dr Voros noted he was unfamiliar with the research on candidiasis and the growing link between endometriosis and chronic candidiasis. (This is not a reflection on Dr Voros—most of the medical profession is unfamiliar with this research because it is so new, and even those familiar with the rapidly enlarging body of research data on candidiasis are not familiar with the links to endometriosis, since those are being made primarily through the Association. For more on candidiasis, see the articles earlier in this section.)

Because so little is known about mitral valve prolapse and because it *is* known that antibiotics can play a strong role in the development of candidiasis, particularly in susceptible individuals such as women with endometriosis, antibiotics used preventively (as opposed to use for actual infection) seems premature at this time. Dr Voros suggests that women with endometriosis should have a cardiac consultation before surgery so that the defect, if present, is noted and attending physicians can be made aware of it.

It was, in fact, surgery that brought the defect to the attention of Dr Voros and his colleagues. Dr Voros said that anaesthesiologists working with the doctors at the Institute were the first to notice and question why they were seeing surgical complications with anaesthesia in young women—patients in whom one would normally not expect these complications. After investigation, they discovered the mitral valve prolapsedefect in *all* the women with endometriosis and also in some women with IUD scarring and other pelvic problems related to infertility.

Dr. Voros feels that the presence of mitral valve prolapse should perhaps be a warning sign to physicians that future fertility problems may occur in that patient. 'It is an absolute must that menstrual problems in teens be investigated for endometriosis,' Dr Voros said. Physicians must start diagnosing endometriosis earlier, he said, so that the disease could be treated medically and then maybe surgery, with the complications possible due to mitral valve prolapse, could be avoided later. 'When we see these teen girls with terrible pain and serious menstrual problems, this should be a signpost for physicians for investigation,' he said. He noted this should include both a gynaecologist investigation and cardiac investigation.

A few days after talking with Dr Voros, the author was paging through one of Dr Orion Truss's research studies. Dr Truss is the pioneer who discovered the role of the Candida fungus in chronic yeast-related illness. The study noted the frequent finding of mitral valve prolapse in patients with chronic candidiasis! The author immediately wrote both doctors about this fascinating link since the two are in separate research fields and unlikely to follow closely the work of the other field. (Due to the proliferation of research studies, most researchers are unable to keep up with everything in their *own* field of study, and clinicians even less so!)

Finally, in a caution that certainly affects women with endometriosis, Dr Synder writes in the *Postgraduate Medicine* article that there is an increased incidence of strokes in young patients with mitral valve prolapse, and therefore oral contraceptives (birth control pills) are relatively contraindicated in those with mitral valve prolapse, because oral contraceptives also increase risk of stroke. A contraindication is a condition that forbids a particular course of treatment, but a 'relative' contraindication means that the birth control pill would not be absolutely ruled out in women with mitral valve prolapse, but that it should be taken into consideration when adding up the risks and benefits for that particular form of treatment.

Synder mentions aerobic exercise conditioning as possibly being useful for those with mitral valve prolapse. And treatment for chronic candidiasis improves mitral valve function, according to speakers at the Yeast-Human Interaction Conference held in San Francisco in March 1985.

13
A Blood Test to Diagnose Endometriosis?

By Sue Deutsch

[Editor's Note: Recently we reported that work was underway on a possible blood test to diagnose endometriosis in the future. The situation is more complicated and controversial than one would assume, given the nature of blood tests. Here's the background.]

Research is currently taking place on the possible utility of CA-125, a cell surface protein, as an indicator of endometriosis when found in the bloodstream. CA-125 is usually found in the uterus, fallopian tubes, and ovaries. An elevated level of CA-125 is found in the bloodstream of women who have ovarian cancer. Current studies also indicate that it is elevated in the bloodstream of pregnant women, menstruant women, and women with pelvic inflammatory disease and with certain other problems of the reproductive system.

There is also evidence of a higher level of CA-125 in some women who have moderate or severe endometriosis. This does not appear to be as much the case with mild endometriosis. The classification of cases used in the studies is that of the American Fertility Society. The reason for the elevated level of CA-125 in all these conditions is as yet unknown.

A study conducted by Dr Robert L. Barbieri and associates under the auspices of Brigham and Women's Hospital, Harvard Medical School, Boston, Massachusetts, and Duke University School of Medicine, Durham, North Carolina, seemed to have mixed results. The study group consisted of 147 consecutive patients. The data presented indicated that

CA-125 was elevated in one-half of the patients in the study group who had advanced endometriosis. This led the researchers to state 'Measurement of serum CA-125 concentrations is not recommended as a screening device for endometriosis because of its low sensitivity.'

Dr. Donald Pittaway and associates, under the auspices of the Bowman Gray School of Medicine, Winston-Salem, North Carolina, came to a somewhat different conclusion as a result of the study of 414 consecutive patients. They found an elevated level of CA-125 in 73 percent of the women who had moderate endometriosis and 100 percent of the women who had severe endometriosis. Dr Pittaway also found a reduced level of CA-125 in those women who have already been treated for endometriosis. As a result of this study, he feels, 'A serum marker such as CA-125 may offer much needed assistance to the clinician.'

The researchers of the Harvard-Duke study also feel that even if CA-125 is not a useful indicator of endometriosis, other cell surface proteins might prove to be useful markers, and 'development of a blood test for endometriosis is feasible.'

The conclusions are somewhat different, but both studies seem to indicate that, in the future, diagnosis of endometriosis will be made much easier for both patients and physicians.

References

Barbieri, R. L.; Niloff, J. M.; Bast, Jr., R. C.; Schaetzl, E.; Kistner, R. L., and Knapp, R. C. Elevated Serum Concentrations of CA-125 in Patients with Advanced Endometriosis. *Fertility and Sterility*, 45:630, 1986.

Pittaway, D. E., and Fayez, A. The Use of CA-125 in the Diagnosis and Management of Endometriosis. *Fertility and Sterility:* in press; preprint copy.

Section V.
Research Recaps

One of the most popular features in the Endometriosis Association newsletter is a column called 'Research Recaps.'

People who are unfamiliar with endometriosis or the work of the Association are sometimes surprised that scholarly, scientific articles should inspire such enthusiasm. Women with the condition know that it is research that will finally provide the answers to this baffling disease.

This section highlights a number of studies that have important implications in connection with the disease. Each 'Research Recap' covers one subject, as a general rule, reviewing all of the most recent articles noted in the *Index Medicus* on the subject. When there are case reports that are poorly constructed, questionable, or just based on one case, the 'Research Recap' reviews and summarizes the most comprehensive article. Suzanne McDonough, our columnist and the author of five of the articles included, has a special skill in wading through dense research materials in order to find conclusions that are meaningful to women with endometriosis.

She tackles a particularly tough and frightening subject in the first 'Research Recap.' She summarizes a comprehensive report on cancer and endometriosis. The Endometriosis Association has been receiving an increasing number of questions on this subject, and we felt the time had come to address it. Fear often stems from lack of knowledge. We hope that Ms. McDonough will help to dispel all unnecessary concerns.

Also in this section, Kay Hurlbutt shares the information gained from her original study on pain control.

14
Cancer and Endometriosis

By Suzanne McDonough

The common belief is that endometriosis is a very distressing disease—but you don't die from it. Yet doctors have known for over 50 years that some rare cases of endometriosis develop into cancer and in recent years have begun to give this difficult aspect of endometriosis more attention. The thought of endometriosis developing into cancer is a very frightening one for every woman with the disease. Just what is the connection between endometriosis and cancer? How concerned should we be?

As Mostoufizadeh and Scully clearly point out in their article, associating cancer with endometriosis is a very formidable and not always objective task. Evidence associating cancer with endometriosis is only definite when a type of cancer or tumour can be seen to be growing from an already existing endometriotic implant. In other words, a tumour or an implant must be in a transition stage between normal endometriotic tissue and abnormal cancerous tissue. In this case a biopsy of the implant probably would show it to be part endometriosis, part tissue with cells in transition, and part cancer.

This continuity (being able to see the actual transition of endometriosis into cancer), however, does not exist in many cases. In other cases the evidence linking endometriosis with cancer is only circumstantial. A laparoscopy may show that a patient has both endometriosis and cancer, but not one growing from the other. One can safely think that it is more than just coincidence, say Mostoufizadeh and Scully, if 'the endometriosis is in the same site as the cancer, if the two . . . coexist at an unusual site or age, or if the patient has a long history of endometriosis with the eventual development of a malignant (cancerous) tumour that could have arisen from it.' (p. 951)

Determining whether cancer has actually developed from endometriosis is further complicated by the fact that not all cancerous tumours removed for biopsy can be studied thoroughly to determine if a part of the tumour may contain endometriotic tissue and very few endometriotic implants are removed (understandably) to see if they contain cancerous cells. (I'm definitely not suggesting that all endometriotic implants should be removed for biopsy since the chance of them being cancerous is *highly* unlikely if they resemble normal endometriotic tissue.) Most studies tend to report only that endometriosis was found in the general pelvic area at the same time as cancer and not if one may have grown from the other.

Also, the authors point out, the cancer may have already destroyed the endometriotic tissue from which it grew, making it totally impossible to associate the cancer with endometriosis. Furthermore, one has to prove that the cancer found with or near the endometriosis has not metastasized (traveled by various means) from another cancer in another part of the pelvis or body that is actually the original site of the cancer.

The two types of cancer typically found in both the conclusively proved cases and the suspected cases are, according to the authors, endometrioid cancer and others of the epithelial group (cancers usually found on the cellular coverings and linings of body surfaces). Endometrioid carcinomas (cancers), as the name suggests, are cancers found outside of the uterus but that very closely resemble cancers found in the endometrium or lining of the uterus.

Of the other cancers in the epithelial group the most common by far are the clear cell carcinomas. Mostoufizadeh and Scully break down their discussion of these types of cancers (as do most other experts) into two groups: cancers arising from endometriosis on the ovary and cancers arising from endometriosis in other areas of the body.

Cancers arising from endometriosis on the ovary are by far the most common cancers in all studies. Because of the difficulties in diagnosing the origin plus other difficulties with classifications of cancers (some of which are a mixture of types of cancer), it is hard to quote an exact figure as to how many cases of endometrioid cancer of the ovary tend to develop directly from endometriosis. Mostoufizadeh and Scully quote studies whose percentages range from 0 to 24 percent of the patients with ovarian cancer. (p. 952) Chances are the 'true' number of cases that develop from endometriosis is somewhere in between.

The mean age of the patient who has endometrioid cancer of the ovary that developed from endometriosis, according to the authors, is under 40 with a range from 25 to 60 years—a decade or more younger than those women who have endometrioid cancer of the ovary that has not developed from endometriosis. The survival rate of those women who have endometrioid cancer of the ovary that resulted from endometriosis, however, seems to be better than that of endometrioid carcinoma in general due to the fact, say Mostoufizadeh and Scully, that the cancers are frequently of a 'small size and low grade . . .' (p. 954)

Evidence of clear cell carcinoma (an epithelial carcinoma) of the ovary arising from endometriosis is even stronger than it is for endometrioid cancer of the ovary. (One researcher found a 49 percent frequency of biopsy-proven pelvic endometriosis in 33 cases of clear cell carcinoma of the ovary; other researchers have found lower frequency rates.) However, it is often found mixed with endometrioid cancer of the ovary. 'The clear cell carcinomas that have arisen in endometriosis were found in women from 38 to 60 years of age with an average age of 51 years, probably somewhat younger than that of patients with clear cell carcinoma in general.' (p. 954) The authors felt that the available data were insufficient to try to evaluate the survival rate of women who have clear cell carcinoma of the ovary developed from endometriosis. Other types of epithelial cancer of the ovary arising from endometriosis are extremely rare.

According to one source Mostoufizadeh and Scully quote, a quarter of the cases dealing with endometriosis and cancer are in sites other than the ovary. The most common nonovarian site is the rectovaginal septum (the tissue that separates the rectum from the vagina). Other less common areas include the vagina, the urinary bladder, the fallopian tubes, areas of and surrounding the uterus, the cervix, the vulva, the uterosacral area, the large or small bowel, and the umbilicus (the navel). The average age of the women who had nonovarian endometrioid cancer arising from endometriosis was 48. Clear cell carcinoma is much less common than endometrioid cancer in nonovarian sites. (Sarcomas—a different type of cancer not belonging to the epithelial group that are usually found in connective tissue—were more common in the studies than clear cell carcinomas but less common than endometrioid cancer in the cases in which sarcomas developed from endometriosis in nonovarian sites.)

In the conclusion of their article, Mostoufizadeh and Scully emphasize that proven incidence of endometriosis developing into cancer is very low. They quote two studies: one in which only three proven cases of cancer (meaning the transition from endometriosis to cancer was actually seen) occurred in about 900 cases of ovarian endometriosis and the other in which only eight were identified in approximately 950 cases of ovarian endometriosis. (p. 962) However, as was explained earlier, many cases are probably missed or impossible to diagnose, so an exact number is not known. But because of the low frequency of relationship to cancer, endometriosis is not considered to be a significant precancerous condition. What is clear, however, is that 'any type of malignant tumour that can arise from the uterine endometrium may also develop in endometriotic tissue.' (p. 961)

So, should *you* be worried? With all the other issues and problems confronting a woman with endometriosis, cancer and endometriosis probably should be very low on the list. You *should* become concerned about the possibility of cancer in your own case if a sudden, unexpected, or otherwise unexplainable change (i.e., not due to medication) occurs in your endometriosis symptoms. With pain being the most common symptom, an abrupt increase in pain with this increased pain becoming more or less continuous or pain that begins after menopause *may* be an indication of cancer. (pp. 952–53) A comparatively rapid increase in the size of an endometriotic mass or implant, hyperplasia (overgrowth of endometrial tissue that is sometimes a precancerous condition), or a change to an unusual appearance or rupture of an endometriotic cyst (which with normal cysts is rare, according to the authors) should alert your gynaecologist to the possibility of cancer. (pp. 953, 962)

Mostoufizadeh and Scully also feel that gynaecologists should be very careful in recommending oestrogen replacement therapy to their patients with a history of endometriosis, due to the link between estrogens and endometrial cancer. A woman with endometriosis has more to risk than other patients who might receive oestrogen replacement since she not only has her intrauterine endometrium to worry about but also endometriotic implants in more difficult places to observe and diagnose that are also subject to the effects of estrogen. (p. 962) Even postmenopausal women and women who have had hysterectomies and removal of the ovaries and who have a history of endometriosis should carefully consider the option to take oestrogen since it *may* activate both microscopic spots of endometriosis and cancer. (However, the risk of osteoporosis, associated with lack of estrogen, is also a serious risk. For additional discussion of this issue, see Section III of this book.)

Cancer developing from endometriosis is *very* rare—but it does occur. Every woman who has endometriosis should carefully monitor her symptoms and report any sudden, unexplainable change in symptoms to her gynecologist. All gynaecologists should be cautious and thorough in diagnosing and treating their patients with endometriosis. Though cancer developing from endometriosis is rare, its potential cannot be taken lightly since the consequences of ignoring its possibility can be quite serious.

Article Reviewed

Mostoufizadeh, Mahpareh, and Scully, Robert E. Malignant tumors arising in endometriosis. *Clinical Obstetrics and Gynecology*, 23: 3 (Sept. 1980): 951–963.

15
Prostaglandins and Endometriosis

By Suzanne McDonough and Mary Lou Ballweg

Prostaglandins are substances produced throughout the body that control contraction and relaxation of smooth muscles, as well as many other functions. They play an important, but unclear, role in endometriosis. Prostaglandin research is at the very forefront of research on endometriosis. We decided it was time for an article on endometriosis and prostaglandins for a number of reasons. Among them:

1. So many women with endometriosis appear to have a history of primary dysmenorrhoea (painful periods due to an overproduction of one type of prostaglandin) preceding the endometriosis, sometimes from early in their menstrual history. Of course, until better diagnosis of endometriosis occurs, we can't be sure that endometriosis isn't present from the start, but descriptions from the women and in our data registry lead to an informal conclusion that primary dysmenorrhoea occurred before endometriosis.

2. Many women with endometriosis report symptoms associated with prostaglandins: severe cramping; vomiting, nausea, and diarrhoea with periods; dizziness and fainting with periods; headache, hot and cold flushes with periods.

3. Frequent reports by women with endometriosis that they pass clots of blood in their menstrual flow. Prostaglandins are involved in blood clotting, though it's not clear if the ones that most affect endometrial tissue are the ones most involved in blood clotting. Prostaglandins, by causing hard contractions, could also theoretically cause more of the

206

endometrial wall to be tearing away than should be and/or tearing it away prematurely.

4. The fact that women with proven endometriosis *sometimes* obtain some relief from symptoms with prostaglandin inhibitors. However, the pain and discomfort of endometriosis have many causes, so relief is seldom complete. The pain can be due to irritation and inflammation caused by the endometrosis growths, scar tissue and adhesions, and location of growths near sensitive areas.

5. The description of pain by some women with endometriosis (being 'caught in a vice,' 'like being squeezed from inside,' 'contractions') sounds like the action of prostaglandins. (But many women with endometriosis also experience other types of pain, described as 'stabbing,' 'like a hot poker,' and so on.) Prostaglandin-induced contractions have been measured at levels equal to or greater than labour on a mercury manometer—a fact you can point out to anyone who seems to underestimate the level of pain possible with periods.

6. The heavy bleeding (long, heavy flow) sometimes associated with endometriosis.

7. The higher miscarriage rate of endometriosis. This tendency toward miscarriages could be related to prostaglandins that cause contraction of endometrial tissue. In fact, prostaglandins have been used experimentally to induce abortion. Vaginal suppositories of prostaglandins are said to induce bleeding in three to six hours and to work very effectively in the weeks just following the first missed period. If the endometriosis growths continued to produce certain prostaglandins in early pregnancy, perhaps the same thing is happening to women with endometriosis.

8. The higher ectopic pregnancy (implantation of a fertilized egg in any location other than the uterus, a very dangerous condition that can lead to rupture, internal bleeding, and sometimes even death) rate of women with endometriosis could also be related to prostaglandins if, as the authors of some of the studies reviewed here suggest, prostaglandins produced by the endometriosis growths could perhaps upset fallopian tube function. If, for instance, prostaglandin ratios were incorrect at the time of or following ovulation, they could theoretically cause the smooth muscle tissue of the fallopian tube to spasm or contract irregularly rather than in smooth, rhythmic motions that might be essential for moving the egg through the tube correctly. Then the egg could perhaps become caught in the tube rather than smoothly pushed through it. (Of course, a kinked or adhered tube could also cause ectopic pregnancy, but doctors have often noted that women with endometriosis who have no observable physical problem such as this still experience infertility.)

9. Finally, it's possible that severe prostaglandin-induced contractions could trap menstrual debris in the uterus and contribute to retrograde flow of endometrial tissue.

Prostaglandins are types of naturally occurring fatty acids that are thought to perform a number of functions, including the stimulation and inhibition of uterine and other smooth muscle contractions and the ability to lower blood pressure, to control inflammation, to regulate the functions of some hormones, and to regulate body temperature. They are formed from essential fatty acids (EFAs)—nutrients not naturally produced in the body that must be provided by the diet to maintain good health.

Prostaglandins were discovered in the 1930s and named such because they were first thought to be derived only from the secretions of the male prostate gland. Since then, prostaglandin production has been established in both sexes, in many different parts of the body, and in some animals as well. In recent years, the functions of approximately 20 different prostaglandins (PGs) have been studied. The most important prostaglandins for our purposes belong to the E and F families and one member of the I family.

Prostaglandin study is still essentially in its infant stage. How and in what combinations all of these prostaglandins work is not yet known. It seems that it is important to maintain certain ratios of prostaglandins that work together to perform various functions and that an imbalance in the ratio can contribute to health problems.

Prostaglandin function, therefore, is a highly complex subject in which some experts disagree and in which some studies conflict. Certainly with this topic, prostaglandins and endometriosis, no definitive studies have been done, and what has been researched is open to much questioning.

In the past decade, the role of prostaglandins in the menstrual cycle has been researched in varying degrees. The greatest amount of prostaglandin in the female reproductive tract is produced by the endometrium, the inside lining of the uterus,[1] but the ovary also is thought to produce some.[2]

The endometrium seems to produce prostaglandins of the E and F families throughout the menstrual cycle. Prostaglandin E seems to have more influence in the first two weeks of the cycle and prostaglandin F in the second two weeks of the cycle.[3]

It is also thought that members of the E family have the ability to decrease uterine and cervical contraction, while the F family increases these contractions.[4] An increase in prostaglandin F_{2a}, one of the F family of prostaglandins, during the menstrual period is thought to account for most of the pains and cramps of primary dysmenorrhoea due to increased hard contractions of the uterus. Primary dysmenorrhoea is defined by medical people as highly painful periods that occur in women with apparently healthy, 'normal' reproductive organs and menstrual cycles (although consistent pain hardly seems 'normal'!). Women with endometriosis who experience painful periods are said to suffer from *secondary* dysmenorrhea, meaning the painful periods result from the disease.

In recent years, anti-inflammatory drugs with names such as Motrin, Ponstel, Anaprox, Advil, Nuprin, and others have been effective in treating some cases of primary dysmenorrhea. They supposedly act by reducing contractions of the uterus and other smooth muscle tissue. These drugs seem to have been successful because of their ability to suppress prostaglandin F_{2a} activity. A fascinating account of how a doctor who suffered from menstrual cramps herself discovered how to combat them with these drugs appears in the book *No More Menstrual Cramps and Other Good News* by Dr Penny Budoff (see Appendix).

In relation to endometriosis, prostaglandins have been theorized to affect the two problems associated most frequently with endometriosis: infertility and pain. The articles listed in the references at the end of this article discuss prostaglandins and their speculated effect on the pain and infertility of endometriosis. Whereas some of the articles find similar results, others seem to contradict them and draw different conclusions.

The Weed article (Article 1) is a very general one that reviews the basis for evaluating prostaglandins in relation to endometriosis and points to directions to be taken in setting up experiments to determine the exact functions of prostaglandins in endometriosis, It quotes studies in which increases in prostaglandin levels were recorded in the blood, endometrium, and urine of women with primary dysmenorrhoea, as well as in women with endometriosis.

'Since the endometrium is the site of production of prostaglandins, increased prostaglandin secretion from endometrial transplants [endometriosis] may be a factor in increasing the amount of venoconstriction [contraction of the blood vessels] in the uterus, in the intensity of uterine contractions, and in severe dysmenorrhea,' writes Weed.[5] He suggests in his article (published in 1980) that the peritoneal fluid (fluid from the membranes that line the walls and organs of the abdominal and pelvic cavities) of women with and without endometriosis be sampled and studied to evaluate prostaglandin levels. This was done by other researchers who reported their findings in articles 2–6. Weed also suggested that control studies be done to rate the effects of anti-inflammatory drugs on women with endometriosis, but this has been done only in one study, conducted in Finland and reported in articles 6 and 7.

Article 2 reports a study of prostaglandin levels in the peritoneal fluid of infertile women with and without endometriosis. The study involved 29 women not undergoing hormonal therapy. Fifteen were infertile women who either had been surgically sterilized or had adhesions of the tubes or ovaries not caused by endometriosis. Fourteen were women with laparoscopy-proven mild to severe endometriosis.

A sample of the peritoneal fluid of all of the women was taken during laparoscopy. Two key prostaglandin compounds (PGI_2 and thromboxane A_2—thromboxane is a breakdown product of prostaglandins) were found significantly increased in the peritoneal fluid of the women with endometriosis. The source of the compounds was not determined in this study, and the authors appear to conclude it was the peritoneum itself. But the compounds could be produced by the endometriosis implants themselves, since normal endometrium produces prostaglandins, or they could have been produced by both.

From their findings and other studies of prostaglandin functions they cite, the authors suggest a possible mechanism for endometriosis-induced infertility. First, the authors suggest, the endometriosis implants cause inflammation and irritation of the peritoneum. Then the peritoneum, as a reaction to this, releases prostaglandins, which increase the peritoneal fluid. The increased prostaglandins and fluid act on the smooth muscle tissue of the fallopian tubes and interfere with the transport of the egg, thus rendering the patient infertile.[6] [Editor's Note: We wonder if this increased fluid volume is the culprit in the uncomfortable abdominal bloating many women with endometriosis and PMS experience.]

As a possible result of their findings, the authors feel that perhaps some patients with endometriosis should undergo a different type of treatment from what is usually advised. 'Current therapy for endometriosis associated with infertility or pelvic pain involves suppressing and/or removing the endometriotic lesion. On the basis of findings in the present study, it is possible that an alternative method of treatment of this condition would be regulation of prostaglandin synthetase activity. Further studies examining the efficacy of inhibition of synthesis in patients with endometriosis and infertility seems to be warranted.'[7]

In article 3, the authors report findings of a study in which they found that the endometrial tissue outside of the uterus contained *higher* concentrations of prostaglandin F than normal endometrium inside the uterus. They also found that this tissue produced higher amounts of prostaglandin F in normal culture.

In article 4, 25 women were studied: 15 infertile women with various stages of endometriosis, 5 women with unexplained infertility and with no evidence of pelvic disease on laparoscopy, and 5 women who served as a normal control group. Samples of the peritoneal fluid of all the women were taken and analyzed for two prostaglandins (F_{2a} and E_2). (Interestingly, the women in the control group and the women with unexplained infertility had little or no peritoneal fluid, so to obtain a sample, the cul-de-sac [the area between the uterus and rectum] was washed with a normal saline solution and evaluated.)

The women with endometriosis showed wide variation (compared to each other) in the levels of both prostaglandins and no correlation between the stage of endometriosis or the stage of the menstrual cycle. However, the prostaglandin levels in the women with endometriosis were, overall, higher than those of the control group. The women with unexplained infertility also showed a wide variation in levels of the two prostaglandins in their peritoneal fluid with prostaglandin F_{2a} higher than in the control group but prostaglandin E_2 not significantly higher than in the control group.

As a result, the authors suggest that prostaglandin F_{2a} seems to be a more important factor than prostaglandin E_2 in patients with endometriosis and unexplained fertility. They, like the authors of Article 2, feel that endometriosis leads to a peritoneal reaction that results in an increase in prostaglandins and also an increase in the amount of peritoneal fluid. They also state that the variability of concentration of prostaglandins in the peritoneal fluid has no relation to the stage of the menstrual cycle but might represent differences in peritoneal reactions due to the presence of endometriosis or variation in the individual woman's body response.[8] The infertile patients without endometriosis in their study, they speculated, also may have had microscopic endometriosis that went undetected at the time of laparoscopy.

With regard to prostaglandins' direct effect on fertility, the authors feel that an increase in the concentration of prostaglandin F_{2a} may lead to improper formation of the egg follicles or could lead to luteal phase inadequacy where the ovulatory process is incomplete. Also, the presence of prostaglandin E_2, known to occur elsewhere in the body to decrease the effects of immune reactions, might indicate that endometriosis causes an immune reaction in the peritoneum that may lead in part to infertility.

Article 5 deals with a study of 21 infertile women and the levels of prostaglandin F_{2a} in their peritoneal fluid. Of the 21 women, 10 had mild to severe endometriosis, 7 had pelvic adhesions not due to endometriosis, and 4 were normal with no sign of any disease. Laparoscopies were performed during the follicular phase (part of the ovulation phase) of each woman's cycle.

Of the women with endometriosis, only those with moderate or severe endometriosis showed measurable amounts of prostaglandin F_{2a} in their peritoneal fluid (that is, three of four women with moderate endometriosis and two of three women with severe endometriosis showed evidence of prostaglandin F_{2a} activity). Prostaglandin F_{2a} was *not* detected in the peritoneal fluid of the three women with mild endometriosis or in most of the women with adhesions not due to endometriosis or in the women classified as normal. However, one woman without endometriosis who had blood-tinged peritoneal fluid and pelvic adhesions did have an elevated level of prostaglandin F_{2a} in her peritoneal fluid. The women who had endometriosis and evidence of prostaglandin F_{2a} in their peritoneal fluid also had blood or chocolate-coloured fluid in the peritoneal fluid. It was proven that the blood had not been caused by the surgical procedure but probably by hemorrhage from the endometriosis implants or adhesions.

The authors of Article 5 feel that hemorrhage in the abdominal cavity is associated with an increase in the levels of prostaglandin F_{2a} in the peritoneal fluid of patients regardless of whether they had endometriosis or not. 'It is not surprising that blood in the peritoneal fluid affects prostaglandin F_{2a} levels since the clotting mechanism itself generates prostaglandins.'[9] They quote a study that observed that 'the highest levels of prostaglandin F_{2a} in endometrial tissue [in the uterus] are found in patients with excessive vaginal bleeding.'[10]

They feel it is unlikely that prostaglandins in the peritoneal fluid are responsible for infertility in women with mild endometriosis because the three women in their study with mild endometriosis did not have detectable levels of prostaglandin F_{2a}. They state that the F_{2a} levels may be increased in more advanced endometriosis and perhaps could alter functions of the fallopian tubes or uterus and contribute to infertility or perhaps not be related to the infertility of endometriosis at all.[11]

Article 6 discusses the findings of a study in which samples of endometriosis tissue removed during surgery from six women with endometriosis were studied for their levels of two prostaglandin compounds (prostaglandin I_2 and thromboxane A_2). Samples for study were taken from ovarian and nonovarian sites of endometriosis. The results showed the compounds were present in all the samples, but the samples from the nonovarian sites had a greater amount of both than those from ovarian sites. The authors feel that 'this finding, if confirmed in future studies, may perhaps provide one explanation for the puzzling clinical phenomenon that the patients with tiny endometrial lesions on the pelvic peritoneum often suffer more intense pain than patients whose ovaries are even badly affected by endometriosis.'[12]

Article 7 reports on the one study in which prostaglandin inhibitors were used for women with endometriosis—with rather surprising results. Eighteen women with laparoscopy-proven endometriosis who were not on any medication were each given one of four drugs to be taken from day 20 of their cycles through menstruation for two consecutive menstrual cycles. These drugs were a placebo and three proven prostaglandin inhibitors—acetylsalicylic acid (common aspirin), indomethacin (brand name Indocin, 25 mg × 3), and tolfenamic acid (brand name Clotam, available only in Finland, 200 mg × 3). The women evaluated pain symptoms (pelvic pain, lower back pain, pain during walking, painful sex), gastrointestinal complaints (nausea, vomiting, diarrhoea), and psychic complaints (insomnia, nervousness). The authors included symptoms other than pain because 'the possible involvement of prostaglandins in endometriosis could explain also the appearance of gastrointestinal and psychic complaints, fever and headache which are characteristic of prostaglandin administration.'[13]

Premenstrually, none of the prostaglandin inhibitors showed any success over the placebo. Menstrually, only tolfenamic acid had a better effect on the patients' symptoms than the placebo, and its success was rather limited. The results, considering the findings of prostaglandins in endometriotic implants, seem counterintuitive. The only explanation the authors could supply for the very limited success was 'the tissue concentrations of prostaglandin inhibitors were not always high enough to inhibit or antagonize prostaglandins, since blood circulation can be impaired in endometriotic lesions' and that the high rate of side effects with indomethacin could have contributed to the poor results with that drug.[14] It must be noted, though, that studies of antiprostaglandins in other fields have also found similar puzzling results with great success in some studies and little success in others. This is most likely due to the fact that all the functions of prostaglandins and the antiprostaglandin drugs themselves simply are not yet well understood. Precise dosages, timing, specific types of inhibitors, and certain ratios may be necessary.

[Editor's Note: Later studies have found that another prostaglandin inhibitor, ibuprofen, seems to have a greater effect. See Hurlbutt study, reported in Chapter 20, and the studies by Witkin reported in Chapter 11. Witkin also found that the ibuprofen was effective only in a narrow range—too little or too much—and it did not work.]

It must be emphasized that, although these studies are certainly very interesting and help to define theories of the relationships between prostaglandins and endometriosis, they are merely preliminary studies whose findings need to be confirmed over and over again in future studies to have any real bearing on the study of endometriosis. The studies are not without fault and problems (we're sure their authors would readily agree), with probably the most serious being the small number of women studied. Studies that involve only 6 to 29 women cannot by any means be considered statistically sufficient. One can only look at these articles and draw *very* general conclusions.

Prostaglandins *do* seem to affect the pain and other discomforts associated with endometriosis along with the infertility of some patients with endometriosis to some undetermined degree. For those of us with endometriosis, this means that prostaglandin inhibitors such as Motrin and Ponstel (or aspirin, which is a mild inhibitor) *may* help with the pain and discomforts of endometriosis—a blessing for those of us who have not been able to tolerate narcotics or were afraid we might become addicted to them. But these prostaglandin inhibitors also may not work. (Try a number of them before giving up—if one doesn't work, another might. Also, be sure to take them *before* the pain begins, at the very first sign of impending pain or even before your period is due, as the inhibition effect must begin early before the chemical reactions of the prostaglandins have gone too far.)

If they do not work, it does not mean that the pain is 'all in your head.' As stated earlier, studies with prostaglandin inhibitors with other diseases have also had mixed results because exactly how these drugs work is not well understood. The prostaglandin inhibitors, since they are thought to inhibit most prostaglandins in the body to some extent, also may be disturbing the delicate balance that some prostaglandins seem to need to function in ways beneficial to the body.

With regard to the infertility associated with endometriosis, some prostaglandin inhibitors may possibly be beneficial, helping to quiet the system down where there is too much prostaglandin F activity so that ovulation, fertilization, and implantation occur more easily. But there also is the possibility that prostaglandin inhibitors could interfere with ovulation by suppressing the prostaglandin actions that seem to be a part of the ovulatory function.

Exactly which prostaglandins are affecting women with endometriosis, in what combinations and ratios they are acting, and the exact mechanisms by which they cause pain or infertility simply is not known. Prostaglandins may cause some of the pain of endometriosis by causing inflammation or muscle contractions or both. They may be a factor in infertility by affecting the process of ovulation or by causing the fallopian tubes or uterus to function inadequately or both. To end on a positive note: great progress is being made in the study of prostaglandins in general. Hopefully, this progress will be applied someday to extensive studies of women with endometriosis to discover the true role of prostaglandins in endometriosis.

Articles Reviewed

1. Weed, John C. Prostaglandins as related to endometriosis. *Clinical Obstetrics and Gynecology* 23:3 (September 1980): 895–900.

2. Drake, Terrance S.; O'Brien, William F.; Ramwell, Peter W.; and Metz, Stephen A. Peritoneal fluid thromboxane B_2 and 6-keto-prostaglandin F_{1a} in endometriosis. *American Journal of Obstetrics and Gynecology* 140:4 (June 15, 1981): 401–404.

3. Moon, Y. S.; Leung, P. C. S.; Yuen, B. H.; and Gomel, V. Prostaglandin F in human endometriotic tissue. *American Journal of Obstetrics and Gynecology* 141:344, 1981.

4. Badawy, Shawky Z. A.; Marshall, Linda; Gabal, Ahmed A.; and Nusbaum, Murray L. The concentration of 13, 14-dihydro-15-keto prostaglandin F_{2a} and prostaglandin E_2 in peritoneal fluid of infertile patients with and without endometriosis. *Fertility and Sterility* 38:2 (August 1982): 166–170.

5. Sondheimer, Steven J.; and Flickinger, George. Prostaglandin F_{2a} in the peritoneal fluid of patients with endometriosis. *International Journal of Fertility* 27:2 (1982): 73–75.

6. Ylikorkala, Olavi; and Viinikka, Lasse. Prostaglandins and endometriosis. *Acta Obstetrics and Gynecology Scandinavia* 113 (1983): 105–107.

7. Kauppila, Antti; Puolakka, Jukka; and Ylikorkala, Olavi. Prostaglandin biosynthesis inhibitors and endometriosis. *Prostaglandins* 18:4 (October 1979): 655–661.

Notes

1. Weed, p.896.
2. Weed, p.897.
3. Weed, p.896.
4. Weed, p.897.
5. Weed, p.898.
6. Drake, p.401.
7. Drake, p.403.
8. Badawy, p.168.
9. Sondheimer, p.75.
10. Sondheimer, p.75.
11. Sondheimer, p.75.
12. Ylikorkala, p. 107.
13. Kauppila, p.659.
14. Kauppila, pp.659–60.

16
Teenagers and Endometriosis

By Suzanne McDonough

Traditionalists have viewed endometriosis as a problem only for women in their thirties and forties. Though today some of these traditionalists have modified their views to include women in their twenties, endometriosis in teenagers is still thought to be rare.

These traditionalists support the retrograde menstruation theory to explain the origins of endometriosis. We're all familiar with this theory (see previous articles in this book). Variations on this retrograde menstruation theory have occurred over the years. Some new theories have developed due to such findings as endometriosis in the lung and kneecap, but most doctors still believe that endometriosis is a problem only in older, physically mature women.

However, results of the Endometriosis Association's first 365 questionnaires in the computerized data registry housed at the Medical College of Wisconsin showed that 36 percent of the women had their first symptoms before age 20, with 14 percent of these experiencing their first symptoms before age 15. Is endometriosis in teenagers really rare, or is this yet another myth about endometriosis that needs to be dispelled? The authors of the articles reviewed here discuss endometriosis in adolescents and, as we have seen with other topics, come to interesting but varied conclusions.

Huffman, in Article 3, takes a traditional view of the topic and mentions that, in his opinion, endometriosis is rare in teenagers. However, he comes to this conclusion by dividing teenagers into two groups: young teenage girls (between 13 and 17 years of age) and older teenage girls (18-and 19-year-olds). 'The two age groups are dissimilar as regards the degree of their sexual maturation, their reproductive capabilities and performances, and their psychological attitudes toward many aspects of life.' (p. 44) He feels that older teenage women should be classified with older, physically mature women in such gynaecological matters and chooses to concentrate on the cases of endometriosis in 13- to 17-year-olds.

After a survey of literature on endometriosis up to the time he was preparing his article (not including Goldstein's article), Huffman found that 'patients under 17 years of age suffering from it [endometriosis], with one exception had proven retrograde menstruation . . . an obstruction to the natural vaginal discharge of some or all of their menstrual fluid. The fluid was, therefore, forced to reflux through one or both uterine tubes into the peritoneal cavity.' (p. 44) According to Huffman, these obstructions were caused by such abnormalities as rudimentary horns of the uterus that were not connected with the endometrial cavity of the uterus; cervical stenosis (a narrowing or complete blockage of the cervix); cervical atresia (in which the cervix is malformed or absent); vaginal agenesis (in which a vagina is not formed at birth) coupled with a functioning, menstruating uterus; and an imperforate hymen (in which the hymen, or the tissues at the opening of the vagina, are partially or entirely blocked).

The author states that endometriosis in older teenagers '. . . can be explained by the fact that they, like mature women, have had many menstrual periods uninterrupted by pregnancy.' (p. 45) He notes cases of endometriosis in 18- and 19-year-olds who had all started menstruating before their 12th birthday. 'With the downward trend in the age of the menarche it is probable that an increasing number of girls less than 20 years of age will develop endometriosis.' (p. 45)

When discussing symptoms, Huffman notes that most young teenage girls with endometriosis have cyclic abdominal or pelvic pain '. . . that simulates dysmenorrhea; some however, have no pain at all.' (p. 46) The second most common symptom is a pelvic mass, with an occasional girl who is sexually active complaining of dyspareunia. Obviously in our society, 'infertility is not a problem for this age group.' (p. 46) He also notes that 'Endometriotic nodulations in the uterosacral ligaments, fixed retrodisplacements of the uterus, and symptoms caused by endometriotic invasion of the bowel, rectum, ureter, or bladder are extremely rare in young girls.' (p. 48)

Since these young girls' endometriosis, Huffman feels, is caused by a physical abnormality, treatment is carried out to correct the abnormality if possible and thus stop the retrograde flow. If a correction is not possible in a severe abnormality, hysterectomy is recommended with preservation of ovarian function. In either case, if some residual endometriosis remains, Huffman advises hormonal therapy to control it.

Huffman feels that, while not every girl with dysmenorrhoea should undergo laparoscopy, young teenagers who have not yet started their periods, who have monthly or periodic abdominal pain without visible genital abnormalities, or '. . . whose menstrual periods are accompanied by increasingly severe dysmenorrhoea that is refractory [resistant] to treatment' (p. 48) should be carefully monitored, with laparoscopy seriously considered.

In Article 2, Goldstein and his colleagues report on their study in which 140 teenagers, 10 to 19 years old, underwent laparoscopy for chronic pelvic pain from 1974 to 1979 at Boston Children's Hospital Medical Center. Sixty-six of the patients (47 percent) had biopsy-proven endometriosis. These patients' symptoms included both pain at the time of menstruation and pain at other times of the month (36 percent had pain so severe that they had to stop normal activities), irregular periods, painful intercourse, gastrointestinal problems, abnormal vaginal discharge, and urinary problems. Their average age of menarche was 11.8 years, with a range of 9–16 years. Pain began an average of 3 years after menarche. However, the youngest patient, 10 years old, had her first period only 5 months before symptoms occurred. Forty patients (56 percent) noted that their symptoms had improved somewhat with the use of birth control pills, analgesics, or anti-inflammatories prior to the laparoscopy.

Most of the patients (38 or 57.5 percent) were classified as having mild endometriosis. The other patients were classified as having moderate or severe cases. Some endometriotic implants were atypical and required microscopic study to diagnose endometriosis. Goldstein et al. note that '. . . severity of pain did not correlate well with the extent of the disease as found at laparoscopy. For example, the presence of gastrointestinal and bladder symptoms were not, invariably, associated with involvement of these organs. Similarly, patients who reported irregular menses did not necessarily have extensive ovarian involvement.' (p. 39) Retroversion of the uterus was found in 7 (11 percent) of the patients.

Surgical treatment varied from case to case depending on the extent of the endometriosis. Some patients had only diagnostic laparoscopy. Other procedures performed in other cases included fulguration ('burning') of implants, cutting of adhesions, uterine suspension, ovarian resection, and presacral neurectomy. Some of these patients who were treated surgically were also treated hormonally for ovulation suppression.

The hormonal drugs used were oral progestogens, danazol, or injections of medroxyprogesterone acetate (Depo-Provera). Sixteen (30 percent) of the 53 patients who received hormonal therapy had to discontinue one or more of the drugs due to side effects.

The follow-up period in this study ranged from three months to five years with 43 patients (65 percent) responding favourably to therapy with no clinical evidence that their endometriosis had returned. The other 23 patients either failed to respond to treatment, had symptoms recur after discontinuing treatment, or had to stop treatment due to side effects. Goldstein and the others state that '. . . it appears that medroxyproge-sterone acetate is the most acceptable hormonal agent from the point of view of side effects and effectiveness.' (p. 40) But they also note that 'surgery . . . achieves the highest initial remission rates.' (p. 41) [Editor's Note: Be aware that at the time of Goldstein's study, danazol was not yet much-used, so is not included in these comparisons.]

In a discussion of their findings, they consider the traditional theory that obstruction of the reproductive tract leads to retrograde flow or 'regurgitation implantation,' which in turn causes endometriosis to develop: '. . . This theory does not seem to be equally applicable to those patients who develop their disease within a few months after menarche. In these individuals, it would appear that the disease may be congenital and that the onset of ovulatory cycles leads to the stimulation of inactive endometrial tissue in the pelvic peritoneum or to the differentiation of totipotential cells [cells that can give rise to other cells of all types].'(p. 41) The authors of this study did not find any congenital malformations or abnormalities, i.e., cervical stenosis or vaginal agenesis, as reported by Huffman in his article. As noted earlier, though, seven patients did have retroflexed uteruses, and therefore retrograde flow could be *possible* in these patients.

Goldstein and his colleagues emphasize that it is important that the presence of endometriosis be confirmed by biopsy: '. . . many of the lesions are atypical, which is no doubt the reason that surgeons performing laparotomy for chronic pelvic pain were unable, in most instances, to make this diagnosis.' (p. 41)

In the closing of their article, they conclude that '. . . endometriosis is an important disease in the teenage female. Early diagnosis and treatment may help preserve reproductive potential and may improve the quality of life in our young patients. Teenage patients with increasing dysmenorrhoea should be thoroughly examined and laparoscoped rather than reassured and treated symptomatically with analgesics and/or other agents.' (p. 41) In a follow-up letter in a later issue of the *Journal of Adolescent Health Care*, Dr Goldstein makes it clear he is not advocating laparoscopy for every teenager with painful periods, but only those whose pain did not respond to medical management (such as anti-inflammatories/antiprostaglandins) or who had abnormalities found on pelvic exam.

In Article 1, Chatman and Ward report on their effort to determine the extent to which endometriosis may affect not only white teenagers, but also teenagers who are black. Black teenagers were chosen to help dispel the myth that endometriosis occurs only in white women. In their study 43 symptomatic black teenagers who complained of disabling pelvic pain and/or abnormal vaginal bleeding were laparoscoped. Preoperatively many of the patients had palpable masses or tenderness in areas such as the cul-de-sac and the uterosacral ligaments. Chatman and Ward emphasize the importance of rectovaginal examinations especially during the patients' menstrual periods when the endometriosis is likely to be especially 'active.'

At the time of laparoscopy it was found that 28 teenagers (65 percent) had endometriosis. The others either had pelvic inflammatory disease (PID) or adhesions not caused by endometriosis, or nothing could be detected. Sixteen (57 percent) were 18 to 19 years old. Seven (25 percent) were in the mid-teens, and 5 (18 percent) were in their early teens (12 to 15 years old). The most common symptom was acquired dysmenorrhoea (74 percent) that was increasing in severity. (*Acquired dysmenorrhea* means the girl started her periods without pain but then the periods became painful.) Chronic pelvic pain was also reported in 43 percent, with 36 percent having abnormal vaginal bleeding. 'Bowel changes in the form of diarrhoea, painful bowel movements or both with menstruation was a significant symptom in 29 percent.' (p. 157) The posterior cul-de-sac was the most common site of endometriosis in these teenagers, followed by the uterosacral ligaments (which Huffman felt was a rare site of endometriosis in teenagers), broad ligaments, utero-ovarian ligament, uterine wall, and the bowel. Most cases were mild or moderate. Only 3 patients had severe endometriosis.

None of the patients had any congenital malformations of their reproductive organs that could have led to retrograde menstruation. 'Because the average interval between menarche and diagnosis was only 4.5 years in our patients [many years of uninterrupted menstruation had not occurred] and because of lack of obstructive phenomena evident on evaluation, it is difficult for us to accept retrograde menstruation as an aetiological factor in these cases. The embryonic-cell-rest theory that endometriosis forms from embryonic reproductive tissue that begins to grow after menarche seems more consistent with our patient group.' (p.158)

Chatman and Ward conclude, 'We have found that increasing dysmenorrhoea (usually acquired) is a very important symptom in endometriosis. Dysmenorrhea is a significant cause of disability, lost work hours and missed school days. We do not want to allow an early, theoretically treatable disease to progress without recognition to a later and more severe stage. Endometriosis can be a progressive disease and seems to occur in the adolescent with previously unrecognized frequency ... diagnosis and treatment of endometriosis represents preventive medicine at its best in gynaecology." (p. 159)

COMMENTARY

The evidence of endometriosis in teenagers as found in the Goldstein study and the Chatman/Ward study suggests that traditionalists need to do some 'rethinking' not only about endometriosis in teenagers, but about the causes of endometriosis as well. The two subjects are undeniably interconnected. The traditional retrograde menstruation theory, while not denying that endometriosis is possible in teenagers, makes it seem rare and of less importance than endometriosis in older women. It seems to imply that endometriosis is only really endometriosis when it becomes a 'problem'—when it becomes palpable or disabling or causes great problems with infertility. The implication is that only after endometriosis has built up year after year can it be diagnosed and dealt with. With the development of the laparoscope and with studies such as the ones discussed above, we now see that endometriosis can occur and produce symptoms soon after menarche without years of buildup; that one tiny spot of endometriosis can produce disabling pain in teenagers or in older women; that endometriosis may be rendering women infertile (in mild or severe cases) when they are young teenagers long before they are ready or socially able to conceive (long before the 'career woman' label can be applied); and that young teenagers who were told they had primary dysmenorrhoea that eventually would just 'go away' actually had endometriosis that should not have gone untreated. One cannot help wondering how many women, including the older teenagers in Huffman's article, had endometriosis that began years before it was diagnosed, years before symptoms started or were severe enough for them to feel it was 'all right' to seek help or perhaps even years before they could convince a doctor that their symptoms were really a 'problem.'

It is encouraging that doctors and researchers are doing studies. Many more like them need to be done. They strongly indicate that endometriosis is more common than was ever suspected in teenagers. For many of us who have suspected that our endometriosis began when

we were very young, it is unfortunately 'too late'—we have already
suffered through years of pain and problems without help. What we can
do now is help spread the word that endometriosis is 'not just for older
women' and try to make our relatives and friends aware that a young
girl who complains of increasingly painful periods should not be ignored.
Hopefully more and more people will take notice of the findings like
those discussed here to help these teenagers with endometriosis avoid
much unnecessary pain and suffering.

Articles Reviewed

1. Chatman, Donald L., and Ward, Anne. Endometriosis in adolescents.
The Journal of Reproductive Medicine 27:3 (March 1982): 156–160.

2. Goldstein, Donald P.; De Cholnoky, Corinne; and Emans, S. Jean.
Adolescent endometriosis. *Journal of Adolescent Health Care* 1:1 (September
1980): 37–41.

3. Huffman, John W. Endometriosis in young teen-age girls. *Pediatric Annals*
10:12 (December 1981): 44–49.

17
Ultrasound in Diagnosis of Endometriosis

By Suzanne McDonough

Undoubtedly, many of us have thought at one time or another, 'Isn't there some way to diagnose endometriosis or check on the progression of the disease without having to go through a laparoscopy?' Though laparoscopy is generally an uncomplicated outpatient procedure, it is not the most pleasant of experiences for most of us and one that we would like to avoid if we could—especially those of us who have had repeated laparoscopies. *Is* there another procedure?

Ultrasound has been used increasingly over the past three decades in the diagnosis and/or treatment of a number of diseases. Very simply, in ultrasonography (ultrasound) sound waves at a frequency higher than a human ear can detect are projected through a portion of a person's body. When the waves hit and bounce off certain soft tissues in the body, the image of the tissue, its density and form, is projected either onto a monitor or directly to film—much like an incoming flight is seen by an air traffic controller with the help of radar. Unlike conventional x-rays, ultrasound does not involve potentially harmful ionizing radiation. Because of this, ultrasound is thought by most experts to be generally risk-free at the normal diagnostic frequencies used by clinicians today. It has been used extensively in the past few years to monitor the growth and development of foetuses in the womb.

The use of ultrasound in gynaecology has been rapidly increasing. It is used primarily to help confirm an already suspected problem. Typically, the gynaecologist has felt a mass in a patient at the time of a

223

pelvic exam and sends the patient to be evaluated by ultrasound to determine the size, location, and probable composition of the mass or masses. Because of a patient's medical history and symptoms, the gynaecologist may suspect that the mass is endometriosis, another benign (noncancerous) mass, or cancer. In quite a few cases, he or she is unsure what to suspect.

Ultrasound is usually a pain-free procedure with the only possible discomfort coming from the fact that the bladder must be very full in order to show up clearly on the ultrasound screen, not be confused with a cyst, and, most important, push the bowel away from the uterus. Often women who go in for ultrasound in the morning are told not to urinate after midnight—this could present a problem for women with cystitis problems or 'touchy' bladders. The only other possible discomfort could come from lying on a hard examining table. However, most women go through ultrasound without any pain or discomfort. Most pelvic ultrasound evaluations are done with the patient lying on her back. Occasionally, there is a need to have a patient lie on her side to get a better 'picture' of the mass. A small scanning device is run over the skin of the pelvic area with the images then appearing on a screen. The actual procedure takes minutes with scans from certain angles occasionally repeated.

The composition of the mass as seen through ultrasound and evaluated by a competent physician (either a radiologist or another physician trained in evaluating ultrasonograms) often gives the gynaecologist more clues to the exact nature of the mass.

Masses are generally divided into three categories. One category of masses will follow a *cystic* pattern and appear on the ultrasound monitor as a clear-cut and well-defined shape, usually spherical, with no inner walls or divisions—like a balloon. Sometimes it appears filled with fluid (blood, etc.). Another type of mass is described as *solid* and usually spherical—like a rubber ball. The third type of mass seen during ultrasonography is labeled as *mixed* or *complex*. In this case the mass contains both solid and cystic components.

Some experts have tried to associate these types of masses with benign and malignant (cancerous) conditions. Masses with a cystic pattern are generally considered noncancerous, indicating endometriosis, pelvic inflammatory disease, or some other benign condition. Mixed and solid patterns in masses are considered more suspicious, possibly indicating cancer. However, there is much disagreement about this, and many findings conflict with these generalities, as the articles reviewed here discuss.

Ultrasound was able to detect masses ranging from 2 cm (1 cm is

0.39 inch) to 18 cm in diameter as reported in these articles. The masses could not be seen clearly in most cases where the endometriosis was very severe, the whole pelvic region was involved with many implants and adhesions, or masses were attached to the uterus. In cases such as these, the ultrasound reading is definitely 'abnormal,' but the masses cannot be distinguished clearly from other pelvic organs and tissues.

In Article 1, 10 patients whose masses were detected during a pelvic exam were examined with ultrasound. Their ages ranged from 26 to 63 years old. All had endometriosis as confirmed by surgery following the ultrasonography. In five patients, the mass appeared to follow a cystic pattern. However, '. . . none had the smooth well-defined wall and totally echo-free appearance [indicating no dividing walls in the cyst] characteristic of a simple cyst. Instead, the wall was shaggy and somewhat irregular, and there was some evidence of septation [inner dividing walls].' (p. 230) Some of these cysts were quite large, with the largest being 18 cm in diameter.

Two masses fell into the mixed category and contained both solid and cystic parts. Cancer had been considered as a possibility. However, because the patients were relatively young, pelvic inflammatory disease was considered more likely. As it turned out, the masses were actually endometriosis. 'In a mixed lesion of this type, it probably is not possible to distinguish endometriosis from pelvic inflammatory disease . . . The symptoms of pelvic inflammatory disease and endometriosis may be similar.' (p. 230)

Three of the masses were solid as seen by ultrasound. Because the masses were solid, cancer could be suspected. Each of the masses was found to be endometriosis during surgery, with one mass being a thick-walled cyst containing brown, thick fluid that had mimicked a solid mass during ultrasound.

It should be pointed out that, in five of seven patients, some endometriosis implants were missed because 'these lesions were too small to be seen by ultrasound.' (p. 230)

Article 2 reports on a study involving 13 women who already had surgically confirmed endometriosis and underwent ultrasonography after the surgery to evaluate the accuracy of ultrasound. The ages of the patients ranged from 21 to 66, with masses detected in 7 cases during pelvic examinations prior to surgery. In 4 cases the pelvic examinations had been normal.

Ultrasound showed masses in all 13 patients ranging from 2 to 11 cm in diameter. Eight masses were cystic. Two were solid, and three were mixed with mostly cystic parts. 'The surgical findings correlated well with the ultrasonic character of the lesions.' (p. 747) In cases in which the masses could not be defined clearly or in which the masses were very irregular in shape, extensive endometriosis was found with the uterus heavily involved and adhesions present. In one case in which the mass was very irregular, the bowel and bladder were also involved as suspected.

According to Coleman et al., 'The results of this study indicate that the ultrasonic appearance of endometriosis is more specific than previously appreciated ... Most of the masses encountered were either cystic or complex [mixed] and the majority possessed a predominantly echo-free central core [indicating no walls] with scattered echoes confined to the periphery [outer edges of the mass]...' (p. 748) The authors proceeded to go into a lengthy discussion of how other masses, benign and malignant, do not usually follow the description given above for endometriosis.

The authors concluded that '... our ability to recognize the disease [endometriosis] improved considerably. This enables us to inform the surgeon of the most likely diagnosis of endometriosis prior to operation in our most recent cases.' (p. 748) However, they feel that a patient's history is extremely important, too, and must be taken into account along with the ultrasound findings.

In Article 3, Walsh et al. report on their study of 25 patients with pelvic masses who underwent ultrasonography. Their ages ranged from 22 to 46, with endometriosis proved in all cases during surgery following ultrasound. A total of 31 masses were seen during ultrasonography.

The masses fell into the three traditional categories (cystic, mixed, and solid), with a fourth, polycystic, pattern added. Seventeen cystic masses were found in 13 patients. Ten of these cystic masses had shaggy and irregular walls as also described in Article 2. Seven cysts had smooth, well-defined walls typical of the classic cystic pattern. Only two of these cystic masses had dividing walls inside the cyst (septation). Four patients had polycystic masses in which a number of small cystic masses were clumped together. Three patients had a mixed pattern. Five patients had solid masses. In conclusion, the authors feel, '... ultrasound is a valuable tool in evaluating patients with endometriosis.'

Article 4 discusses a study of 26 women who underwent ultrasonography followed by surgery that confirmed endometriosis in all cases. The patients' ages ranged from 20 to 44. Thirty-seven masses were evaluated. Ultrasound identified 12 cystic masses, 18 mixed masses, and 7 solid masses.

'The cystic lesions were usually not completely smooth and often multiple ... often described as having shaggy walls.' (p. 179) Mixed and solid masses were identified by ultrasound when the endometriotic implants were composed of 'various degrees of organized blood and fibrin [an insoluble protein that is essential to blood clotting].' (p. 179) As in the other articles, when the uterus or other pelvic organs could not be distinguished easily from the mass or masses during ultrasonography, the patient usually had extensive endometriosis with adhesions. However, in one case, endometriosis was found only on the ovary with the uterus having a large fibroid (noncancerous, nonendometriotic) tumour.

In their summary, Goldman and Minkin question the conclusions drawn by the authors of some of the previous articles. 'Our most common pattern was mixed rather than cystic or solid' (p. 180), they reported, referring to the predominantly cystic findings of the previous studies. They also emphasize that they could not diagnose adenomyosis (a disease in which the endometrium, the lining of the uterus, seems to 'grow into' the muscular part of the uterus) or even extensive endometriosis for certain. They agree that 'ultrasound is extremely accurate in determining the size, shape, and location of the endometriosis. The major question remaining is whether one can diagnose endometriosis preoperatively purely from the ultrasonic appearance.' (p. 180)

They point out that, '. . . our surgeons were usually no more specific in their preoperative diagnosis than to suggest a pelvic and/or adnexal (ovarian) mass.' (p. 181) 'The major value of ultrasound lies in its ability to demonstrate the extent of disease.' (p. 182)

The final verdict on endometriosis and ultrasound is not yet in, and the debate as to how accurate a picture of endometriosis ultrasound can show continues. It seems safe to say that ultrasound is useful in searching out masses prior to surgery (giving a physician an indication of where some 'trouble spots' may be) and helping to monitor the progression of larger endometriotic cysts after a diagnosis of endometriosis, either by laparoscopy or laparotomy, has been made.

Because 2 cm seems to be probably the smallest average mass that ultrasonography will detect (allowing for differences in individuals), many of the typically tiny endometriotic implants could be missed as reported in Article 1. Only large cysts can be detected. And, even then, ultrasound is not 100 percent accurate. Therefore, ultrasonography could miss endometriosis in many patients prior to surgery and fail to monitor the progression of the disease after surgery when new tiny implants could form or until the previously viewed implants had reached sizes of 2 cm or more. Also, though all of these articles remarked on the 'shaggy-walled' cystic appearance of many endometriotic implants, there seem to be enough exceptions to this 'typical' appearance to make a definite preoperative diagnosis of endometriosis impossible at this time.

There have been a number of reports concerning the safety of ultrasound, especially when it is used to monitor the foetus in the uterus. None of the articles reviewed here discussed the safety of ultrasound. However, R. L. Brent reports in the article 'The Effects of Embryo and Fetal Exposure to X-Ray, Microwaves, and Ultrasound' (*Clinical Obstetrics and Gynecology* 26: 2 [June 1983]: 506) that, so far, epidemiologic studies (studies of the frequency of diseases) involving infants who were exposed to ultrasound as foetuses have not shown any significant biological effects. 'There is [sic] some data on the biological effects of ultrasound involving DNA repair, cytogenetic alterations (chromosome changes), and teratogenesis (deformities in the foetus). At the present time, the results would indicate that low exposure to ultrasound presents minimal risks or none at all.' It is presumed that this would also apply to women with endometriosis undergoing ultrasonography, though, as Brent points out, studies on the subject of safety are continuing.

In summary, ultrasound in relation to endometriosis appears to be a useful way of preoperatively detecting large masses of unknown origins and helping to monitor the progression of larger endometriotic cysts after the endometriosis has been diagnosed through surgery. It cannot, by any means, replace laparoscopy for the diagnosis of endometriosis or monitoring of smaller implants. We can all hope that future developments will someday find a safe and effective way of diagnosing endometriosis without surgery.

Articles Reviewed

1. Sandler, Michael A., and Karo, James J. The spectrum of ultrasonic findings in endometriosis. *Radiology* 127: 4 (April 1978): 229–231.

2. Coleman, Beverly G.; Arger, Peter H.; and Mulhern, Jr., Charles B. Endometriosis: clinical and ultrasonic correlations. *American Journal of Roentgenology* 132: 5 (May 1979): 747–749.

3. Walsh, James W.; Taylor, Kenneth J. W.; and Rosenfield, Arthur T. Gray scale ultrasonography in the diagnosis of endometriosis and adenomyosis. *American Journal of Roentgenology* 132: 1 (January 1979): 87–90.

4. Goldman, M.D., Stanford M., and Minkin, M.D., Sanford I. Diagnosing endometriosis with ultrasound: accuracy and specificity. *The Journal of Reproductive Medicine* 25: 4 (October 1980): 178–182.

18
Endometriosis in Men

By Suzanne McDonough

Picture this: you are sitting at the next meeting of your local chapter of the Endometriosis Association, talking with a friend before the meeting begins. A man walks in. He is alone. He hasn't come as someone's husband or friend. He isn't a reporter or even a doctor or another medical professional there to give a lecture. Who *is* he? His answer: he's come for support and information—he has endometriosis.

Crazy? Impossible? Actually, it *is* highly unlikely—but not impossible. The common description of endometriosis always includes that it is a disease affecting women in their childbearing years. However, there are a few, *very* rare cases of endometriosis occurring in men.

Article 1 reports on a case of 68-year-old man who was found to have cancer of the prostate. (The prostate is a gland in males that surrounds the urethra at the bladder and produces the milky fluid released with sperm during ejaculation.) The cancerous part of the prostate was removed, and because cancer of the male reproductive organs is thought to be somehow hormonally related, both of the man's testicles were removed. He then was placed on oestrogen therapy in hopes that this would suppress any new cancerous cells. Five years later the man was hospitalized again after having blood in his urine. Surgery found that a lesion was present on the right side of his bladder near the entrance to the ureter (one of two tubular passageways from the kidneys to the bladder). Biopsy of the lesion revealed that it was composed of cancerous prostatic cells and one tissue fragment that was indistinguishable from endometrium. Examination of the bladder two weeks later revealed more tissue obstructing the entrance to the ureter. Biopsy showed that the tissue again was part prostate cancer plus two tissue fragments of cells identical to endometrium—endometriosis.

Article 2 describes a very similar case. A 50-year-old man was found to have a small hard mass in the prostate during a routine physical exam. Surgery with biopsy of the mass revealed that the man had cancer of the prostate. The entire prostate and seminal vesicles (two saclike glands that secrete fluid during ejaculation) were removed. Thirteen years later the man was readmitted to the hospital because of rectal bleeding, pain, and diarrhoea. It was found that he had cancer in the rectal wall identical to the cancer found previously in his prostate. At this point both testicles were removed, and the patient was put on oestrogen therapy.

Four years later the patient was readmitted to the hospital with blood in his urine. Surgery revealed a tumour on the left side of his bladder. Biopsy showed that the tumour was prostatic cancer. The patient's oestrogen was increased. Three years later the man was hospitalized again with blood in his urine. Surgery revealed a large lesion on the left side of the bladder blocking the opening to the ureter. Biopsy revealed endometriosis. 'At this time, all previously resected tissue was reexamined and the presence of endometriosis in the 1972 [three years previous] specimen was first identified.' (p. 1565)

The rest of the lesion was then removed, with biopsy showing only endometriosis with no prostatic cancer. The oestrogen therapy was discontinued, and '. . . the patient was placed on a regimen similar to that used in the treatment of endometriosis in the female, consisting of an oral contraceptive agent . . .' (p. 1565)

This therapy was not successful, however, with the patient experiencing more blood in his urine and finally being unable to urinate, at which time the lesion was fulgurated. From that point until the writing of the article, the patient remained well with cystoscopy (viewing of the urethra and bladder by way of a small scope passed through the urethra) showing that 'the mass in the region of the left ureter had diminished remarkably in size.' (p. 1565)

How could a man develop endometriosis? Experts aren't sure why, though the remarkable similarity in all reported cases (only three at the time of the writing of Article 1) leads them to some theories.

The reproductive systems in both males and females develop from the same type of tissues in the embryo (the fertilized egg in the first three months of development before the embryo becomes a foetus). Most of the male reproductive organs form from wolffian or mesonephric ducts in the embryo. The female reproductive organs form from Müllerian or paramesonephric ducts. The Müllerian ducts are also present in the young male embryo but undergo regression with the only visible remnants after birth being the appendix testis and the uterus masculinus or the prostatic utricle. The prostatic utricle is a small pouch in the prostate. These structures are described as corresponding to the fallopian tube (appendix testis) and the uterus or vagina (prostatic utricle) in the female due to their similar embryonic origins.

Further support for how much these structures may correspond is gained from a few recent reports of endometrial cancer arising in the area of the utricle. This endometrial cancer appears to be identical to endometrial cancer of the uterus in women.

It is presumed that the rest of the Müllerian ducts and tissue along the pathway between the utricle and the testicles completely disappears. However, according to Pinkert et al., '... it is not unreasonable to suppose that cell rests may persist, at least in some individuals.' (p. 1566) In other words, some cell remnants of the Müllerian ducts may still be present in the reproductive organs of some men.

Two main theories have developed from the knowledge of the embryonic origins of the male reproductive system and the incidence of endometriosis in males. They are similar to theories that have been proposed for the origins of endometriosis in the female. The first theory, the implantation theory, states that the endometrial tissue is present in the prostatic utricle and gets transferred to other areas, i.e., the bladder, during genital surgery. Pinkert et al. Point out that, while endometriosis in men has occurred after surgery, in two cases '... the nature of the surgery, radical perineal prostatectomy [removal of the entire prostate], implies that the utricle ... was removed in its entirety by the surgery.' (p. 1566) This makes the transplantation theory less likely in these cases.

The second theory of the origins of endometriosis in males is thought to be more plausible by most experts. This theory, the embryonic cell rest theory, states that in certain men there are spots of 'left over' Müllerian cells that give rise to endometriosis. According to Pinkert et al., 'The location of the endometriosis in the trigonal area [an area of the bladder] is very near to the proposed Müllerian cell rests ...' (p. 1566)

'All three of these unusual cases were associated with prolonged oestrogen therapy which appears to be a prerequisite for the development of endometriosis in the male. If so, it is strange indeed not to have seen the phenomenon more frequently, in view of the relatively common occurrence of prostatic carcinoma [cancer] treated with oestrogens for prolonged periods. Perhaps an additional factor is necessary.' (p. 1566) The researchers explain that this other factor could include transplanted tissue from the utricle or the presence of Müllerian cell rests. 'The latter factor seems to be the most likely explanation at this time.' (p. 1566)

The time when we will see male victims of endometriosis appearing at our local Endometriosis Association meetings probably will never come. However, the knowledge that endometriosis *can* occur in males and further study of these rare cases hopefully will help add a few more missing pieces to the puzzle of endometriosis.

Articles Reviewed

1. Schrodt, G. Randolph; Alcorn, Merritt O.; and Ibanez, Jose. Endometriosis of the male urinary system: a case report. *Journal of Urology* 124:5 (November 1980): 722–723.

2. Pinkert, Ted C.; Catlow, Charles E.; and Straus, Reuben. Endometriosis of the urinary bladder in a man with prostatic carcinoma. *Cancer* 43: 4 (April 1979): 1562–1567.

19

Report on Pain Management in Women with Endometriosis

By Kay Ellen Hurlbutt, R.N.-C., M.S.N., F.N.P.

[Editor's Note: This research report is a summarization of the findings of a study done as part of a clinical paper entitled 'Assisting the Client with Endometriosis in the Self-Care Aspects of Pain Management' by Kay Hurlbutt, R.N., M.S.N.]

The purpose of this paper was to develop a protocol for use by nurse practitioners to educate and assist women with endometriosis in the self-care aspects of pain management. A questionnaire that examined such variables as characteristics of the pain, effect on lifestyle, coping methods, effectiveness of pain relief measures, and perceived needs in regard to pain management was distributed randomly to 100 members of the Endometriosis Association. Of the 100 questionnaires distributed, 73 were returned from all geographic areas of the United States and 2 from Canada. Five of the returned questionnaires were eliminated from the study as they lacked criteria established for inclusion in the study (diagnosis of endometriosis by pelvic exam, laparoscopy, or abdominal surgery). Therefore, 68 percent actually participated in the study.

Pain was reported as a symptom by 100 percent of the respondents. Pain occurring one to two days prior to or at the time of menstruation was reported by 71 percent of the women participating in the study, at mid-cycle by 47 percent, and at other times in the menstrual cycle by 40 percent. Pain occurring throughout the entire menstrual cycle was reported by 20 women. Intermittent pain throughout the menstrual cycle having no identifiable pattern was reported by 5 women, or 7 percent. Since the time of initial onset of the pain, 81 percent of the sample reported that the pain had become progressively worse.

The pain was most commonly abdominal in location. In addition, pain in the lower back was reported by 63 percent of the women, pain in the legs by 31 percent, and chest pain by 7 percent. Other locations, which were reported rarely, included vagina, rectum, upper back, buttocks, groin, and coccyx.

The respondents were asked to rate the intensity of their pain at its *worst* on a scale of one to five. No one reported the pain to be mild, 1 percent reported the pain to be discomforting, 10 percent distressing, 31 percent horrible, 56 percent excruciating. The respondents were also asked to rate the intensity of their pain at its *least* on a scale of one to five. Thirty-five percent reported the pain to be mild, 44 percent discomforting, 16 percent distressing, 3 percent horrible, and no one reported the pain to be excruciating.

Pain was reported to interfere in some way with all aspects of activities of daily living. Most frequently reported, 78 percent, was interference with sleep. Women frequently reported difficulty falling asleep because of the pain or being awakened from sleep by the pain. This finding is significant because fatigue tends to potentiate the severity of pain.

Interference with social activities was reported by 72 percent. Women frequently reported pain and fatigue as major factors in the lack of desire to be with friends and family and participate in social events and recreational activities formerly enjoyed.

Interference with work or school was reported by 69 percent, and days lost from work or school because of pain was reported by 66 percent. The most frequent response, 62 percent, was one to two days per month lost from work or school. Of the 26 percent who did not report days lost from work or school, many commonly responded that they felt a noticeable decrease in the quality of their work during the times they were experiencing pain. Interference with ability to do common household chores because of pain was reported by 68 percent.

Interference with sexual activity was reported by 63 percent. Many commonly reported pain with sexual intercourse and a resulting decrease in sexual desire, although none verbalized a strain in a relationship because of this factor. Difficulty with urination was reported by over half of the subjects (59 percent). Decrease in appetite because of pain was reported by only 38 percent, but still over a third of the sample.

It was reported by 21 percent of the sample that the pain had had no effect on family and/or marital relationships, while 25 percent reported a slight change, 29 percent a moderate change, and 19 percent an extreme change. This finding indicates some degree of stress on relationships with significant others as a result of the pain experience. It is interesting to note that a common response was that many felt that significant others were very supportive in helping to cope with the disease and its associated pain. In friendships with people other than family, a slight change from before pain was reported by 38 percent, a moderate change by 21 percent, and extreme change by 6 percent.

Respondents were asked to describe their moods and feelings when experiencing pain. Eighty-four percent reported feeling depressed, 75 percent irritable, 63 percent experienced mood swings, 54 percent reported feeling anxious, 53 percent angry, 51 percent negative, 43 percent helpless, 35 percent fearful and powerless, 32 percent worried, 31 percent insecure, and 19 percent hopeless.

Pain medications were being used at some time by virtually all respondents. Sixty-six percent reported use of aspirin for pain, and three-fourths (75 percent) used Tylenol. *Commonly used medications for pain included the nonsteroidal anti-inflammatory agents. Of these, Motrin was used for pain by 60 percent and was the most beneficial for pain relief.* Tylenol with codeine was the most frequently used narcotic analgesic. The majority reported that pain medication frequently did not relieve the pain, but rather made it more tolerable. Narcotic analgesics were frequently associated with unpleasant side effects such as drowsiness, depression, and nausea. Many had used pain medications over a period of many years. There seemed to be no pattern as to how many days per month pain medications were used.

Respondents were asked to relate other things they did to help relieve or manage their pain and comment on usefulness. Frequently mentioned were many of the noninvasive pain relief techniques. Heat in the form of heating pads and hot baths was by far the most frequently used for pain. One had tried cold packs over the abdomen and felt them to be more effective than heat. Other methods mentioned include body positioning, distraction techniques, relaxation techniques, breathing exercises, and massage. These methods were felt by all who used them to promote relaxation and were effective in helping the individual to cope with the pain. Again, these measures did not eliminate the pain and were helpful only for short periods while employing the technique.

Only a small number of women had learned of various pain relief techniques from health professionals. Nurses were listed least often. Only three related that they had learned of pain relief measures from a nurse. Physicians were most often mentioned among health professionals for providing information about pain relief. The second most common source of information was listed as mothers and close friends or family. The most common response was that individuals had learned of and tried pain relief techniques as a result of their own searching and reading.

When asked what they thought health professionals could do to help them with their pain, a great majority felt a need for more education and information about all aspects of endometriosis. Many also felt a need for health professionals to be more understanding and supportive. They felt that in many cases health professionals were not sympathetic toward the problems of endometriosis. For example, some had been told that they suffered from 'painful periods' or had a low pain tolerance. Many felt that their pain was not taken seriously by health professionals. Mirrored throughout was a perceived need for pain relief measures without surgical intervention and without the side effects associated with hormonal treatments and pain medications. Many expressed a need for more information about alternative resources such as a holistic approach to pain relief. The study demonstrated that a need exists for assistance in learning to cope with and manage the disease and its associated pain.

Kay Hurlbutt, R.N.-C., M.S.N., F.N.P., received her B.S.N. from Marian College in Fond du Lac, Wisconsin, and her M.S.N. from the University of Wisconsin in Oshkosh, Wisconsin. She is certified by the American Nurses' Association as a Family Nurse Practitioner.

Section VI.
Working Together to Overcome Endometriosis

'I didn't know there was anyone else who shared this problem . . .' How often we've had members tell us that! Perhaps the most important thing we've done for women with endometriosis is to let them know that there are millions of other women who share the suffering caused by the disease and not only that they are not alone with the disease, but that others with it are working together to overcome it. Nowhere is this effort more evident than in our research. In this section the story of the development of our data registry is presented as well as a sampling of its data.

We're also not alone in these efforts worldwide. The U.S./Canadian Endometriosis Association was delighted to hear of sister efforts in Great Britain and Australia. We exchange newsletters, information, and the support that comes with creating the start of what we hope will someday be a worldwide network of organizations.

This section gives the reader a historical perspective on the U.S./ Canadian Endometriosis Association, the British Endometriosis Society, and the Victorian Endometriosis Association, which is the Australian organization. There are differences between the three groups, but there is similarity in purpose and dedication. Working together worldwide, we know we can overcome endometriosis.

20
Research: Where Information on Endometriosis Begins

By Mary Jou Ballweg

'I am willing to participate in research on this disease. Although I have learned to cope with my infertility and am fortunate to have two beautiful children through adoption, I willingly would help share my experiences in hopes of sparing someone the pain and trouble I have had.'

Yolanda, Berkeley, California

'Enclosed is the questionnaire for your research. It is my hope that you are able to receive enough information and funding to put the pieces together to prevent more suffering and help those who now suffer.

'The literature I received gave me support by knowing that the problem is recognized and being looked into. It truly touched my heart. Much of the information is hard to absorb all at once ... what is so great is that I can now study it. Learning in itself is a great deal of support.

'I look forward to receiving the newsletter, and if I can be of help in any other way, please don't hesitate to ask.'

Donna, Clear Lake, Wisconsin

'Just keep the research going. As I said, I'll keep my dollars coming in and you keep the research going and stick with the great job you're all doing. Just thanks for being there.'

Barbara, Spencer, Wisconsin

'*Here are my dues—plus a contribution. Your work is excellent!
I am a premedical student and, as such, see much in terms of
study results. Seldom do I see such in-depth reporting as I do in
your newsletters.*'   Laura, New Mexico

In 1980, when the Endometriosis Association was founded in Milwaukee,
we did not know we were the first group of women with endometriosis
in the world to try to find help for treating this frustrating disease. We
did know we all had dozens and dozens of questions about the disease
for which no one had answers—doctors didn't know, researchers didn't
know, and we, the women with endometriosis, didn't know.

Medical textbooks typically described the disease as puzzling, and
the history of treatments showed women with endometriosis were put on
whatever new hormonal drug came along in the hopes that it might work.
No lay books existed. In fact, no lay body of literature existed—only a
fact sheet by Resolve, the U.S. group that helps infertile couples, and a
small pamphlet by the American College of Obstetricians and Gynecolog-
ists. The standard 'wisdom' was to get pregnant—it was said that would
cure the disease. But all we had to do was look around our group to see
numerous women who had been pregnant and still had endometriosis.
And much of the rest of the standard 'wisdom' was clearly contradicted
by the women with whom we came in contact. Could we *all* be exceptions
to the rule?

It didn't take long to figure out that the reason for the misinformation
was that serious ongoing study of women with endometriosis across
patient population groups had never been undertaken. We set out to find
answers. We developed a questionnaire and distributed it to every woman
with endometriosis willing to fill it out. By the fall of 1980 we had
received over 300 completed questionnaires, and with the help of one of
our medical advisors we started working with the Medical College of
Wisconsin to computerize and analyze our data.

From that process, we were able to develop, for the first time in
history, solid information on large numbers of women with endometriosis.
The registry has grown over time to 2,000 cases, and there is an ongoing
influx of questionnaires awaiting coding. These are added to the registry
as funding allows—fortunately generous donations by members and
others have allowed this work and the research analysis that goes with
it to continue unabated for now. (No names or addresses are put in the
computer—all data are described by a number code only, for total
confidentiality of the computerized data.)

Little by little, we established solid information on numerous aspects
of the disease—information that was only a fantasy for the founding

group back in 1980! Best of all, we've been able to generate real interest and enthusiasm for research on endometriosis as was evidenced at the 1986 American Fertility Society/Canadian Fertility and Andrology Society convention in Toronto.

Most of the Association's literature and information has been rooted in our data registry, as well as our informal information gathering. For instance, when we first published our data registry findings on danazol, it was the first large study of women on danazol. With results on a large research group, we were able to determine with accuracy what the results of the drug were, what the side effects and their frequencies really were, as well as other information on it, and then publish an article on it.

In addition to developing our own huge body of lay information on the disease, we began the serious endeavour of scientific research using the registry. Dr Karen Lamb, for many years assistant professor of preventive medicine at the Medical College of Wisconsin, and now director of the research registry programme for the Association, was instrumental in this. Five of the research studies produced by her and others working with her have already been published in medical journals, and quite a number of additional articles are near publication.

The studies already published include 'Data Registry for Endometriosis,' *Wisconsin Medical Journal*, August, 1986; 'Endometriosis: A Comparison of Associated Disease Histories,' *American Journal of Preventive Medicine*, June, 1986; 'Family Trait Analysis: A Case-Control Study of 43 women with Endometriosis and Their Best Friends,' *American Journal of Obstetrics & Gynecology*, March, 1986: 'Tampon Use in Women with Endometriosis,' *Journal of Community Health*, Winter, 1985, and 'The Association of Atopic Diseases with Endometriosis,' *Annals of Allergy*, October 1987. Additional studies Dr Lamb and the Association are pursuing include studies of the links among immune deficiencies, candidiasis, and endometriosis; the pregnancy and miscarriage experiences of members; symptoms and disability of endometriosis; a generational study; and others.

Imagine endometriosis as a huge picture puzzle like the jigsaw puzzles you put together as a kid. But you don't have a picture on the box to tell you what the completed puzzle will look like, and you're allowed to take only certain pieces out of the box at a time. Some of the pieces are trick pieces—they don't really fit in this puzzle at all, but you won't know that till the puzzle is done. On top of that, some of the key pieces in this puzzle may be in *other* puzzle boxes.

Do we have a 1,000-piece puzzle or a 500-piece one? Are the pieces turned up now important ones, or will they be insignificant or not even part of the puzzle in the end? Are we overlooking key pieces that are already turned up or are in another puzzle box and look like something else? *Only more research will tell.*

21
Facts and Figures from the Data Registry: Women Share Their Stories About Living with Endometriosis

By Karen Lamb, R.N., Ph.D.

Medical statistics are simply people with the tears wiped away. The hundreds of case histories provided by members of the Endometriosis Association attest to the frustration and discomfort faced by many of these women and their families.

The team working on the data registry has searched for ways to capture the stories in a fashion that summarizes the common experiences, the differences and similarities among women. In translating these lengthy case histories into numerical tabulations, we hope that we have not detracted from their complexity. The sharing of each woman's unique, very personal, and private experiences with others is greatly appreciated. The tables that follow merely capture a snapshot of the women's journeys through the medical care system.

Women have responded from every state and province of the U.S. and Canada. Several countries are represented. A profile of early respondents indicates that, statistically speaking, the 'average' woman is about 31 years old when she corresponds with us. Most are married, and approximately one in three has graduated from college. It should be noted that 'paper and pencil' questionnaires, which require written completion of answers and adequate reading skills, do have a built-in bias. Wording of questions, vocabulary used, and skills required may tend to exclude women who have a limited education or women who use

English as a second language. Although some chose not to share family financial data with us, the data we do have indicate that the median annual income for most families is about $32,000 a year. Single women have access to considerably less family income than married women. Considering that these earnings more typically represent the combined income of both spouses, the data once again do little to support the stereotype of the woman with endometriosis as the career woman. Many are homemakers, and for those women working outside the home, employment opportunities still reflect the traditional occupations of women prior to the women's movement.

TABLE I. CHARACTERISTICS OF WOMEN WITH ENDOMETRIOSIS AT THE TIME OF PROVIDING MEDICAL, SURGICAL, AND SOCIAL HISTORIES FOR THE DATA REGISTRY

Age of Respondents

Average age	31.3
Standard deviation	5.6
Median age	31.0
Youngest	16.0
Oldest	57.0

Marital status

Married	65.5%
Single	25.9%
Divorced or widowed	8.6%

Educational Levels

College-educated	32.3%
Some college, high school, or less	67.7%

Family Income

Median	$32,000
Range	$2,000 to over $98,000

A special study on a sample of members showed that menarche (the age when young girls begin menstruation), occurred at 12.6 years. (The standard deviation, s, was found to be $\pm$ 1.5 years, showing that the majority of these women began menstruation between 11.1 and 14.1 years.) Many reported to us that symptoms appeared soon after. Contrary to previously held beliefs that endometriosis developed in the late twenties and early thirties as a response to women's delayed childbearing, our members' histories simply just do not support this generalization. Over

244 Working Together to Overcome Endometriosis

one-half reported pain before the age of 24. (The statistical average reflects the wide variation among women: average age = 18.5 ± 6.6 years.)

Remarkable percentages of women told us that their symptomatology occurred during their teenage years. Thirty-six percent were under 20. Thirteen percent were younger than 15.

TABLE 2. AGE ENDOMETRIOSIS SYMPTOMS FIRST PRESENTED

Age	Number	Percent
Under 15 years of age	108	13.4
Age 15–19	189	23.4
Age 20–24	182	22.6
Age 25–29	210	26.0
Age 30–34	87	10.8
Age 35–39	31	3.8
Total	807	100.0

No response = 23 (2.7%)

Common symptoms are shown in Table 3. The classic symptom of dysmenorrhoea is reflected in this table, with 9 out of 10 women reporting this complaint. Most women with endometriosis experience a myriad of symptoms. However, a tiny percentage experience no evident sign of the disease, at least as measured by subjective symptoms. In part, this is why the disease has been long characterized as an enigma.

TABLE 3. SYMPTOMATOLOGY OF ENDOMETRIOSIS

Symptom	Number	Percent of Total
Dysmenorrhoea and/or pain throughout the menstrual cycle	772	90.2
Dyspareunia (Painful sexual intercourse)	498	58.2
Infertility	409	47.8
Heavy or irregular bleeding	493	57.6
Nausea, stomach upset at time of menses	424	49.5
Diarrhoea, painful bowel movements, or other intestinal upsets with menses	611	71.4
Dizziness, headaches or pain with menses	451	52.7
Fatigue, exhaustion, low energy	621	72.5
Low-grade fever	213	24.9
Low resistance to infection	275	32.1
No symptoms	23	2.7

The list in Table 3 is far from complete. Fully 34 percent volunteered additional complaints: abdominal bloating, heaviness, skeletal and muscular aches as well as emotional fluctuations were frequently voiced.

By definition, *dysmenorrhoea* refers to pain and discomfort relative to the menses itself. As can be seen in Table 4, fewer than one in five reported their distress to be isolated to this few days each month. More than three out of four (77 percent) experience pain throughout the cycle. When asked to characterize the level of pain, note that approximately 74 percent chose a response indicating that, for them, the pain was at least sometimes severe.

TABLE 4. PAIN PROFILE RELATIVE TO MENSTRUAL CYCLE AND PATIENTS' CHARACTERIZATION OF SEVERITY LEVELS

Occurrence	Number	Percent
No pain *relative to menses*	32	3.9
At time of menses only	143	17.3
At ovulation only	16	1.9
Throughout the menstrual cycle	637	76.9
Total	828	100.0

No pain at all = 28 (3.3%)

Severity	Number	Percent
Mild	35	4.4
Mild to moderate	57	7.2
Moderate	119	14.9
Moderate to severe	260	32.6
Severe	193	24.2
Varies, mild to severe	133	16.7
Total	797	100.0

No response = 31 (3.7%)

We asked if the woman had ever been unable to carry out her normal work and activities. While some reacted with comments indicating that 'women's work . . . is never done,' fully 70 percent reported being disabled by the disease. And some reported lengthy periods of disability involving weeks. Most, however, told us that the incapacitation is limited to two days or less; but when one contemplates the cyclical nature and the chronicity of endometriosis, the magnitude of disability becomes apparent.

One of the attributes of maintaining a data registry for research purposes lies in the complexity of treatment regimes to which women have been subjected. Most authorities accept the most valid method of diagnosing the disease to be via surgical laparoscopy. This procedure lends itself to aspects of therapy per se as the endometriotic implants are often cauterized, excised, and removed simultaneously as the diagnostic phase is initiated.

So, too, data provided by these women offer a wealth of information to researchers. Surgical interventions, medical treatments with both male and female hormonal therapies (including oral contraceptives and danazol), as well as the advocacy of pregnancy-as-therapy have been recommended and used by these patients. Comparable percentages (slightly over 60 percent) of registry respondents have used each of the current major management techniques: surgery, danazol therapy, and birth control medications.

Ironically, for a group in whom infertility is both a significant and heartbreaking problem, 90 percent of the women report their physicians have told them that pregnancy may cause a regression or cure in their diseases. Pregnancy was suggested to 73 percent of the women, and while concern was voiced about pregnancy as therapy—sometimes without regard for marital status of the individual—still some 63 percent have tried or are trying to become pregnant. The success of these endeavours remains the subject of future books.

The types of surgical procedures demanded by endometriosis has been labeled 'the blue plate special.' We attempted to categorize several of the types of surgeries undergone by members of the Association in the analysis shown in the next chart. The data in Table 5 were based on a subgroup of 365 women, 233 of whom had had a surgery that they described in some detail. Of these women, about 15 percent have lost childbearing potential.

TABLE 5. SURGICAL PROCEDURES AND ORGANS REMOVED (N = 233)

	f	%
I. Elimination of Childbearing Potential	35	15
Bilateral oophorectomy (both ovaries removed) and hysterectomy	(22)	
Hysterectomy with one ovary removed	(8)	
Hysterectomy with no ovaries removed	(5)	
II. Maintenance of Childbearing Potential	73	31
Partial oophorectomy:		
1 ovary only removed	(18)	
1 ovary with cauterization	(26)	
2 ovaries partially removed	(6)	

1 ovary + part of other with cauterization (4)
1 ovary + 1 tube removed (1)
1 ovary + other procedures:
  with uterine suspension with cauterization (2)
  with presacral neurectomy (1)
  with appendectomy (6)
  with fallopian tube removal (3)
  with large bowel resection (1)
  with colon repair (1)
  with appendectomy, parts of kidney, bladder, and
    rectum removed (1)
  with uterine resection and cauterization (1)
Fallopian tube removal (partial) with cauterization (2)

III. Other Surgeries　　　118　　51
Removal and cauterization of growths (74)
Uterine suspension with cauterization (15)
  (includes 4 cases with presacral neurectomy and 1 case
  with ovary reconstruction and 1 with ovary resection)
Adhesions and scar tissue removed (11)
  with appendectomy
  with bilateral ovarian cystectomy
Dilation and curettage (D&C)
  with laparoscopy (3)
  with laparoscopy with cauterization (1)
    + uterine suspension
  with uterine suspension and cauterization (2)
Other surgical procedures:
  colon removed (partial resection) (1)
  small intestine removed (partial resection) (1)
  drainage of chocolate cysts (2)
  lancing of vulva (1)
  laparoscopy (2)
  bladder suspension with ovaries 'shelled' (1)
  repair septate uterus (1)
  hydrotubation with cauterization (1)
  appendectomy with cauterization (1)
  microsurgery repair of ovaries and tubes (1)

IV. Multiple and Miscellaneous Surgeries　　　7　　3
Ruptured ovarian cyst; removal of tube due to ectopic
  pregnancy, cauterization, ovarian resection (1)
D&C X 3 with ovary resection and with presacral
  neurectomy (1)
Laparotomy × 2, laparoscopy X3, and wedge resection (1)
Surgery × 7 to repair blocked tubes (1)
Myomectomy with ovarian suspension + removal of cyst (1)

Myomectomy with laparoscopy   (1)
Laparoscopy with tubal ligation + several D&Cs   (1)

That improvements in therapies, the kinds of education and information patients and their families need, and improvements in physician
knowledge and ability to communicate with patients exist is readily
apparent from reading even a small sample of these case histories. Almost
without exception the women acknowledged fears and insecurities in
their present situation. While fear of further surgeries and pain is readily
expressed, as could be expected, the ability to bear children elicits the
greatest anxiety. Embedded in response are fears of cancer and fears of
birth defects, particularly as a result of hormonal therapies. Whether
realistic or not, equally half of all of the first 856 histories analyzed
showed patients were having difficulty making treatment decisions. One
of each three patients reported her physician has not been willing and
fully able to discuss endometriosis with her. Again, over half need more
information, and about 4 in 10 wish to have someone with whom
treatment options can be discussed.

TABLE 6. HOW WOULD YOU SUGGEST THAT MEDICAL PROFESSIONALS IMPROVE THEIR WAYS OF RELATING AND TREATING PATIENTS WITH ENDOMETRIOSIS?

	Number	Percent
Improve attitudes toward patient	186	27.5
Increase professional education	117	17.3
Provide patients with educational materials	119	17.6
Improve communication skills	168	24.9
Give patient choices and treatment alternatives	67	9.9
Make referrals to individual or a group with same problems	19	2.8
Total	676	100.0

No suggestions = 180 (21%)

An open-ended question regarding suggestions to medical professionals elicited often vociferous responses. Many called for an improvement
in physicians' attitudes as well as their communication skills. In their
own voices the women express their sense of frustration and state their
needs eloquently: 'Take endometriosis more seriously and understand
that we are in pain.' 'Stop recommending pregnancy.' And finally:
'Diagnose women earlier!'

The future work of medical practitioners has been well defined.

Karen Lamb, R.N., Ph.D., holds a broad range of interests in medicine and health care: homelessness in America, abused and neglected children, and immune deficiency diseases, including AIDS.

An active practitioner, researcher, and writer, Dr Lamb has been instrumental in improving the quality of care and influencing health policy. Her articles and epidemiological studies have appeared in a variety of national (U.S.) nursing and medical journals.

As a faculty member at the Medical College of Wisconsin, Dr Lamb developed the computerized data registry for the Endometriosis Association. She is currently the director of the Endometriosis Association Research Registry Program and executive director of the Uihlein Family Health Program.

22
Australian Women with
Endometriosis Help Each Other

By Sue Deutsch

'*It has taken us some time to find your address, but we are really pleased to be able to contact you at last.*

'*The Women's Health Resource Collective, a Melbourne-based feminist group, has recently produced an information leaflet about endometriosis.*

'*To our knowledge, no other work has been done on this issue in Melbourne (or Australia) before. Recently a small article about the disease was published in our daily press, to which some 100 women responded immediately.*

'*Each of these women shares the difficulty of having had little access to information about her condition and no contact with other women with the disease. As a consequence, a self-help group is in the process of being established, and the Women's Health Resource Collective is distributing a questionnaire . . .*

'*We are also trying to compile a research file for the use of women with endometriosis, though this is a slow process given the dearth of local information . . .*

'*We'd also love to hear more about your Association, how it functions, and what your plans are. Certainly we'd be really grateful for any information about endometriosis you may be able to send us.*

'*Looking forward to hearing from you, yours in international sisterhood,*'

Di Surgey, for the WHRC

250

Endometriosis doesn't respect national boundaries. The Endometriosis Association receives letters from women all over the world. We are especially pleased when we hear that support groups are being started in other countries.

In 1984, women in Melbourne, Australia, joined their sisters in England, the United States, and Canada in having their own endometriosis self-help organization.

We are working to strengthen the links among the U.S.-Canadian, British, and Australian organizations. The sharing of knowledge can only give us greater strength. Eventually we hope to see groups started in other parts of the world.

Melbourne is one of Australia's largest cities and has proved to be a hospitable site for the Australian group. They got off to a good start with the sponsorship of the Women's Health Resource Collective. This is a Melbourne-based feminist organization that offered help with publicity, a meeting space, and other services.

The collective also produced a leaflet that is a good blend of medical facts, eye-catching illustrations, and direct quotations from endometriosis sufferers. Much of the information applies to women who have endometriosis anywhere in the world. As the leaflet so aptly puts it:

'We may also be tempted to forget about the pain until the next time we feel it. When we do seek help, we are often faced by doctors who are unwilling to take our complaints seriously or who diagnose other causes, such as anxiety, psychosomatic conditions, or "normal" premenstrual cramps. Consequently, diagnosis is often a long-drawn-out process, which leaves us feeling powerless, demoralized, and untrusting of our perceptions.'

This statement is also true of many of the women with endometriosis in the United States and Canada. Indeed, it is the similarity of experience that makes reading the news of the Australian group so fascinating. However, there are differences in word usage (as there are in Great Britain), which remind us that there is diversity as well as unity in the English language. For example, women in the Australian organization speak of wanting to 'fall' pregnant. They almost certainly find some of our idioms just as odd . . .

Despite minor differences in language, there is ample evidence that women with endometriosis in Australia have much to share with us. Their newsletter tells of their use of danazol and the serious side effects that sometimes are the result. Some of the Australian women have gone through agonizing, lengthy surgical and drug procedures but feel they are worthwhile because the end result was a much-wanted pregnancy.

For others there is the sadness of being forced to accept continued infertility due to endometriosis.

A number of women report being told by gynaecologists that they were imagining symptoms—and other equally devastating comments that sound all too familiar. One of the Australian women told of an experience in which she was undergoing terrible pain, bleeding, and other symptoms due to endometriosis. The disease had not yet been diagnosed. Several doctors told her that her condition was due to a rare 'tropical disease.' She was actually placed in a hospital for six days, in isolation, so no one else could catch her 'dangerous' disease!

Research efforts—and interest on the part of physicians—sound even more meager than here in North America. The Australian medical and scientific community has devoted a great deal of time and attention to the problem of infertility. They have done pioneer work in the area of in vitro fertilization. Let's hope that their interest in infertility leads to research on endometriosis.

There are also some notable differences in treatment methods in Australia. Although danazol is used frequently, there is also another commonly prescribed hormonal preparation. It's called Duphaston, and it's a progestin compound. Duphaston is used in England and was used here. The Australians also stress alternative treatments, as do the English. The natural remedies that are used are the same as the ones described in the article on alternative treatments in Section II of this book.

The Australian group has undergone a process of growth since it first contacted us. The first step was the process of becoming an independent organization, rather than an adjunct of the Women's Health Resource Collective. The name Victorian Endometriosis Self-Help Group was selected. *Victorian* doesn't refer to old-fashioned attitudes on the part of the members of the group! The city of Melbourne is located in the Australian state of Victoria.

Lorraine Henderson, who is a member of the Australian organization, attended many meetings of the British Endometriosis Society. She brought her expertise on how to run a successful organization back home to Australia. Ros Wood, who is editor of the *Victorian Newsletter*, has worked hard to create a periodical that meets the needs of group members. Many other women are also responsible for the success of the group.

For a year or so, the Victorian group seemed to be rather loosely organized. No dues were charged, and no efforts were made to gain the Australian equivalent of American nonprofit status. Women could subscribe to the newsletter, but it seems that a number of copies were sent out free. Eventually this generosity had to end. The organization is

A FEW COMPARATIVE FINDINGS: ENDOMETRIOSIS ASSOCIATION, BRITISH SOCIETY, AND VICTORIAN ENDOMETRIOSIS ASSOCIATION

	First Symptoms				First Report to Doctor		Endo First Suspected by Doctor or Diagnosed	
Society	*Society*	*Endo. Assoc.*		*Vict. E.A.*	*Society*	*Vict. E.A.*	*Society*	*Vict. E.A.*
10–15 years	16%	10–14 years	14%	6%	5%	0%	0%	0%
16–20 years	25%	15–19 years	22%	36%	10%	26%	2%	3%
21–25 years	22%	20–24 years	21%	21%	25%	20%	21%	18%
26–30 years	20%	25–29 years	30%	22%	27%	29%	29%	34%
31–35 years	11%	30–34 years	11%	9%	17%	16%	25%	27%
36–40 years	6%	35–39 years	3%	6%	10%	7%	15%	14%
41–45 years	1%	40+ years			3%	1%	5%	3%
46–50 years	0%				1%		2%	

Society = British Endometriosis Society. Number of subjects in this report = 726.

Endo. Assoc. = U.S.-Canadian Endometriosis Association. Number of subjects in this report = 365.

Vict. E.A. = Victorian Endometriosis Association, Australia. Number of subjects in this report = 88.

First Symptoms Chart: 14% of the Society group, 6% of the E.A. group, and 10% of the Victorian group did not answer this question.

First Report Chart: 16% of the Victorian group did not answer this question.

All Charts: Percentages may not always add to 100 due to rounding.

    Age groupings of U.S.–Canadian Endometriosis Association and Victorian Endometriosis Association are the same. E.A. questionnaire did not ask when the woman first reported her symptoms to her doctor. It did ask age at diagnosis, but data were not readily available for this group.

now more formally structured, and the name has officially been changed to the Victorian Endometriosis Association. Members pay yearly dues. The organization is seeking grants for special projects.

Meetings are held on a regular basis and often feature speakers or films. Some meetings are just devoted to discussion and support group programming. There are also a number of pleasant social events such as picnics and dinners.

The Australian group has developed its own questionnaire and is busy compiling results on a regular basis. It will be interesting to compare the data obtained with our own findings and that of the British group. The Australians also publish a book list from time to time, and some of the materials listed are reprints from the U.S.-Canadian newsletter.

So far the Australian group has not become national in its scope. We have heard from two smaller Australian groups. They are located in Chippendale, Australia, and Wentworth Falls, Australia. A national (and now transnational!) model has worked well for the U.S.-Canadian Association and for the British Society, so perhaps the Australians will soon consider it.

At any rate, the Victorian Endometriosis Association seems to be a strong and active organization. We wish them continued success and look forward to working together toward our mutual goal—ending endometriosis.

23
The U.S.–Canadian
Endometriosis Association

By Mary Lou Ballweg

*'I don't intend to sound overly dramatic, but in all of this sharing
I really wish to reach out and extend what help I can to other
women that have been facing the same nightmare. I know the
isolation, the sense of reclusivity as the illness progresses, the
unendurable pain, the lingering doubts about one's own mental
acuity, thanks to the many medical professionals who seem
unwilling to listen to what we are saying . . . Now that my body
is on the mend and my vision has become clear once again, I would
like to express a very active interest in what your organization is
doing to help others along this sojourn of pain and loneliness.'*

Thelma, Madison, Wisconsin

*'I am really happy to hear that there is a place to get information
on a disease that is plaguing women more than the medical
profession knows or admits.'*

Susan, Needham, Maine

*'The Association saved my sanity. When I was in pain, when I
was confused, when I didn't know what choices to make, nothing
else could help—not a friend, not doctors, not a lover.'*

Andrea, Washington, DC, as quoted in
Feeling Great magazine, August 1984

'Our Association is for a disease that is not considered to be life-

255

threatening, but it can, and often does, prevent *life by making a woman infertile. We have no poster child, no telethons, no movie stars (yet!), no nickname or initials for its long name. But the Association has helped to educate and support women from all over the United States and beyond, who have felt isolated, confused, and depressed, besides battling chronic, sometimes disabling, pain and problems with employment, marriage, and/or social life. 'Personally speaking, being a part of this Association, and the caring and sharing that is the heart of it, has made me feel rewarded and proud.'*

Gloria, Wisconsin

'*I am convinced that information, education, and taking charge of your own medical care is the only solution to receive proper treatment for endometriosis.*'

Colleen, Miami, Florida

'*This past Thursday night I was informed by my doctor that she believes I suffer from endometriosis. On Friday, a friend presented me with an article on the subject printed in a magazine, which gave the address of your Association.*

'*I am so pleased to have discovered the Association, because after years of suffering for three weeks of every month, I was casually informed by one specialist that "there's nothing that can be done, except to keep taking a drug called Anaprox, which certainly makes life more livable." I went for a second opinion on the "nothing can be done" decree, and she much less casually informed me that what could be done isn't worth going through until it becomes so bad that the Anaprox no longer relieves the pain and pressure. Can you tell me whether or not this is true?*

'*What truly amazes me is that neither the specialist nor the GP even bothered to test or examine me.*'

Jeanne, mid-Canada

'*Every time I receive one of your newsletters, I am reminded of my terrible struggle with endometriosis and I realize that I must continue to support this Association.*'

Marcia, Florida

'*I think the Endometriosis Association is doing a great job. I only wish I had known about you years ago. Through all the years I suffered with the pain of endometriosis I felt so alone. I thought there must be something wrong with me because I couldn't tolerate the pain. Even though I'm a nurse, I had never heard much about endometriosis except for what the doctor who diagnosed it told me. He said it was very common and would not require any treatment! I never could find much about it in medical books either . . .'*

Judy, Crystal Falls, Michigan

'To my mind, the great accomplishment of the Association is the way it has empowered women.: by legitimizing our pain and anger, by allowing us to pool information and gain from our collective experience, and by giving us concrete reason to hope for a better future. I think this is an amazing accomplishment: to take a group of people who are suffering from, as it now stands, an incurable and debilitating disease and to make this group powerful . . .'

Barbara, Toronto

HOW WE BEGAN

In early 1980, a group of diverse women began meeting at Milwaukee's Bread and Roses Women's Health Center and in our homes to talk about something we all had in common: endometriosis—a chronic, progressive disease that plagues some women from their first to their last periods. Each shared her story, a therapeutic outpouring that brought almost magical relief—just to tell it to others who really wanted to hear it, who truly understood! Each thought her own story was unique—none knew that the sad stories they were pouring out would be repeated and echoed thousands and thousands of times in the next few years from all over the U.S. and Canada.

There was Carol, in her early twenties, who'd lost her job because of ongoing pain and repeated work absences. She'd now been forced to return home to live with her parents, and her sickening bouts with her periods were forcing her to become a periodic shut-in, hanging over the toilet with alternating vomiting, constipation, and diarrhoea. There was Sandra, 36, who'd lost her marriage in part to the ongoing disability, painful intercourse and orgasm, and emotional struggles of infertility, including three miscarriages. There was Mary Lou, 31, who'd lost so many months from work she'd had to go on food stamps to eat. In spite of complete disability, she'd been told her problems were in her head. Finally diagnosed, she was put on the pill and suffered a near-stroke. Now, because no other insurance would cover her, she faced surgery with the same group of doctors who'd told her it was in her head.

There was Jean, whose ovaries, within a year and a half of each other, had grown to grapefruit and orange size. By 22, she'd had them out and a hysterectomy. Now in her early thirties, she was concerned about the long-term consequences of the oestrogen she would be on for more than 30 years. There was Sharon, who couldn't walk two and a half weeks of every month. She'd had a hysterectomy, but now the disease was back. Not well-educated, she had a hard time with the medical terms. The doctors had never explained things to her, not even that she'd go into menopause after the hysterectomy or that the disease could come back.

There was Tina, a lesbian woman whose severe menstrual cramps started at age 11. Now in her mid-twenties, she'd stayed in a low-paying, boring job for years because she needed the health insurance and knew she wouldn't be covered if she switched to a new job ('preexisting condition'). Continually exhausted, she collapsed into bed every night immediately after work, no energy left for any social life or the theater work she loved. She'd been begging doctors to do a hysterectomy for years to end her misery, but they refused, saying she was too young and should preserve her childbearing capability even though she told them she didn't want children. (She couldn't, of course, tell them she was gay.)

There was Charlene, whose husband was dead-set on their having their own child. She developed a sudden abscess in one of her endometrial cysts and went into emergency surgery with her husband on standby outside the operating room in case the doctors decided she needed a hysterectomy while 'under.' They would have had to do some fast talking, convincing him that she was near death, before he would ever have OK'd a hysterectomy, she said. There was Adele, a black woman in her early thirties, who'd had a hysterectomy. She didn't want anyone to know she was involved with us because she'd been rejected by men who walked out on her when they found out she couldn't bear 'his' child. She desperately wanted a family.

And there were the 'lucky' ones like Jane, who had no painful symptoms but couldn't get pregnant, and Lorraine and Diane, who were able to get pregnant and temporarily put the disease in remission. But their doctors had no answers for them except to get pregnant again after they and their husbands had the two children they wanted.

Each felt great relief in being able to share her story. Each thought she was partly at fault for her problems: if only she'd been more assertive with the doctors; if only she hadn't ignored the symptoms for so long; if only she hadn't been too embarrassed to tell someone when she was a teen and the disease was setting in; if only she'd stood up to her husband when sex hurt too much; if only she'd tried a few more doctors; if only, if only, if only . . .

But in hearing each other's stories, we realized we'd all had similar problems and perhaps weren't individually at fault. The commonality of experiences was remarkable—reassuring to us as individuals in a way but frightening as we realized the immense scope of what we were up against and how many thousands of women like us must exist around the country.

Within six months, the group had grown to more than 50 members who paid a small sum to publish a newsletter and start producing brochures and questionnaires. Word of mouth was spreading the news that there was a group for women with endometriosis in Milwaukee, and letters started pouring in from around the country. Many told the same sad stories of years of building symptoms; the many different doctors tried; the struggle to get diagnosed; the struggles with difficult treatment decisions; long-term drug usage and side effects; the experience of going into surgery at a young age not knowing what they'd come out with and which organs would be gone—some of the most important decisions about our bodies and lives made by others.

Many had had the experience of symptoms being dismissed by family, friends, or doctors when we were younger (just 'a normal part of being a woman,' which we'd outgrow when we had babies). Many had been told their problems were psychological, had been hurt by the disbelief of others in how debilitating the symptoms could be, and in turn doubted themselves and their own bodies. Many lived part of every month shut in or restricted. Most had looked for information and found little. (*One* pamphlet existed with information for the 'lay' person, and it said basically your doctor knows best and pregnancy cures the disease—a myth.)

At first the Milwaukee women answered the letters individually. But pretty quickly that became impossible because of the number of letters we were receiving. (We received 700 letters because of a letter to the editor about us in *Ms. Magazine*, for instance.) So we developed pamphlets and fact sheets to help answer the letters. Some of us became Crisis Call listeners. Some started working to get our literature distributed and articles in the media. A few gave talks in the community.

The information for our pamphlets and fact sheets came from our sharing, our study of the medical literature (by those who could comprehend it and share it with the rest), and our own systematically compiled data. We had determined within a few months of starting that the information most of us needed did not exist. So we decided to gather it ourselves. We designed a questionnaire, printed it, and started distributing it. Soon, we had hundreds of completed questionnaires and couldn't compile all the data manually. Through some of our medical advisors, we went to the Medical College of Wisconsin to see if we could get some advice and use their computer. There we found a fairy godmother—Dr. Karen Lamb, a professor and researcher in the Department of Preventive Medicine. She has worked with us ever since. Combining the resources of the college and the volunteer power of our members (just to code the first 365 questionnaires took over 900 hours of volunteer time!), we were able to start our data registry, the only data bank of information on endometriosis in the world.

By the end of 1981, women we had helped in other parts of the U.S. had decided they wanted to do in their own areas what we had done in Milwaukee and asked us how to go about it. So we wrote 'Guidelines for Starting an Endometriosis Support Group' and later other materials. After developing as support groups, some wanted more formal affiliation with the 'mother' group, and we started more conscious efforts to develop the organizational components of the Association. Still, an enormous amount of work needs to be done in this area of our work.

Today, we have chartered chapters, groups, and networks across the U.S. and Canada.

Every part of our work has grown out of the experiences and work of women with the disease themselves, and the structure of the entire organization is self-help, governed by women with endometriosis. We have felt tremendously empowered by our work and our networking. We have seen woman after woman evolve through contact with the Association from a 'victim,' entrapped by fear, pain, lack of information, lack of support, and medical confusion about this puzzling disease, into a woman able to take back at least some control in her life and a part of her self-esteem. Still, we are but a speck in the face of the power of this disease, the taboos and myths surrounding it, and social and medical traditions about women's bodies. *Our work has only just begun.*

WHO WE ARE

We invite you to join us. The Endometriosis Association is a self-help group of persons with endometriosis and others united to:

- establish a means for women with endometriosis to provide support and help to each other with the problems of endometriosis;
- educate the public and medical community about the disease;
- conduct and promote research on the disease and related concerns.

Our Self-Help Philosophy

The basic philosophy of the Endometriosis Association is one of self-help, that is, those with the disease helping themselves and others with the disease. This philosophy embodies in it the concepts of self-responsibility (to inform yourself and take action in order to make the best decisions for yourself) and the right to be treated with dignity, to be informed, to choose and make decisions yourself regarding your health, body, and spirit. We believe that—because of the extremely personal nature of this disease with its serious effects on health, sexuality, fertility, and self-image—no one (medical professionals, Association individuals, or anyone else) should make the important life decisions that often face a woman with endometriosis except the woman herself.

THE ENDOMETRIOSIS ASSOCIATION: OUR ACCOMPLISHMENTS

In seven years (1980 to 1987), the U.S.-Canadian Endometriosis Association, the first organization in the world for those with endometriosis (there are now similar groups in England and Australia) has worked to provide these services:

- The first support groups especially for endometriosis.
- A network of chapters, groups, sponsors, and women with endometriosis all over the U.S. and Canada. It is now possible for most women with endometriosis to find others near them for sharing ideas, emotional support, listening, finding the best doctors in the area, etc.
- The first continuous programme for education related to endometriosis ever. Lectures and workshops are now ongoing for those with endometriosis, the general public, and even the medical community.
- The first accurate and comprehensive lay literature ever for those with endometriosis. Our brochures, fact sheets, newsletters, and reports grow out of the most extensive body of information ever gathered on endometriosis (our data registry, housed at the Medical College of Wisconsin and maintained by the Association). Our literature is highly acclaimed by those with the disease and medical professionals and is in great demand.
- The first (and only) Crisis Call help for those with endometriosis. Members can call on these caring and knowledgeable Crisis Call listeners at any time.
- The first (and only) data registry of information for research on endometriosis. A highly significant and important accomplishment.
- The first Endometriosis Clinic for those with endometriosis without financial resources (in conjunction with Downtown Beekman Hospital, New York City).
- A massive educational project involving mailings to every gynaecologist, hospital, and college health service. Our letter to gynaecologists

sent under the signature of leading experts, including Dr Robert Kistner of Harvard Medical School. Response to the mailings was so enthusiastic that we had to print an extra 200,000 brochures!

- A large public education effort to teach people about endometriosis and hopefully get women and teens with symptoms in for earlier diagnosis. This campaign, funded by Winthrop Laboratories, ran in over 20 women's and news magazines.

Our Goals:

- A support group or chapter in your area.
- Our data registry in wide use by researchers.
- A cure for endometriosis and preventive measures for endometriosis.

Appendix

Readings to Assist the Woman with Endometriosis

We can say unabashedly that the very best lay literature on endometriosis is that published by the Endometriosis Association. If you are a woman with endometriosis looking for information on the disease, treatment information, coping ideas, and a sense of support and understanding from others with endometriosis, start with our newsletters and literature that you can receive by clipping the coupon at the back of this book. Once you have obtained and thoroughly read these materials, you may wish to read more broadly in the areas of women's health or perhaps read some of the medical materials on endometriosis. This reading list was drawn up for that broader reading you may wish to do after absorbing all the Association literature.

BOOKS ON ENDOMETRIOSIS

1. *Endometriosis*, Julia Older, 1984, Charles Scribner's Sons. This was the first book on endometriosis written for the general public. It still provides a good, basic introduction to the disease for family, friends, and others who do not have endometriosis; but the material on treatments is too basic and outdated for women with endometriosis now, as the manuscript was completed at the end of 1982.

2. *Living with Endometriosis*, Kate Weinstein, 1987, Addison-Wesley Publishers. A good book, based on thorough research. The writing is carefully balanced and includes an extensive use of Endometriosis Association resources. It focuses

more on the emotional aspects of endometriosis and takes a traditional, individualistic approach to problem solving.

TEXTBOOKS

Recommended only for those prepared for heavy reading and able to contend with the sometimes frightening illustrations. However, we've found that when it concerns our bodies and our need to know, we can learn much from professional sources.

1. *The Atlas of Infertility Surgery*, Grant W. Patton and Robert Kistner, 1984, 2nd ed., Little, Brown and Company.

2. *The Biology of Women*, Ethel Sloan, 1985, Wiley.

3. *Gynecology Principles and Practice*, Robert W. Kistner, 1986, 4th ed., Year Book Medical Publishers.

4. *Laparoscopic Complications*, Max Borten, 1986, B.C. Decker.

5. *Novak's Textbook of Gynecology*, Edward Novak, Howard W. Jones, and Georgeanna Seegar Jones, 1981, 10th ed., Williams & Wilkins.

For the latest scientific studies (some very limited) on endometriosis and very narrow aspects of the disease and treatment, see the annual editions of *Cumulated Index Medicus*, an index to all the medical scientific literature published annually.

BOOKS FOR THE GENERAL PUBLIC

1. *Anatomy of an Illness*, Norman Cousins, 1979, W. W. Norton Company. The author is a former editor of the magazine *Saturday Review*. Several years ago he suffered from a crippling and seemingly irreversible illness. He orchestrated most of his own recovery and decided laughter was the best medicine! An inspiring book that provides a blueprint for some practical methods of self-healing.

2. *The Castrated Woman*, Naomi Miller Stokes, 1986, Franklin Watts. Strongly recommended for any woman considering a hysterectomy. An informative personal account that also tells the story of other women who have been faced with the decision. The book is subtitled *What Your Doctor Won't Tell You About Hysterectomy*, and it lives up to its promise.

3. *Coping with a Hysterectomy: Your Own Choice, Your Own Solutions*, Susanne Morgan, 1982, Dial Press. Best book available on hysterectomy, especially good on decision making, emotional factors, and self-help, including 'home-brew oestrogen' (alternative to oestrogen replacement therapy).

4. *Infertility*, Linda P. Salzer, 1986, G. K. Hall and Company. A guide for those who are infertile and those who want to help them. Gives sympathetic and direct advice that can lead to informed decision making. Also recommended by Resolve.

5. *Infertility: A Guide for the Childless Couple*, Barbara Eck Menning, 1977, Prentice-Ball. Recommended by Resolve, U.S. group for infertile couples.

6. *Menopause: A Positive Approach*, Rosetta Reitz, 1977, Penguin. A very upbeat book about menopause, particularly good on nutrition and self-care. Unfortunately, primarily about natural menopause, not surgery-induced menopause.

7. *The Menopause Book*, Barry Anderson, 1977, Hawthorne Books. Good source on menopause.

8. *The New Our Bodies, Ourselves*, Boston Women's Health Book Collective, 1984, Simon and Schuster.The original and best women's self-help health book.

9. *No More Menstrual Cramps and Other Good News*, Penny W. Budoff, M.D., 1980, G. P. Putnam Publishing Company. Excellent, interesting first chapter on menstrual 'cramps' and primary dysmenorrhoea and treatment with prostaglandin inhibitors (Motrin, Ponstel, etc.). Witty and insightful on medical world's treatment of women, written by a woman doctor.

10. *Our Own Harms*, Jo Hynes Newman, 1976, Quail Street. Fairly good, simple book on menopause and oestrogen replacement. Argues against oestrogen replacement.

11. *Stand Tall: The Informed Woman's Guide to Preventing Osteoporosis*, Morris Notelovitz, M.D., and Marsha Ware, 1982, Triad Publishing Company.

12. *When Bad Things Happen to Good People*, Rabbi Harold S. Kushner, 1981, Avon Books. Rabbi Kushner rejects the theory that we cause or deserve most of the had things that happen to us. Bad things happen as a part of being human and living in the world. This book helps put an end to self-blame. The author had a tragedy in his own life that helped him develop his philosophy.

13. *With Child*, Susan T. Viguers, 1986, Harcourt Brace Jovanovich. A moving story of a couple struggling with infertility combined with the difficulties involved in adoption. There is a happy ending resulting from two successful international adoptions. The author suffers from endometriosis.

14. *Women and the Crisis in Sex Hormones*, Barbara and Gideon Seaman, M.D., 1977. No material on endometriosis, but an excellent resource on birth control pills, IUD, DES, and research on hormones. Very well-researched book.

15. *Womancare*, Linda Madarase and Jane Patterson, M.D., 1981, Avon Books. Informative, thorough, and balanced.

BOOKS ON ALLERGY AND CANDIDIASIS

The following books may help readers understand problems related to allergy and *Candida albicans*-related illnesses better.

1. *The Complete Book of Allergy Control*, Laura J. Stevens, 1983, Macmillan.

2. *The Missing Diagnosis*, C. Orian Truss, M.D., 1984, The Missing Diagnosis, Inc.

3. *The Yeast Connection*, William Crook, M.D., 1984, Professional Books.

PRESCRIPTION DRUG REFERENCES

Check for these books in the reference section of your library.

The People's Pharmacy, Volumes 1 and 2

The Physician's Desk Reference, published yearly; check latest edition

Modern Drug Encyclopedia

Essential Guide to Prescription Drugs

The Medical Letter. Pharmacological industry publication that reviews new drugs and comments on side effects, results, and long-term effects.

Additional Resources

For women with endometriosis in the British Isles, contact:

Endometriosis Society
65 Holmdene Avenue
Herne Hill
London SE24 9LD
England

For all aspects of endometriosis:

U.S.-Canadian Endometriosis Association
Headquarters Office
P.O. Box 92187
Milwaukee, WI 53202
(414) 962–8972
1–800–992-ENDO (U.S.), 1–800–426–2END (Canada)—For first-time callers to give name and address for free brochure, materials order form, description of the Association, information on how to get help, current chapter and support group listings, how to get help in locating good physicians, etc. (Note: First-time callers located in Wisconsin and those callers contacting the Association for business purposes, call: (414) 962–8972.)

For women with endometriosis in Australia, contact:

Victorian Endometriosis Association
C/O 37 Andrew Crescent
South Croydon, Victoria 3136
Australia

Starting New Chapters and Support Groups

Members of the Association are often interested in starting chapters and support groups. The Director of Support Programs, who is on the staff at headquarters, works specifically with chapter organizers. The first step taken is to send the would-be organizer 'Guidelines for Starting an Association Chapter or Support Group' plus an 'Organizing Agreement' to sign.

The return of the signed 'Organizing Agreement' is the signal to the Director of Support Programs that the member is seriously interested in getting a chapter or support group started. Additional helpful printed materials are sent to the organizer, including the following:

- Chapter programme ideas and tips
- Guidelines for facilitating a support group
- Working with local media: a press packet
- Letter to a potential sponsor
- Guide to public speaking on endometriosis
- Literature for distribution to local health care personnel, schools, conferences—and to potential members at meetings
- Chartering packet (which includes steps in chartering a chapter, by-laws, and other important information)

The Director of Support Programmes is also always available to the organizer, by phone or mail, for advice on getting the chapter started, as well as for help once the chapter is actually functioning.

There is also help available for the member who is interested in serving as a volunteer speaker or Crisis Call Helper. Someone interested in public speaking is sent the Guide to Public Speaking and given any additional information needed Assistance is available in preparing a speech.

Crisis Call Helpers are sent a package of materials on how to work with people in crisis. A test is given, and the person then agrees to serve for a year.

Reaching Out to Teach About Endometriosis

Endometriosis is not exactly a household word—but chances are today that far more people you meet will have heard of it than in 1980. That's because of extensive educational campaigns undertaken by the Association. From the beginning, we felt it was important that women with endometriosis obtain earlier diagnosis so that the more devastating effects of the disease could, perhaps, be forestalled. And we wanted the medical community to be more aware of it and diagnose it, where it existed, rather than simply telling women with symptoms that these symptoms were normal. Beyond that, we felt that if the public at large knew something about the disease, they would more readily recognize symptoms in daughters, wives, female relatives and friends, and also be more supportive of them if they did have the disease.

Some of the educational efforts we've undertaken include a mailing to all gynaecologists in the U.S. in 1985. Response was tremendous—we had to print an extra 200,000 yellow brochures to fill the requests we received from doctors for them. Next, we mailed materials to every hospital in the U.S. Response was even greater! Another letter to every college health service elicited similar interest. As this book went to press, we were preparing similar mailings in Canada.

The overwhelming response to our advertising campaign has proven once again how great the needs of millions of women with menstrual problems and endometriosis are, just as the thousands of letters women sent to the Lydia Pinkham Company over 100 years ago did. But this

271

time, women will not let their needs simply be turned into profits for patent medicine and drug companies, doctors prescribing leeches and hormones. This time, we're determined to work together until the real cause and cure are found for endometriosis!

Glossary

Adenomyosis—A disease in which the endometrium, the lining of the uterus, seems to 'grow into' the muscular part of the uterus.

Adhesions—Bands of scar tissue.

Aetiological—Dealing with the cause of disease.

Analgesic—A drug to relieve pain.

Androgens—Male hormones involved in sexual response.

Autoimmune polyendocrinopathy—A disease in which many parts of the endocrine system are attacked by the body's own immune system.

Benign—Noncancerous, when used to refer to a tumour or mass.

Carcinoma—A cancer of epithelial origin.

Cauterize—To burn off with a fine electric charge.

Centimetre—Equals 0.39 inches.

Cervical atresia—Condition in which the cervix is malformed or absent.

Cervical stenosis—A narrowing or complete blockage of the cervix.

Chromosome—A structure in the nucleus (centre) of animal cells containing the DNA that transmits genetic information.

Clinically diagnosed—(Of disease) Identified through direct observation of the patient, as in a laparoscopy.

Coelomic epithelium—Tissue in the embryo that develops into the lining of the pelvis.

Corpus luteum—After ovulation the empty follicle is called a *corpus luteum* (a Latin phrase meaning 'yellow body' and referring to yellow fat in it).

Corticoids—Adrenal gland hormones.

Cyst—A closed cavity or sac, epithelium-lined, usually containing liquid or semisolid material.

Cystoscopy—Viewing of the urethra and bladder by way of a small scope passed through the urethra.

Cytogenetic alterations—Chromosome changes.

Depo-Provera—An injectable form of progestin.

Dysmenorrhoea—Painful periods.

Dyspareunia—Painful intercourse.

Ectopic pregnancy—Implantation of a fertilized egg in any location other than the uterus; a very dangerous condition that can lead to rupture, internal bleeding, and sometimes even death.

Endocrine system—System of glands and other structures that controls hormones; includes thyroid, pituitary, parathyroid, adrenal glands, ovaries and testes, pancreas, pineal body, and paraganglia.

Endometrioma—A mass containing endometrial tissue, often described as a 'chocolate cyst' because of its colour.

Endometrium—Tissue that lines the inside of the uterus and builds up and sheds each month in the menstrual cycle.

Epidemiologic—Pertaining to the study of the relationships of various factors determining the frequency and distribution of disease. Epidemiology is a science that deals with the occurrence, distribution, and control of disease in a population.

Epithelial—Pertaining to or composed of epithelium, which refers to the cellular coverings and linings of the body surface.

Erythrocytes—Red blood cells.

Fibroid—Noncancerous, nonendometriotic tumour.

Fibrosis—A condition marked by increase of tissues resembling fibres in the spaces between organs.

Follicles—Balls of cells with an immature egg in the centre.

Follicular phase—Part of the ovulation process, when the egg is still in the follicle (days 1–14 of a 28-day cycle).

Fulguration—Burning.

Fundus—Large upper end of the uterus.

Fungi—A group of organisms including yeasts, moulds, mildews, smuts, and rusts.

Gland—A group of cells specialized to secrete or excrete materials not related to their ordinary metabolic needs, such as the adrenal or endocrine glands.

Glandular—Relating to glands, gland cells, or their products.

Gonadectomy—Removal of the gonads—ovaries or testicles.

Gonadotropins—Hormones that have a stimulating effect on the ovaries and testes.

Helper T-cells—Immune system cells that are a necessary part of keeping potentially harmful organisms under control.

Hemorrhagic—Pertaining to bleeding from the blood vessels.

Hirsutism—Excessive facial and body hair.

Holistic—An approach to health and healing that considers the body and person as a whole.

Hormone—A substance produced by an endocrine gland and carried in the bloodstream to another organ in which the hormone stimulates some action.

Hyperplasia—Overgrowth of endometrial tissue that is sometimes a precancerous condition.

Hypothalamus—Attached to pituitary gland: controls production and release of hormones in the pituitary.

Hysterosalpingogram—X-ray test in which a dye is injected into the uterus and tubes to determine their condition.

Imperforate hymen—Condition in which the hymen (the tissues at the opening of the vagina) is partially or entirely blocked.

Kegel exercises—Exercises that involve tightening and relaxing the muscles in the pelvic floor to keep them firm.

Laparoscopy—Surgical procedure, generally done on an outpatient basis under general anaesthesia. Small incision is made near the navel, and a lighted, thin tube is inserted, through which the surgeon can view organs in abdomen.

Laparotomy—Incision through the flank, or, more generally, through any part of the abdominal wall. It is a major operation to remove endometrial implants.

Laser—Machine which produces extremely concentrated beam of light that can be directed precisely to destroy diseased tissue.

Macrophages—Immune cells that gobble up invaders.

Macular—Characterized by macules, patches of skin altered in colour, but usually not elevated.

Malignant—Cancerous, when used to refer to a tumour or mass.

Menorrhagia—Excessively profuse or prolonged menstruation.

Metabolism—The sum of all the physical and chemical processes by which living organized substance is produced and maintained.

Metastasized—Travelled by various means, referring to spread of cancer.

Microgram—One-millionth of a gram, abbreviated to μg.

Microsurgery—Surgery using a microscope.

Miliary—Made up of many small projections or lesions.

Milligram—One-thousandth of a gram, abbreviated to mg.

Millimetre—Equals 0.04 inches, abbreviated to mm.

Mitral valve prolapse—A defect in which a valve on the left side of the heart flaps up instead of closing tightly, allowing some blood to backflow.

Modalities—Treatment application methods.

Müllerian ducts—Ducts in the embryo that develop into the ovaries, uterus, and vagina.

Oestrogen—The female sex hormones; including oestradiol, oestriol, and oestrone.

Oopherectomy—Surgical removal of the ovaries.

Osteoporosis—Disease of the bones in which bones become thin and porous and break easily.

Palpation—Pelvic examination by doctor's hands.

Papular—Characterized by papules, elevations of the skin.

Pathologically diagnosed—(Of disease) identified through study of the changes in body tissues and organs, as in a laboratory analysis of tissue taken during surgery from areas presumed to be endometriosis.

Pelvic inflammatory disease—An infection in the pelvic area that can be caused by a variety of bacteria and can attack various pelvic organs; often abbreviated as *PID*.

Petechiae—Minute hemorrhagic spots.

Physiological—Normal organic function.

Pituitary gland—Located at the base of the brain; secretes, regulates, and stores a number of different hormones that affect the thyroids, reproductive organs, and other areas of the body.

Plaque—A localized abnormal patch on a body part or surface.

Premature menopause—Before natural menopause would occur.

Primary dysmenorrhoea—Painful periods and other symptoms due to an imbalance in prostaglandins.

Progesterone—A hormone that prepares the uterus for reception and development of the fertilized egg.

Prognosis—Prospect for recovery.

Prostaglandins—Substances produced throughout the body that control contraction and relaxation of smooth muscles, as well as performing many other functions.

Prostate—Gland in males surrounding the urethra at the bladder. Produces the milky fluid released with sperm during ejaculation.

Seminal vesicles—Two saclike glands that secrete fluid during ejaculation.

Species—A category of biological grouping made up of related organisms which are potentially capable of interbreeding.

Spontaneous abortion—Miscarriage.

Stellate—Resembling a star in shape.

Steroid—Includes many hormones, bile acids, sterols, and other bodily substances.

Stroma—Tissue that forms the framework of an organ; in endometriosis, the foundation of an endometrioma ('chocolate cyst'), the part that bleeds.

Surgical menopause—Menopause brought on by surgical removal of the ovaries.

Symptomatology—The combined symptoms of a disease.

Teratogenesis—Deformities in the foetus.

Testosterone—Part of a group of male hormones known as *androgens*.

Therapeutic abortion—Interruption of pregnancy by artificial means, for medical reasons.

Totipotential cells—Cells that give rise to other cells of all types.

Umbilicus—Navel.

Vaginal agenesis—Condition in which a vagina is not formed at birth.

Index